AF478839

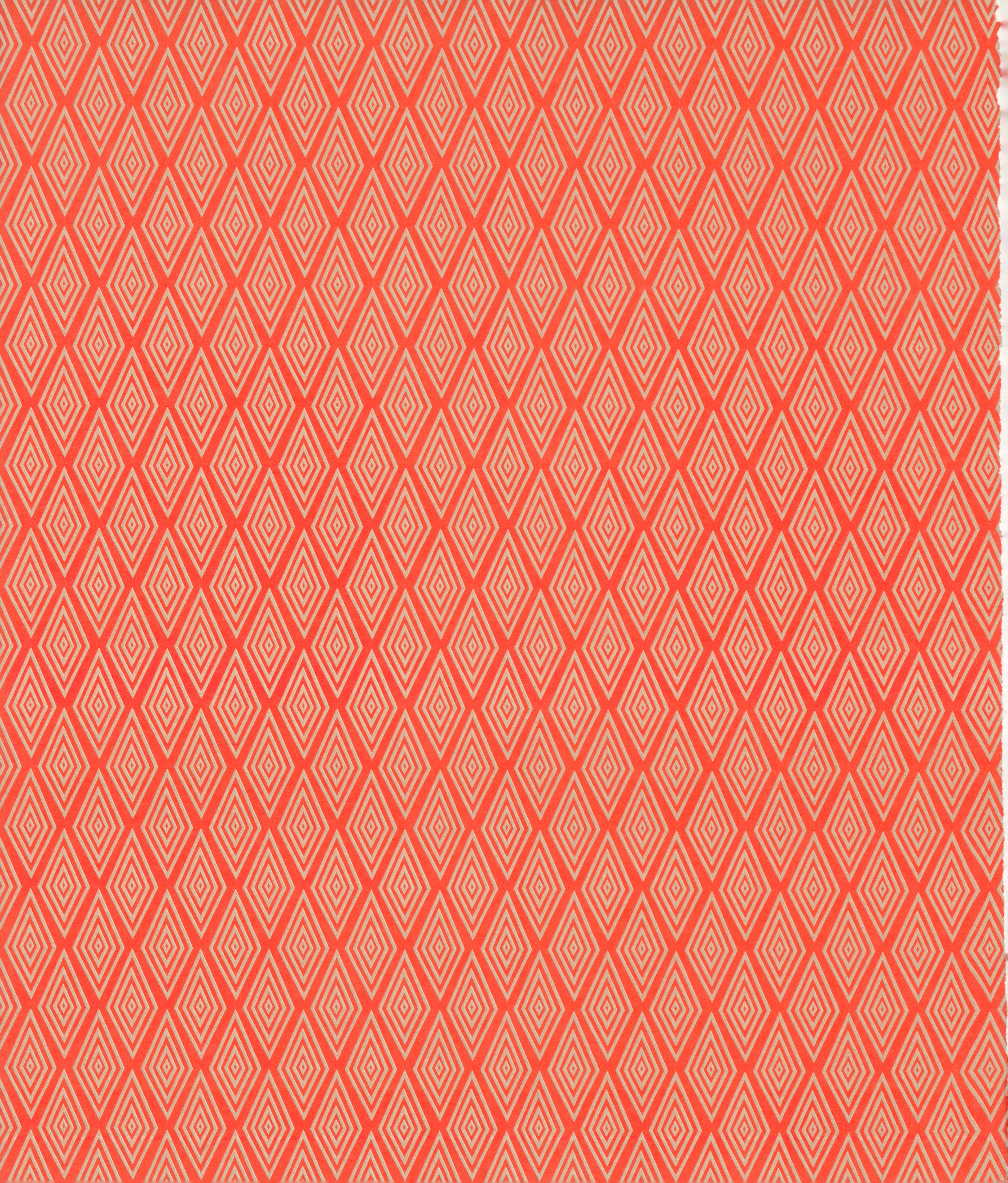

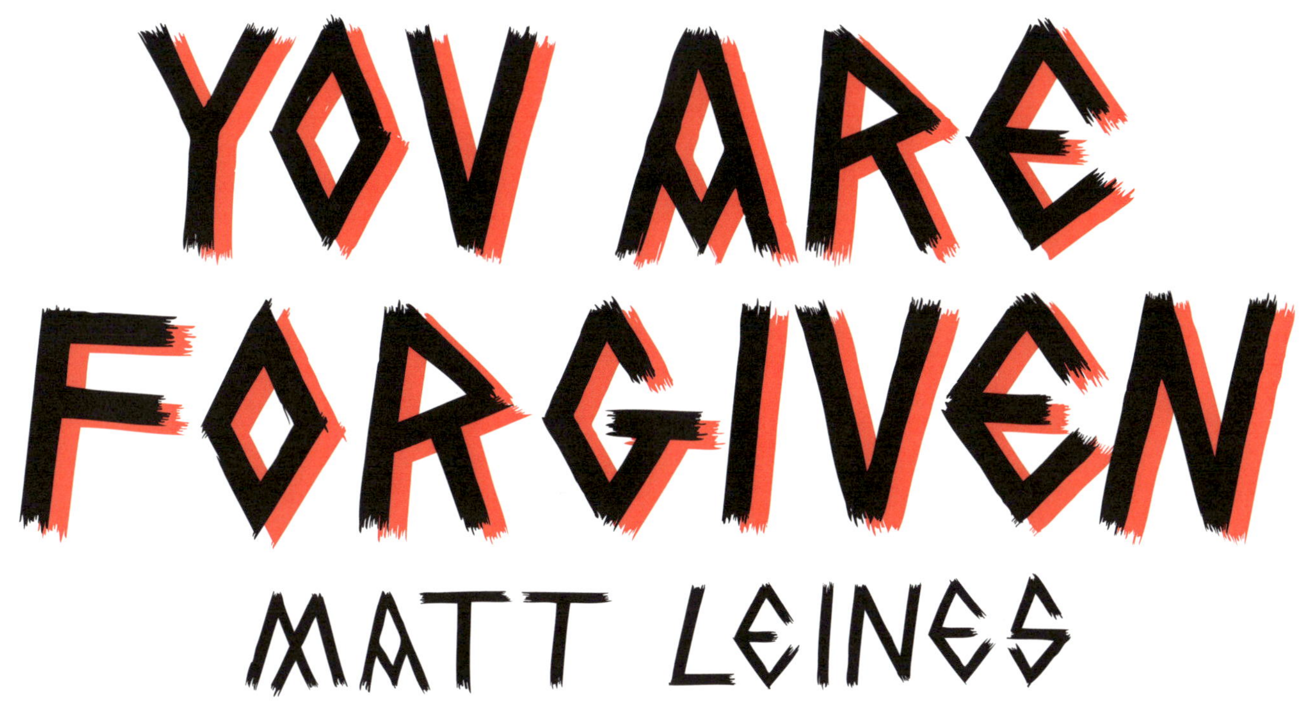

FREE NEWS PROJECTS

First Edition

Free News Projects
1026 Arch Street
Philadelphia, PA 19134
email: info@freenewsprojects.com
www.freenewsprojects.com

First published in the United States of America by
Free News Projects, Publishers

Introduction by Gary Panter
Essay by Taylor McKimens
Executive production by Maximillian Lawrence
Book design by Smyrski Creative
Image retouching by Meg Kemner
Photography by Tom Dubrock, Amy Giunta and Adam Wallacavage
Special thanks to Edmond and Morgan Lawrence

ISBN 0-9776523-5-1
ISBN 978-0-977-65235-8

Printed and Bound in Canada

Available through D.A.P./Distributed Art Publishers
155 Sixth Avenue, 2nd Floor, New York, N.Y. 10013
Tel: (212) 627-1999 Fax: (212) 627-9484.

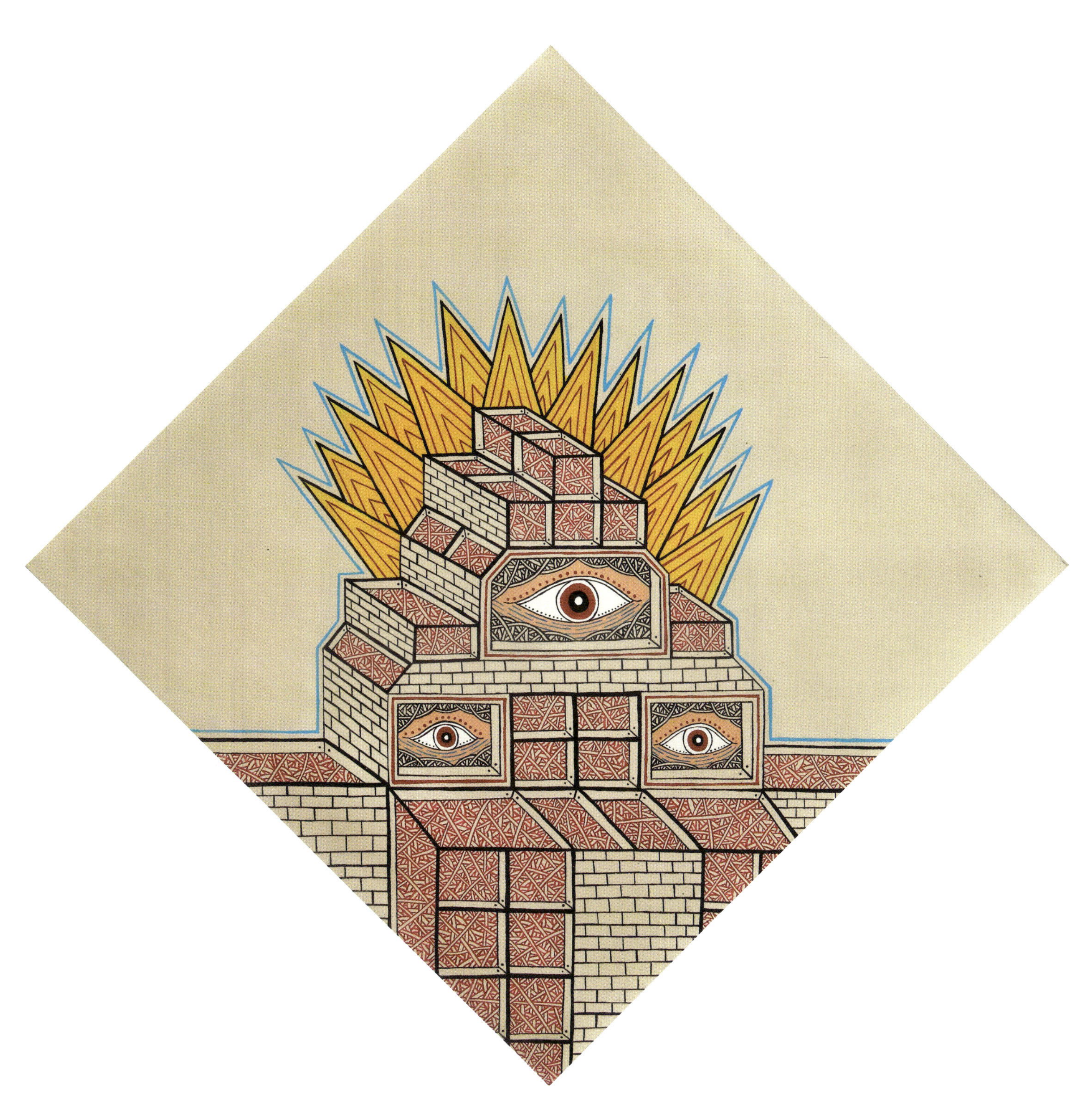

THE CVLTVRE OF MR. LEINES

BY GARY PANTER

The world has gotten so crowded and itchy a lot of us want to get off. But we can't. We can jump only so high. OK. OK. You COULD go into astronaut training and get lucky after 20 years and get off Earth, but you'll have to hold your breath a lot after debarking onto another world.

You can kill yourself, which I heartily do not recommend, because it might turn out very, very, boring, even dull and un-stimulating.

You can sleep all the time and reside in a dream-time world, but as you will find out--if you over-over-sleep your mind starts giving you unpleasant or really boring dreams to prick you back into waking reality on earth with all the itchy people again.

There are those who inhabit game worlds or who dream up worlds. The former, gamers, are cast in a role of hunter slayer quick wily neanderthal shooter mostly by the eighth generation game designers. The verisimilitude increases with memory and the crafts of the new crafters. Shoot. Pile. Burn. You are the hand in someone else's glove. Nice glove? Can you man the glove?

Abusers of hard drugs also escape. Get away you creep. Get a Yoo Hoo. Don't try anything! Get the fuck out of here!

Then, there are the latter mentioned brethren of the gamers, the day dreamers and schemers. The builders of false worlds. That includes most of us, those of us who observe and model our thoughts and aspirations. Or who obsessively rehearse them. To invoke them. To make them more quasi-authentic. This includes such folks as--list makers, model train set builders, dioramists, taxi-dermists, animators, flip-book makers, cinefiles, comic book drawers, short story writers, poets , gravers, gardeners, grotto builders, architects, weavers, baseball trivialists, ceramicists, wood carvers, printmakers, dope smokers, zoo designers, glassblowers, short story writers, stamp collectors, poets, unfo-cussed students staring out windows, kite-flyers, cloud watchers, shadow interpreters, sandwich eaters--all makers of little worlds.

Some of these worlds are fleeting notions, some are careers, some are con-structed of toothpicks , some laboriously wrought of steel, or lines inscribed on paper with ink, or tattooed on extremities. Whatever else they are, they are PHONY AND POWERFUL.

Matt Leines

Often the invented world is a shabby substitute for the detailed richness of our collective material reality. Some implied realities are only lists: baby, egg, flour, wind, phone. As such, they barely exist. You read them--the world blooms open. You stop. The little parachute droops.

Big worlds, little worlds—shiny, dull, phosphorescent, glazed, erratic, monstrous, sophomoric, drunken, pointless, startlingly enlightening fabrications.

Matt Leines' world is very very tidy. A serious and dedicated gardener and team of handy-men all named Matt, stand by, eagle-eyed waiting for a stray leaf to drop. Leaves will drop. An alarm sounds. The truck pulls up quick as a wink and the stray leaf is exiled to a phantom zone. A very tidy world, but with a lot of implied poisonous spiked underbrush and also contrasting implied verdant fields. A synthetic world that implies something beyond what it circumscribes and gains vast glimpsed territory and psychic power thereby.

Matt is mapping the collective art of a none-existent tribe in a no-mans-land far away. Exotic and invincible. A magnanimous people, yet possessed of a fierce and independent spirit, forged and tempered by age after age of adversity or calm, calamity and advantage. Centuries of plenty and eons of famine—everlasting warfare and subterfuge. Maybe he will tell us everything about these nations and maybe not. Yet, we can learn much about them by observing the artifacts produced by so great and tenacious peoples.

A fleet of wood and steel sailing ships is inferred. Also a state-sized corral of yaks and dromedaries. Probably a lavish palace housing tens of competing veil dancing schools adrift with incense and fragrant ointments. Or maybe I have added a room, accidently that is not in the plan. Time and Mr. Leines will fill us in.

CVLT OF DETAIL
BY TAYLOR McKIMENS

There's no small-talking with Matt Leines. He's a stickler for the details… you're gonna need to be able to back up what you say at all times. There'll be no partaking in mindless chatter. No skipping steps, no broad strokes of any sort. It's all in the details.

His memory for detail seems to be an intricately honed machine. No doubt it is not a slick new computer, but instead a complex and mysterious organization. A faction of beings performing an extensive detail gathering ritual as old as time. It is not made up of enslaved workers. All involved have pledged allegiance to the cause. It's a cult of detail. These beings wear strange tunics and robes covered in inexplicable patterns, with images that denote their place in the larger network of devotees to the mission of compiling data. They are constantly making notes of specifics in a peculiar geometric language, and filing them carefully away in a sacred yet easily accessible vault. There they'll sit, waiting to be instantly put into action to clear up Leines' disagreements amongst friends about which color of tights the Japanese wrestler Tiger Mask wears, exactly when that Springsteen song was recorded, or what those unintelligible Misfits lyrics are. The detail cult is always on call, religiously filing away new details and retrieving others. There are no details too small, none too trivial. It's this same sacred vault that contains the endless files of various diamonds, half circles, mini lines and microscopic dots that will be compiled into the super condensed fields of details that make up each of his drawings. Enough microscopic zig-zags and diagonals to fill vast amounts of pictorial space. The flow of pattern variations is unrelenting.

That fanatical quality defines Matt's drawings. They are intricate continuations of artwork he may have made as a child after watching G.I. Joe or He-Man cartoons, where he would likely devise his own evil characters that were so much cooler than the ones on TV. But now these creations have progressed to such a sophisticated and fantastic level. These new characters are light years beyond anything seen on even the most bizarre episode of He-Man. If Matt had been a concept artist creating wrestler identities for the WWF, he would have no doubt been fired for creating inconceivably outlandish characters. In his wrestling federation, rather than having wrestlers wear glitter robes and make-up, they would be forced to reconfigure their heads into severe geometric shapes made of blocks rather than flesh. The number of functional eyes would have to drastically change, as well as the number of mustaches. When injured in the ring, they may need to bleed in equal sized symmetrical goblets of red white and black. Chances are fair that they'll have a limb replaced with a lightning bolt or a rhombus, and it's also possible that they'll need to be able to simultaneously ride on the back of a mutated bear and command a legion of 1,000 stubble faced clouds. There is just no wrestling promoter that is getting behind that. Good thing too, instead he pumps these things straight into his drawings without restrictions.

Matt is relentlessly inventing extraordinary characters and the scenarios that envelop them. The imagery has the strangely familiar look of medieval or archaic artwork. But as much as it appears to have been unearthed in some archeological dig in the ruins of an ancient lost civilization wrought with mysterious powers and gods, very little of it is directly referencing any specific historical artworks or imagery. The intricate line work and patterning lends a timeless quality which is then shaken up by a clash with subject matter that seems to reference multiple times and dimensions.

A look through one of his sketchbooks is a mind dissolving experience. Each page you look at zaps the last page from your memory and impairs your ability to prepare for the jolt of the next. You are blasted by a flood of his ideas, each one seeming fully formed. While turning pages you'll notice the extreme rarity of the failed sketches that usually populate artists' sketchbooks. His sketches are completed with such an accuracy that makes you wonder if his detail cult is sometimes calling the shots, and he's simply carrying out their orders. If you were to ask him, he'd surely complain to you about how bad they are. And when he carries his ideas out on a larger scale, it becomes apparent what his original intentions were. Even as the work becomes larger, the intense patterning remains miniscule. It's as if the whole reason to even make large work is to just create some more room to pack in more detail.

Whatever it is that drives Matt Leines to continue to spew dynamic images of gods, skeletons, beasts and men, and mercilessly abuse all those pen tips filling in the microscopic details, may remain a mystery. But if there is some cult in his head calling the shots, let's pray that they just stick with the pens and paint as a means to conquer.

8

Matt Leines

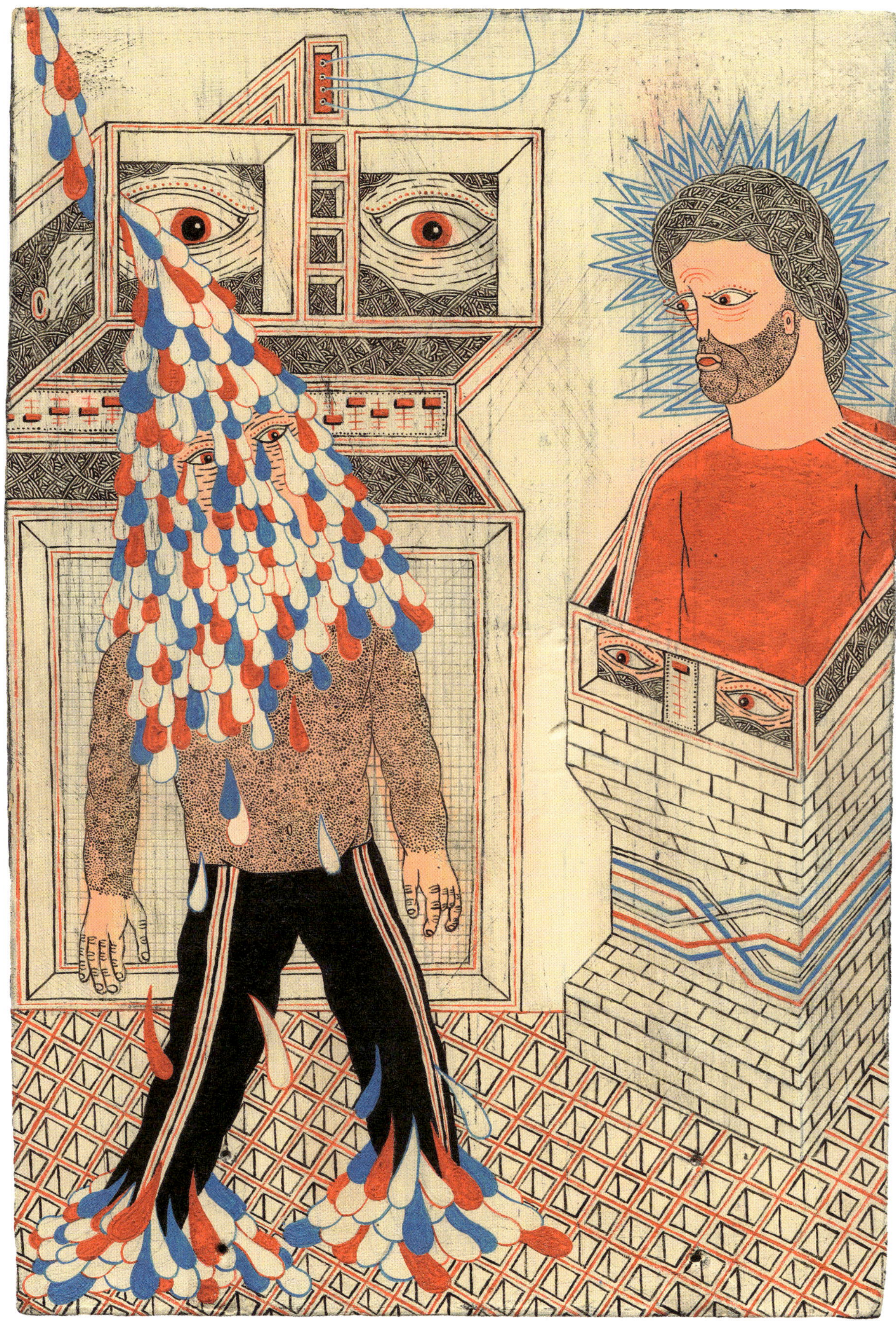

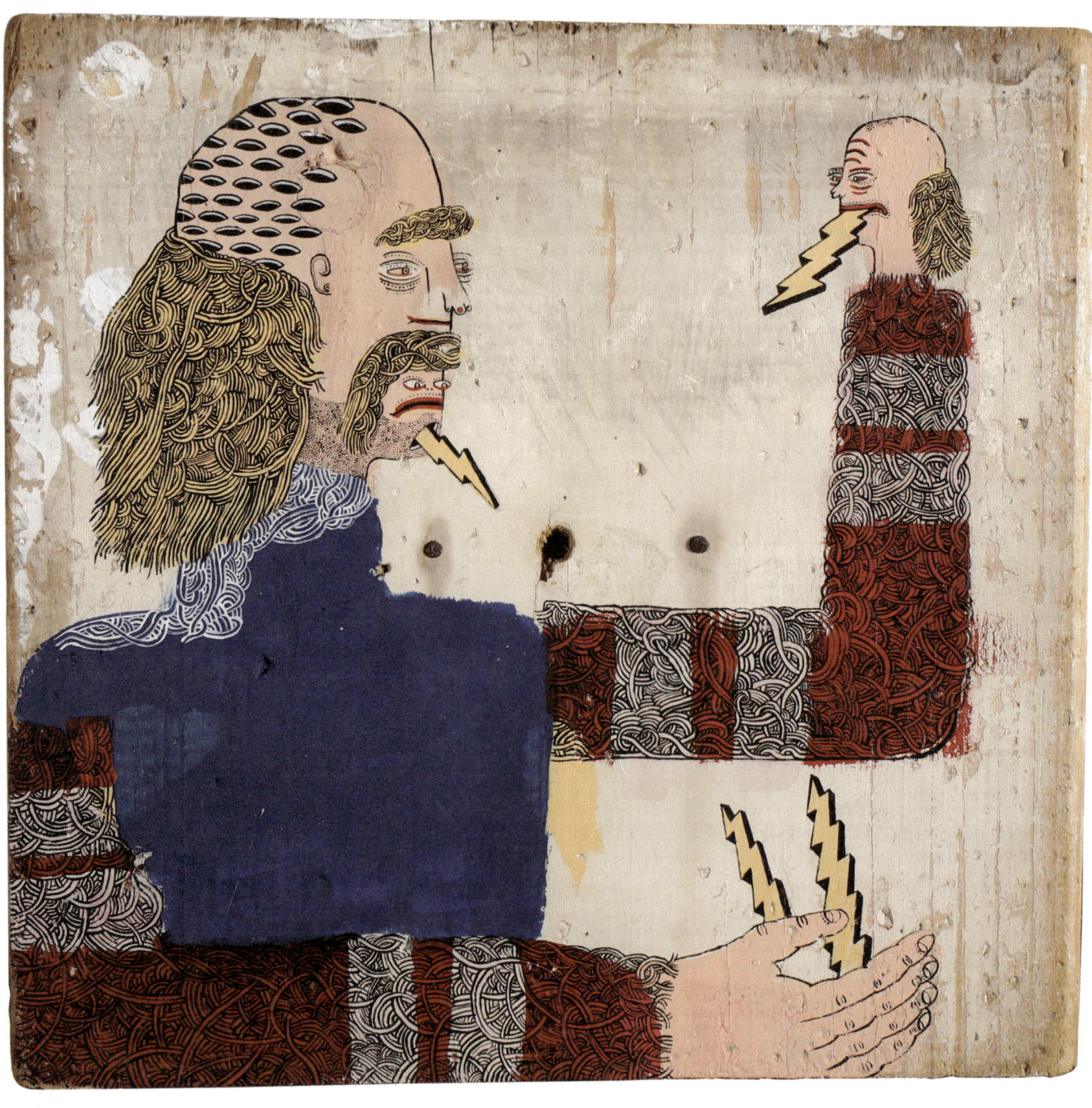

Matt Leines

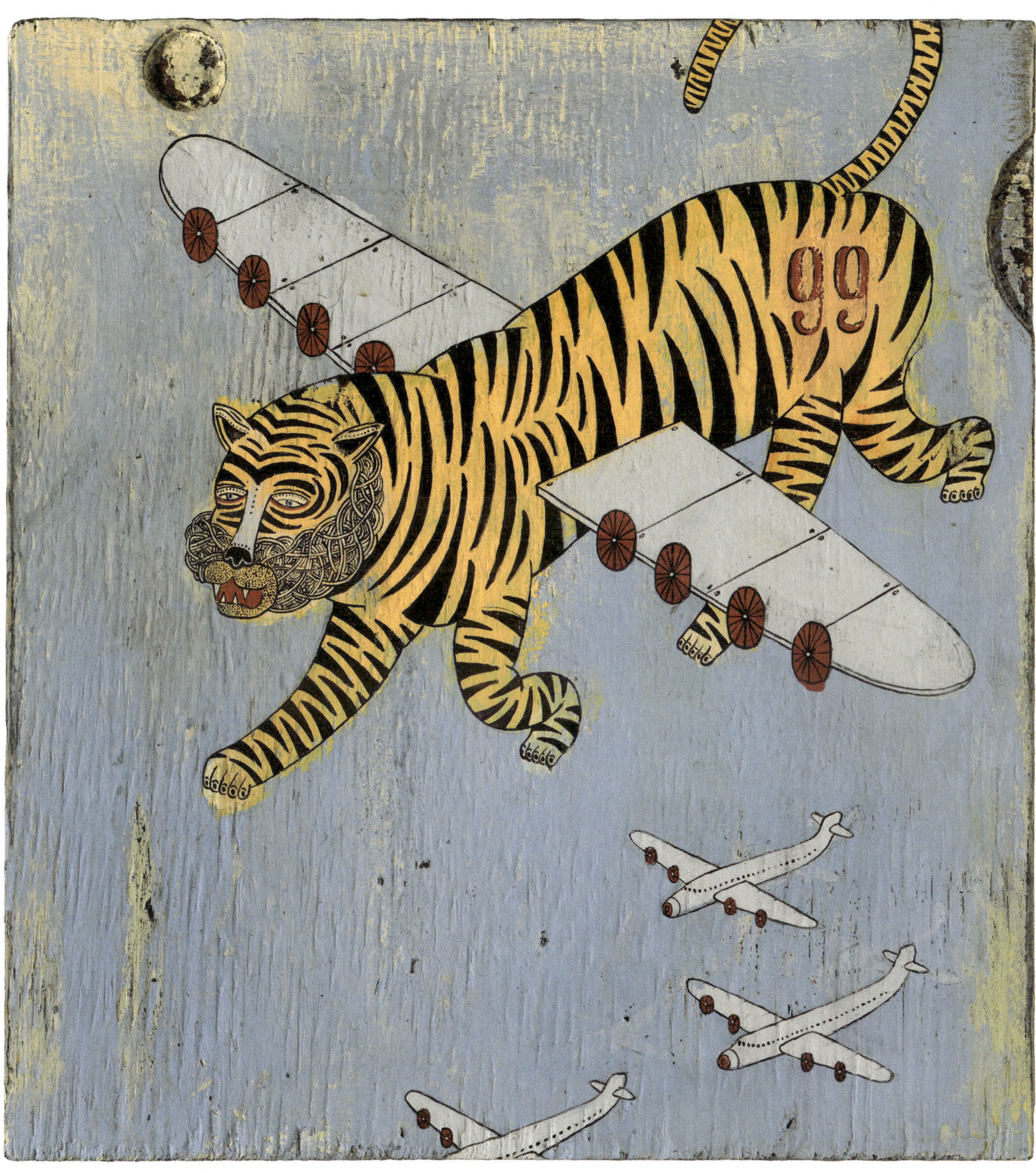

You Are Forgiven

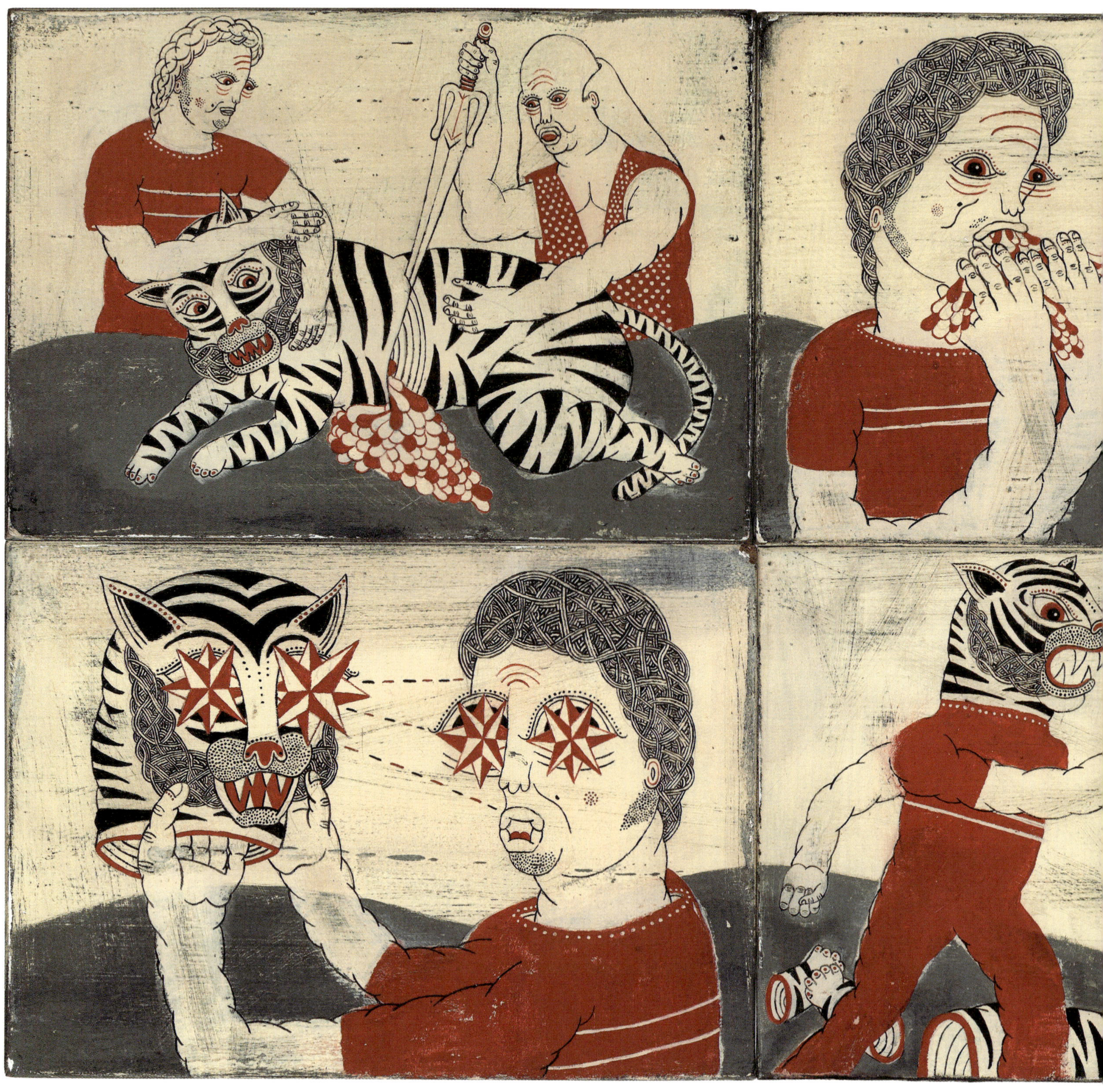

Matt Leines

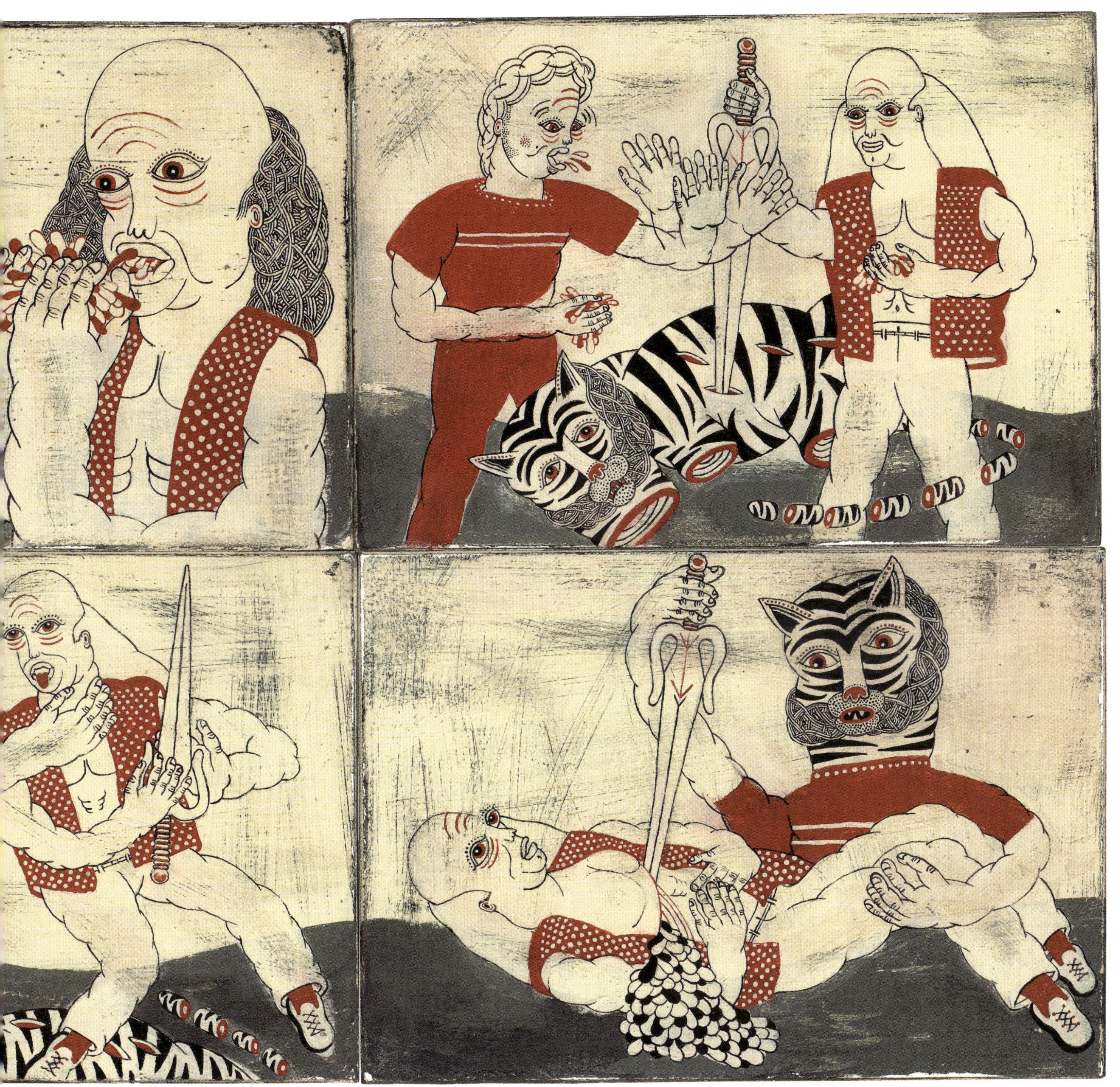

You Are Forgiven

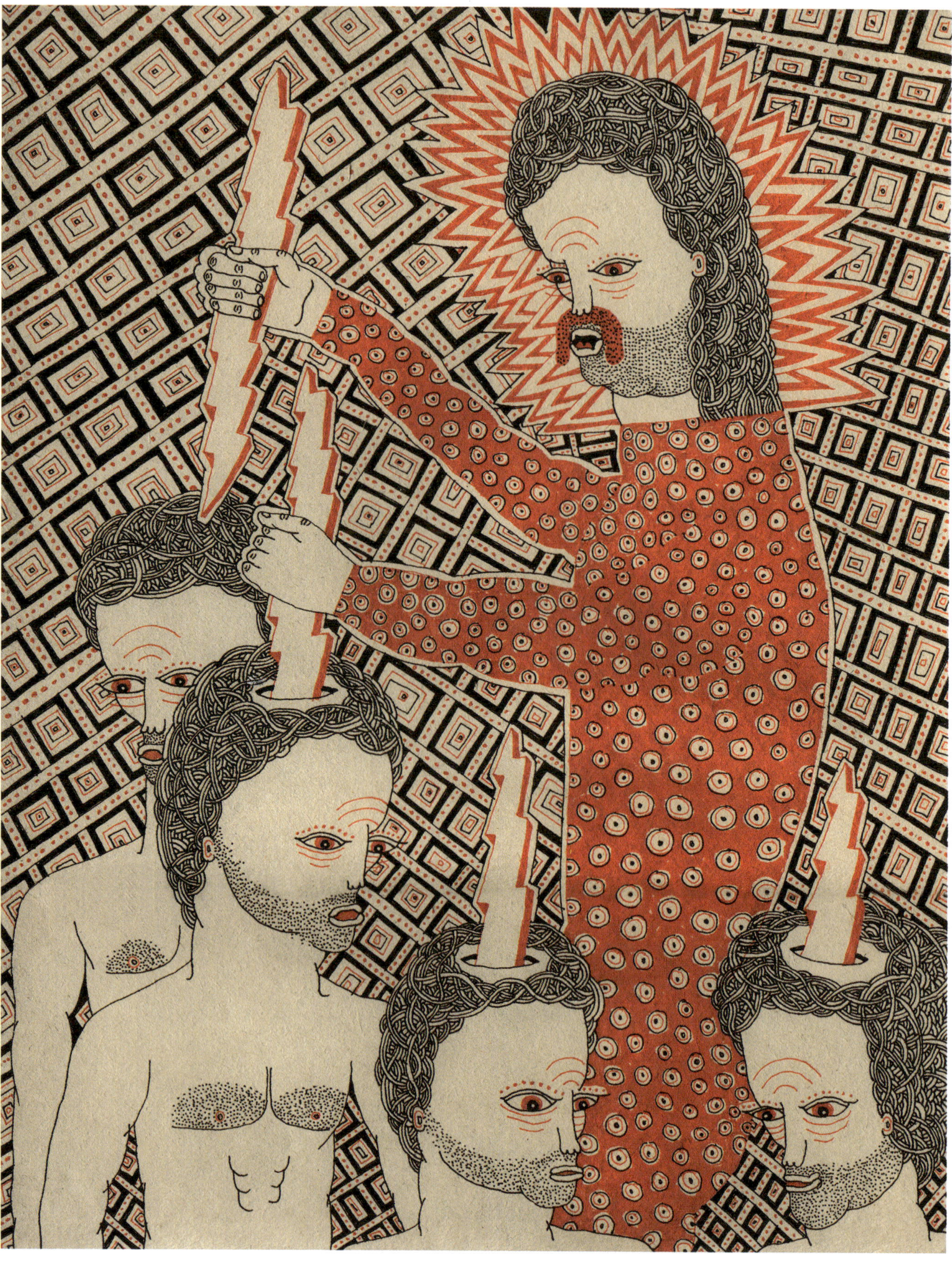

Matt Leines

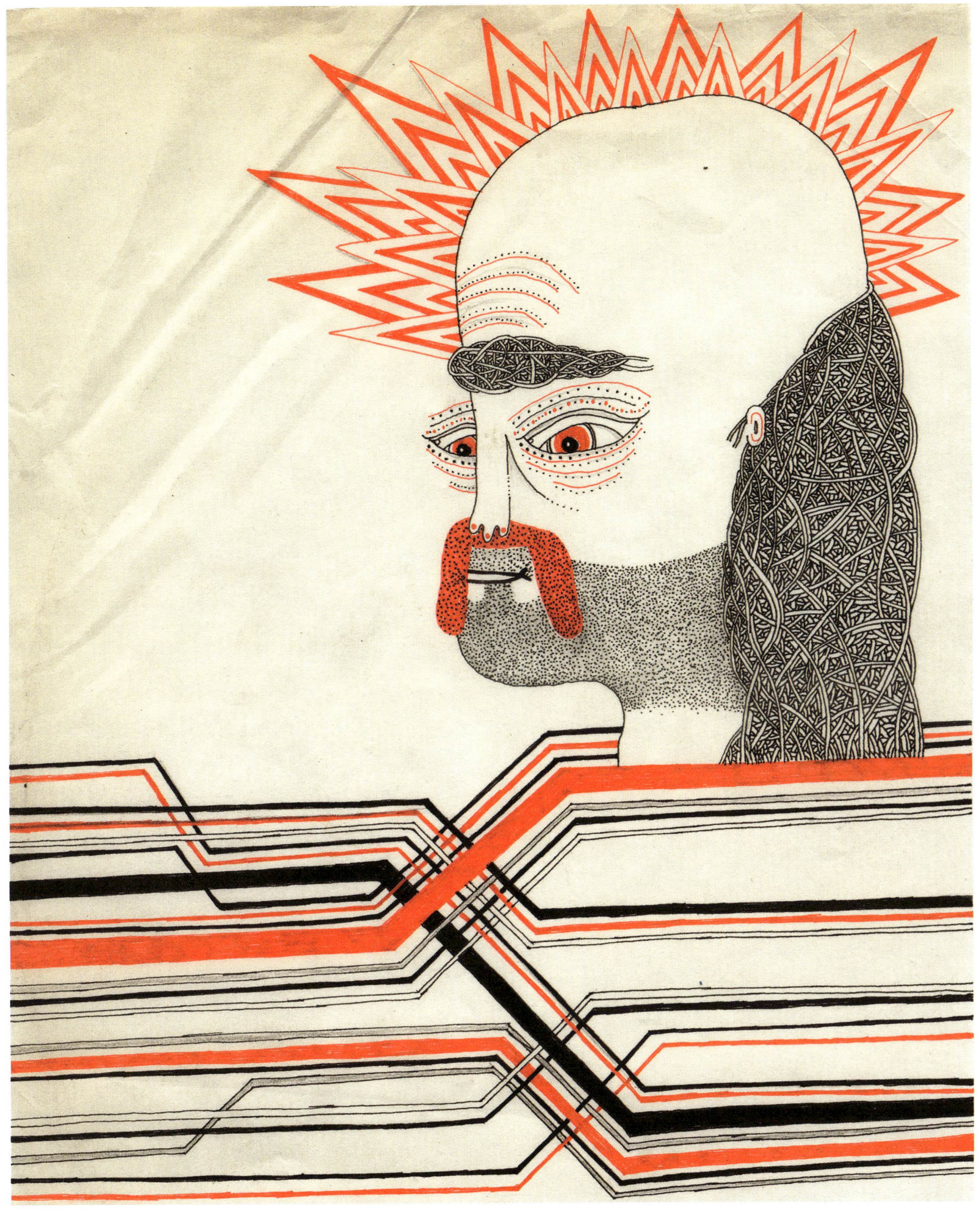

You Are Forgiven

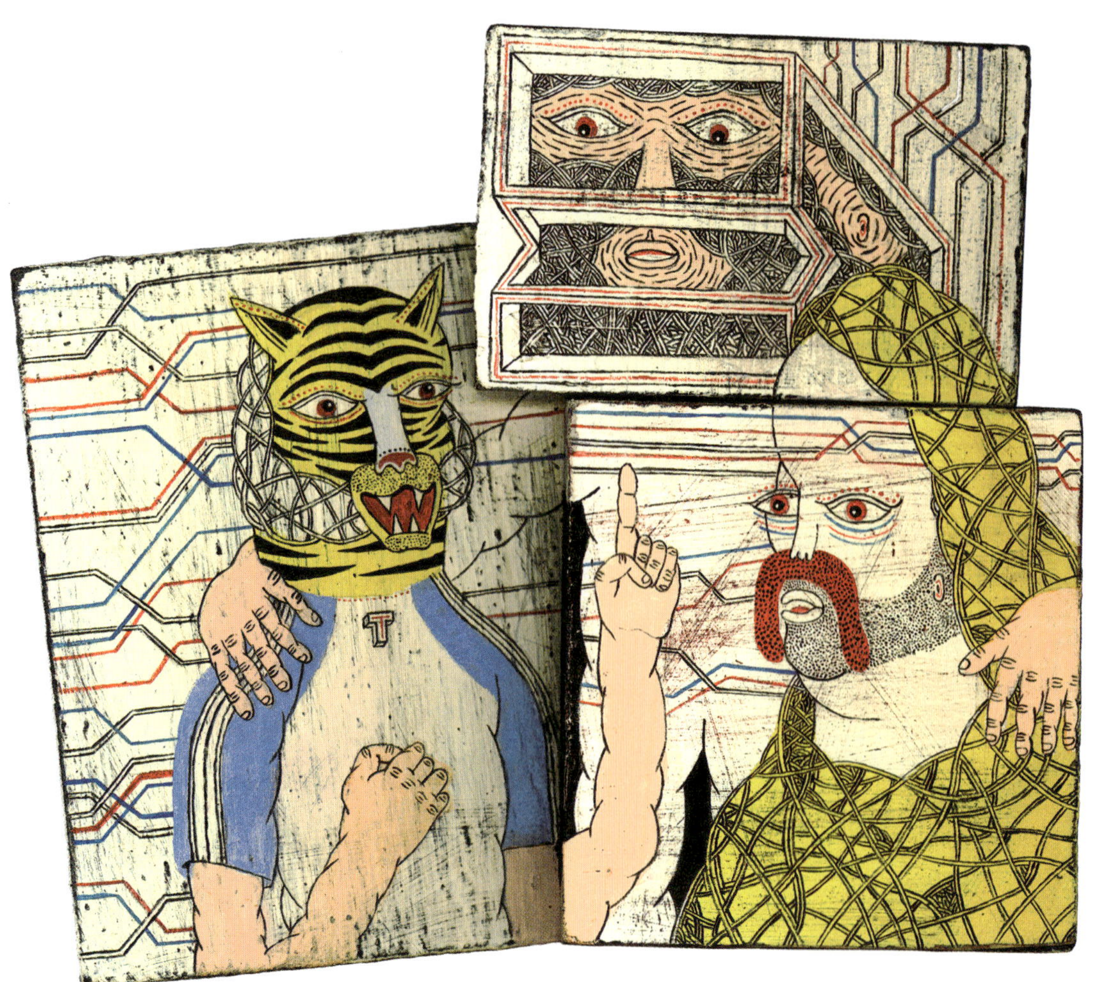

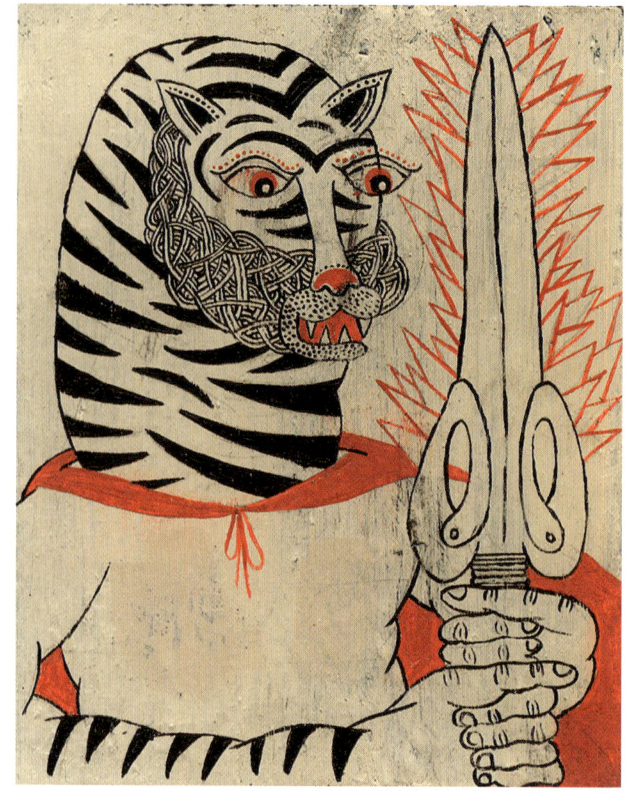

Matt Leines

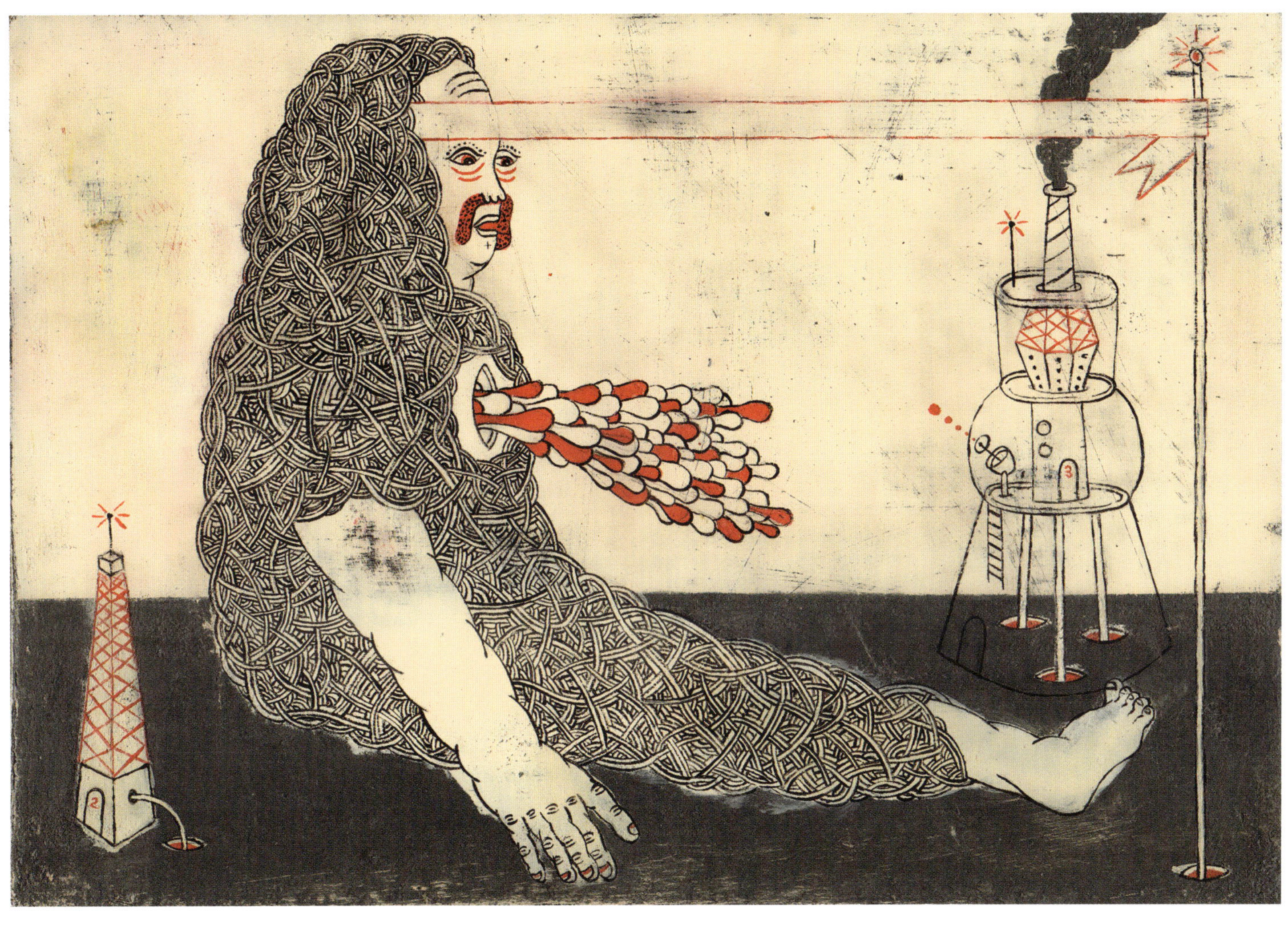

You Are Forgiven

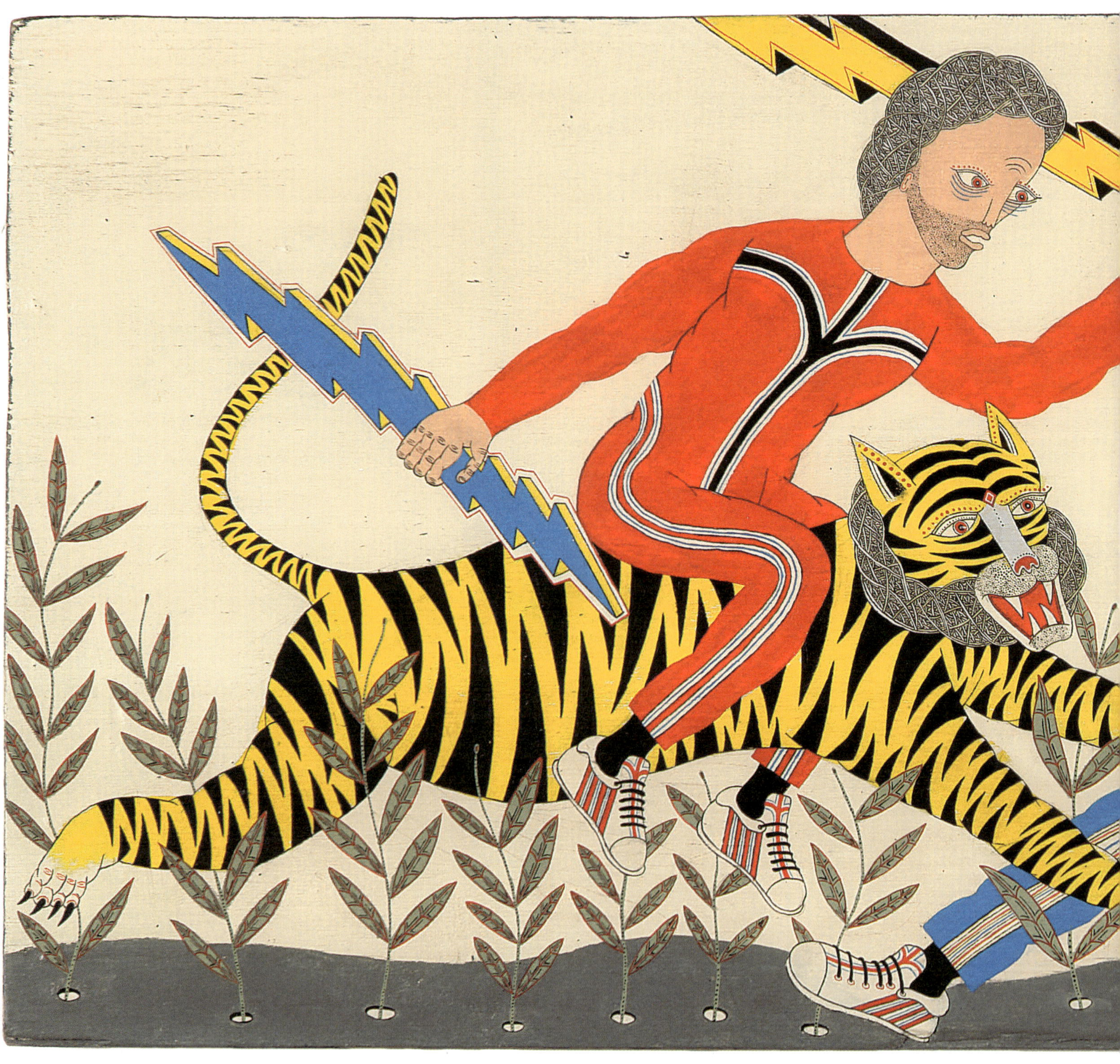

Matt Leines

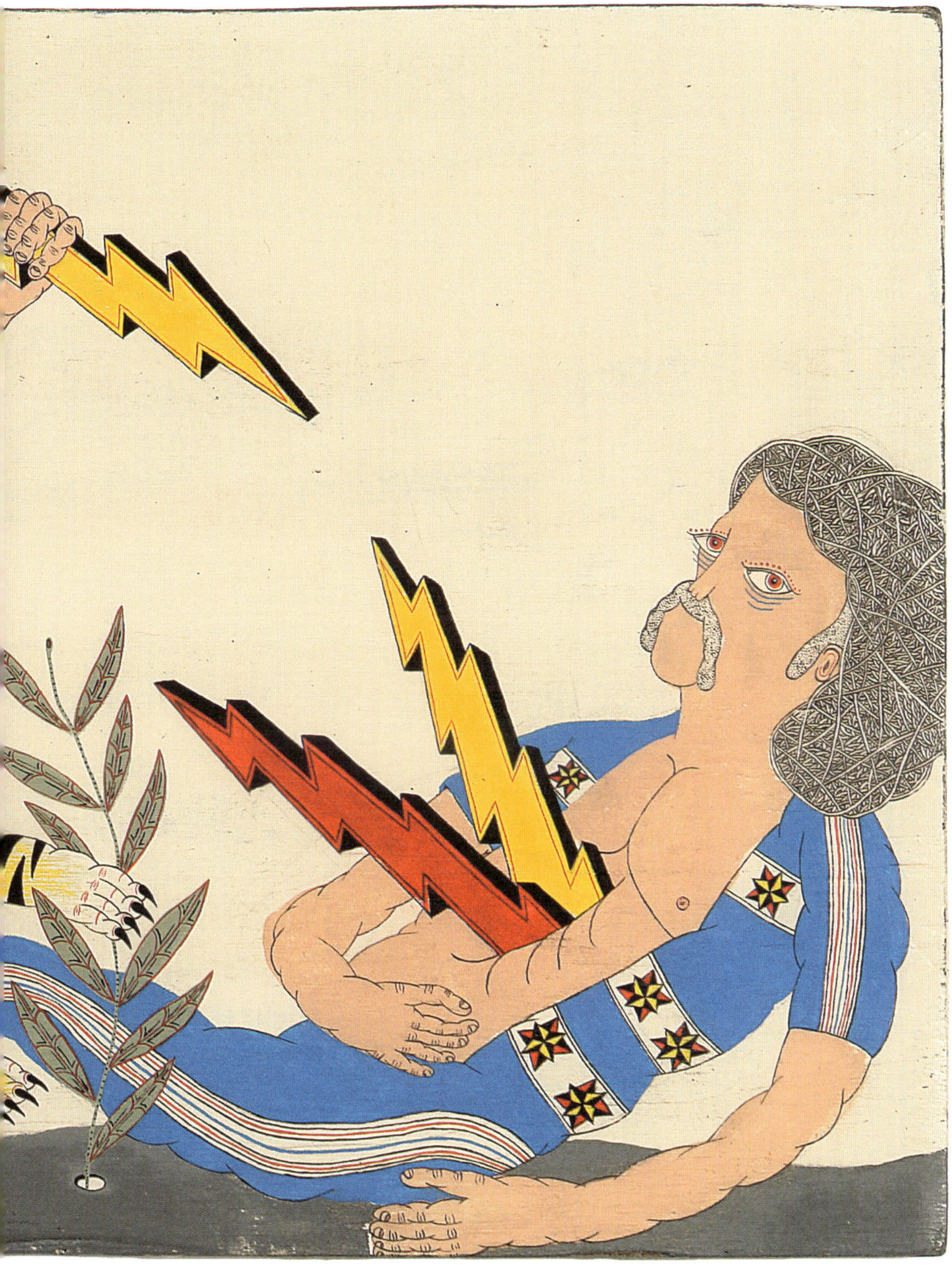

You Are Forgiven

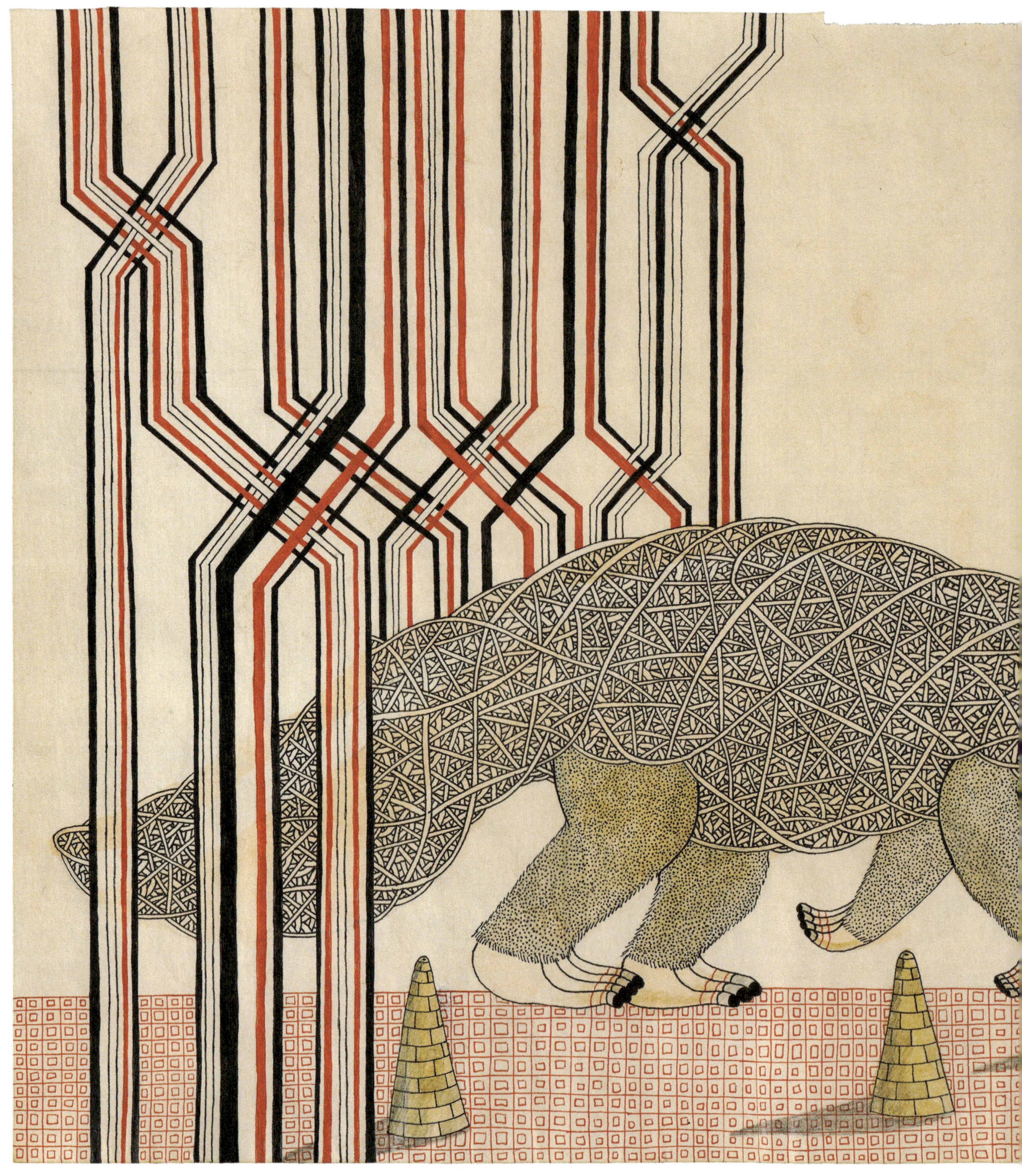

Matt Leines

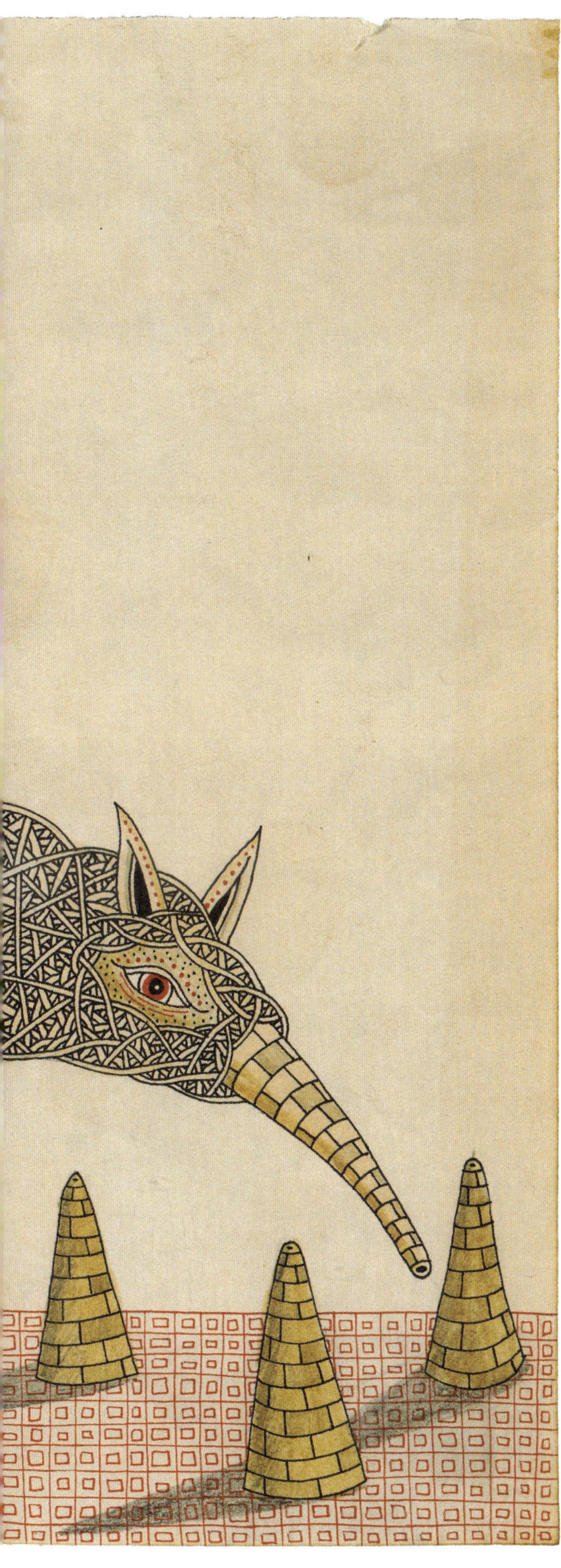

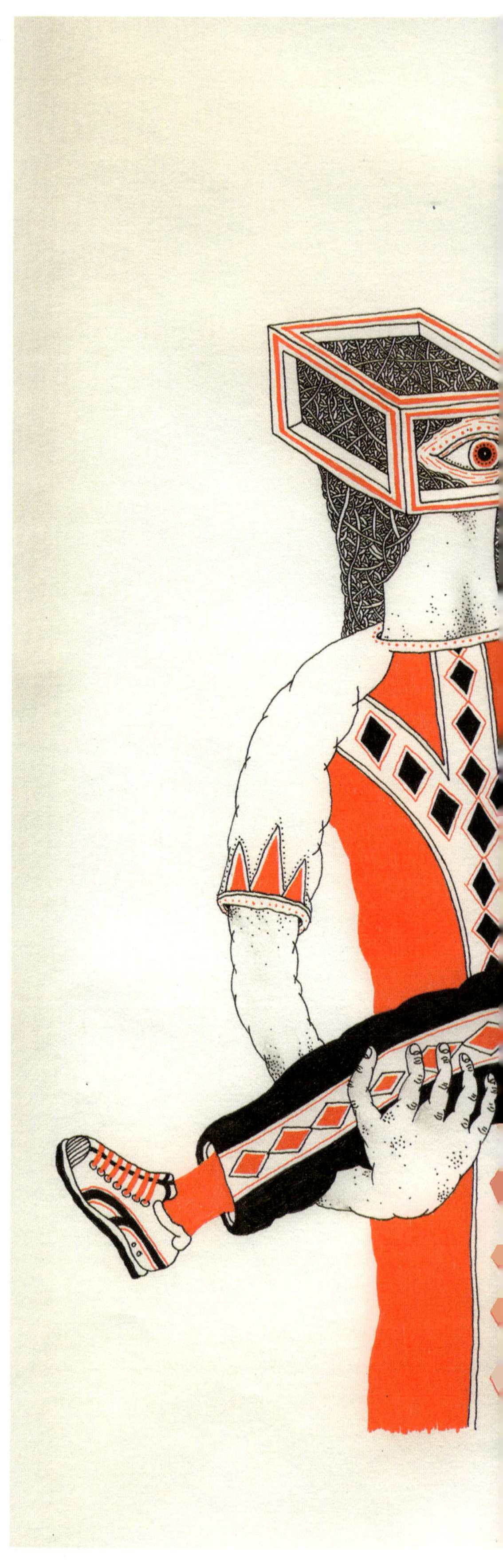

Matt Leines

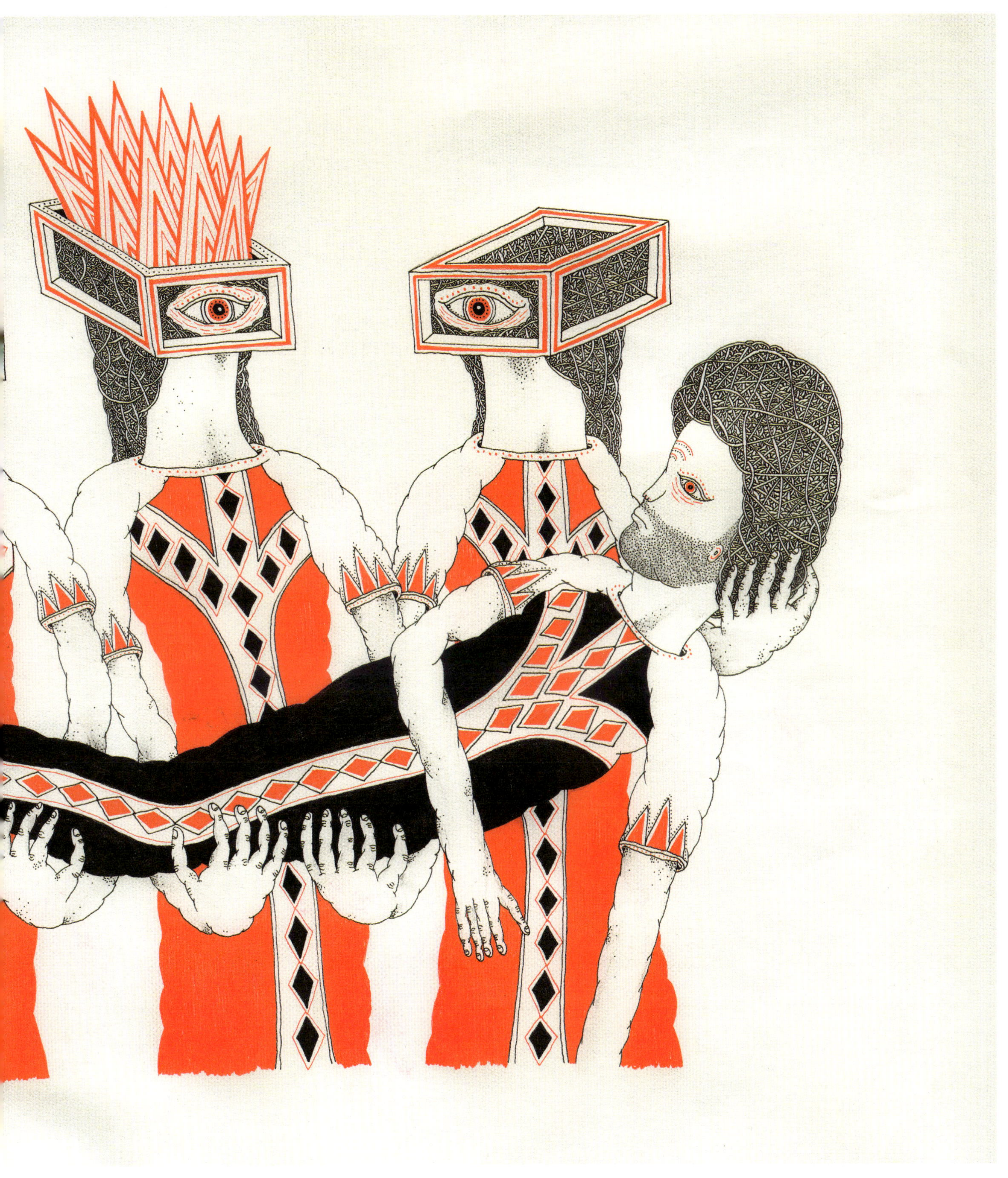

You Are Forgiven

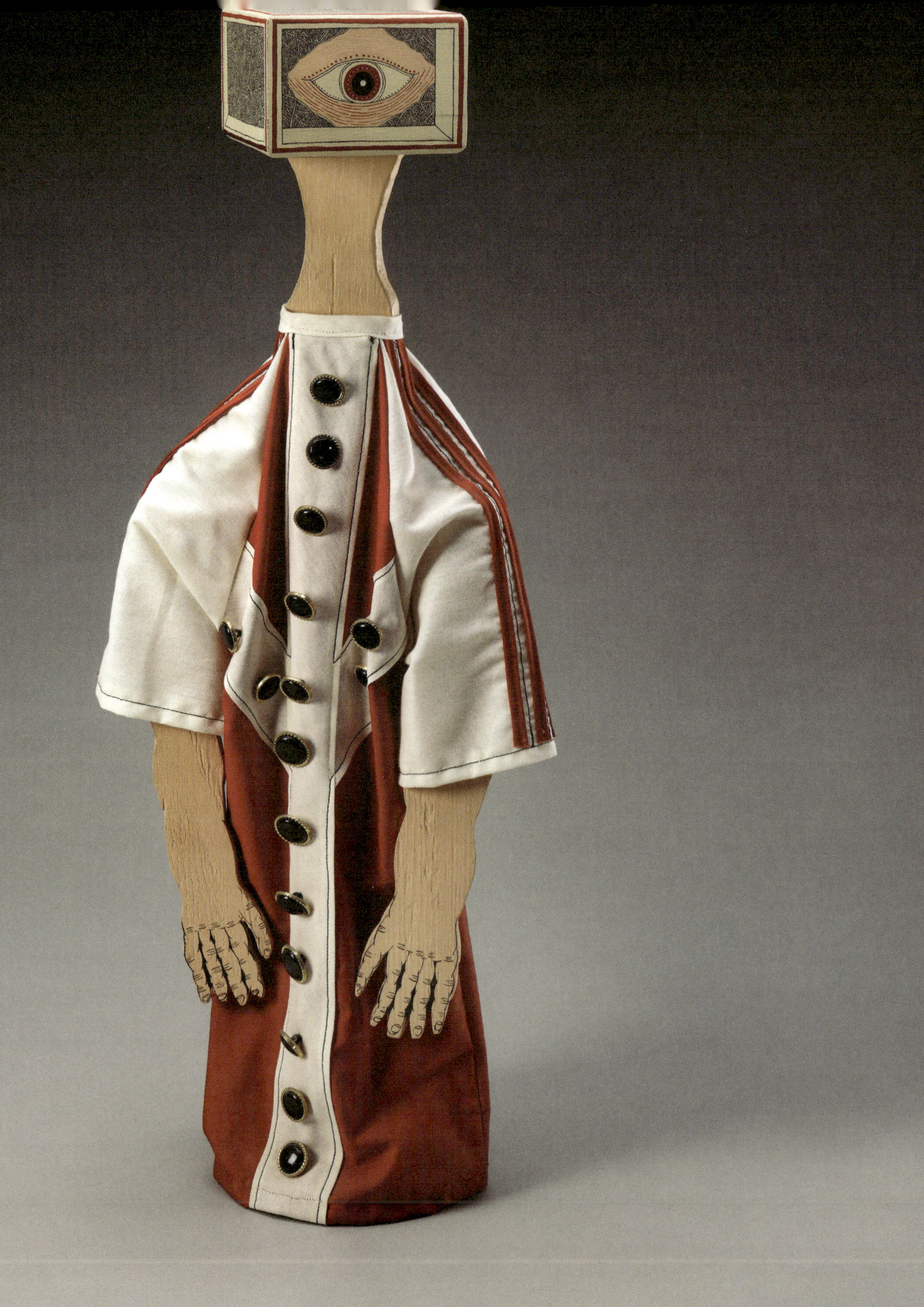

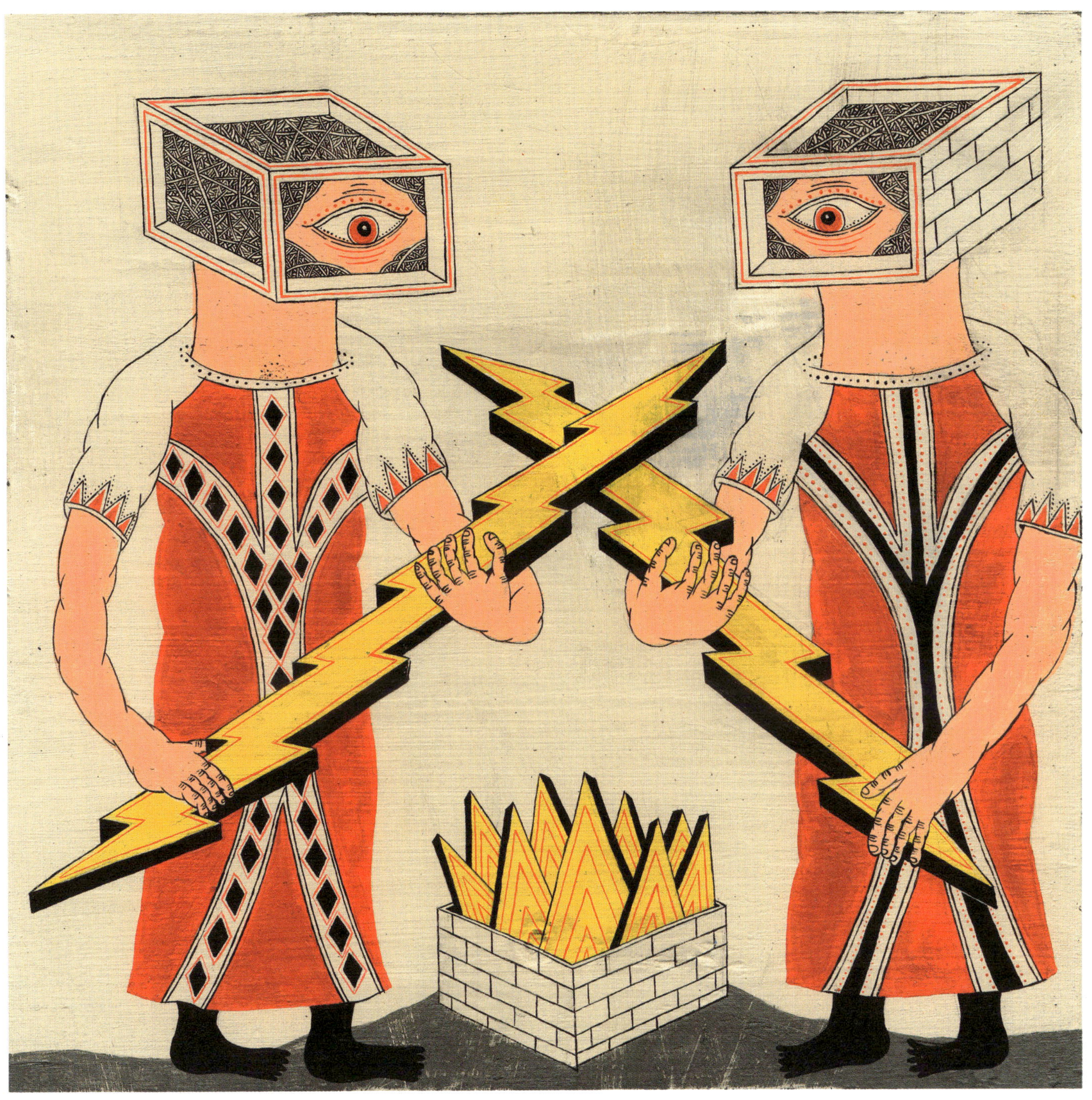

You Are Forgiven

Matt Leines

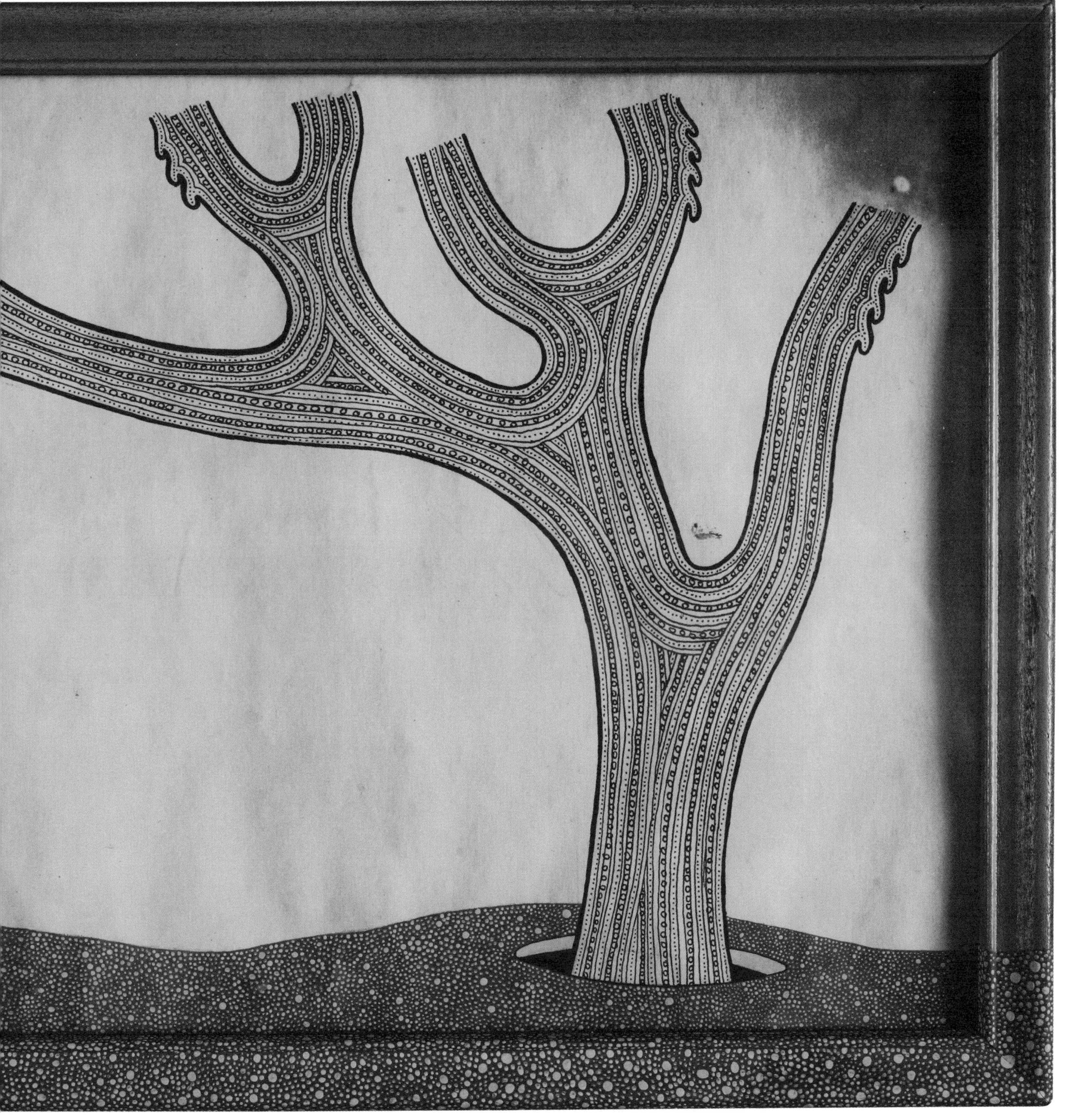

You Are Forgiven

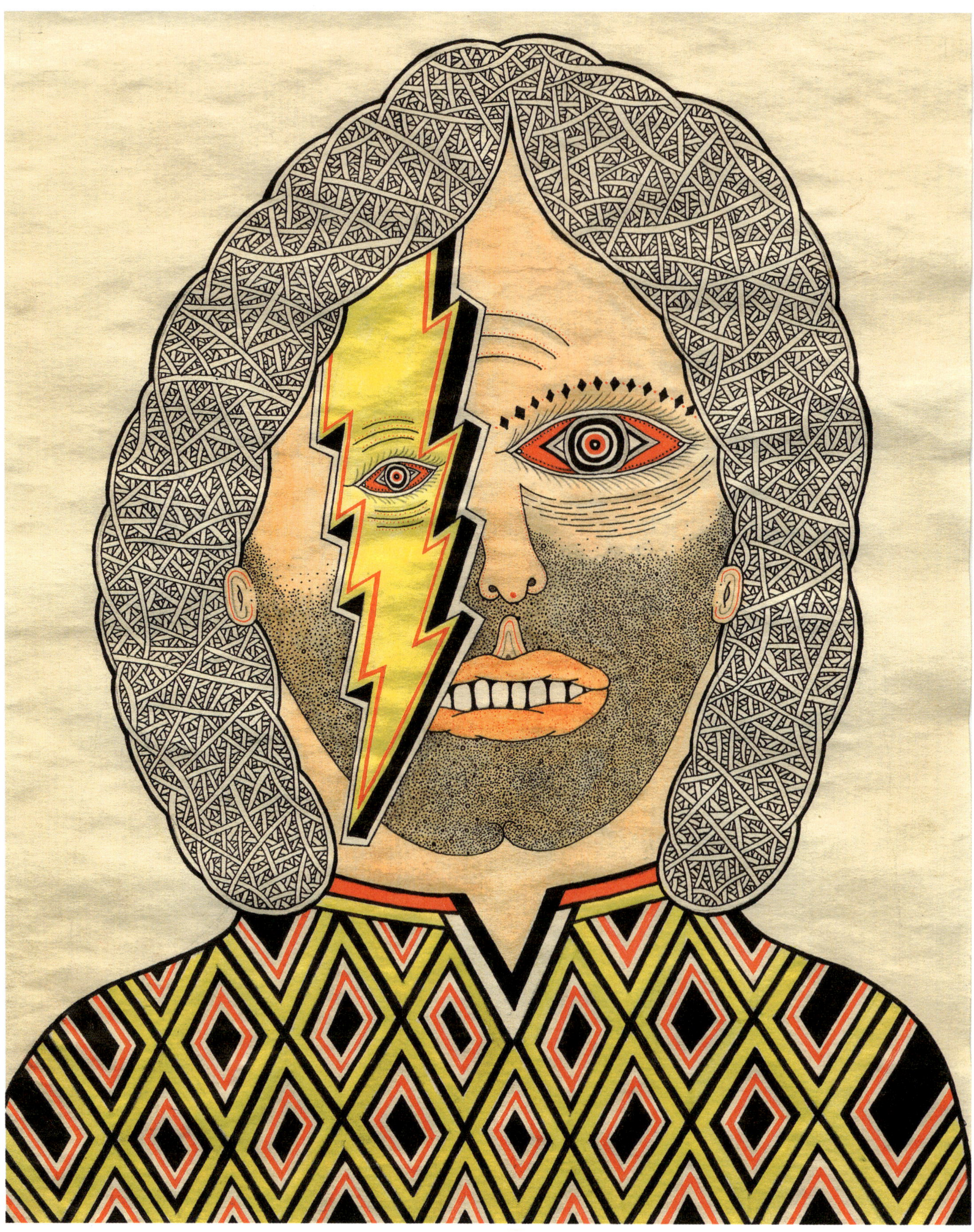

Matt Leines

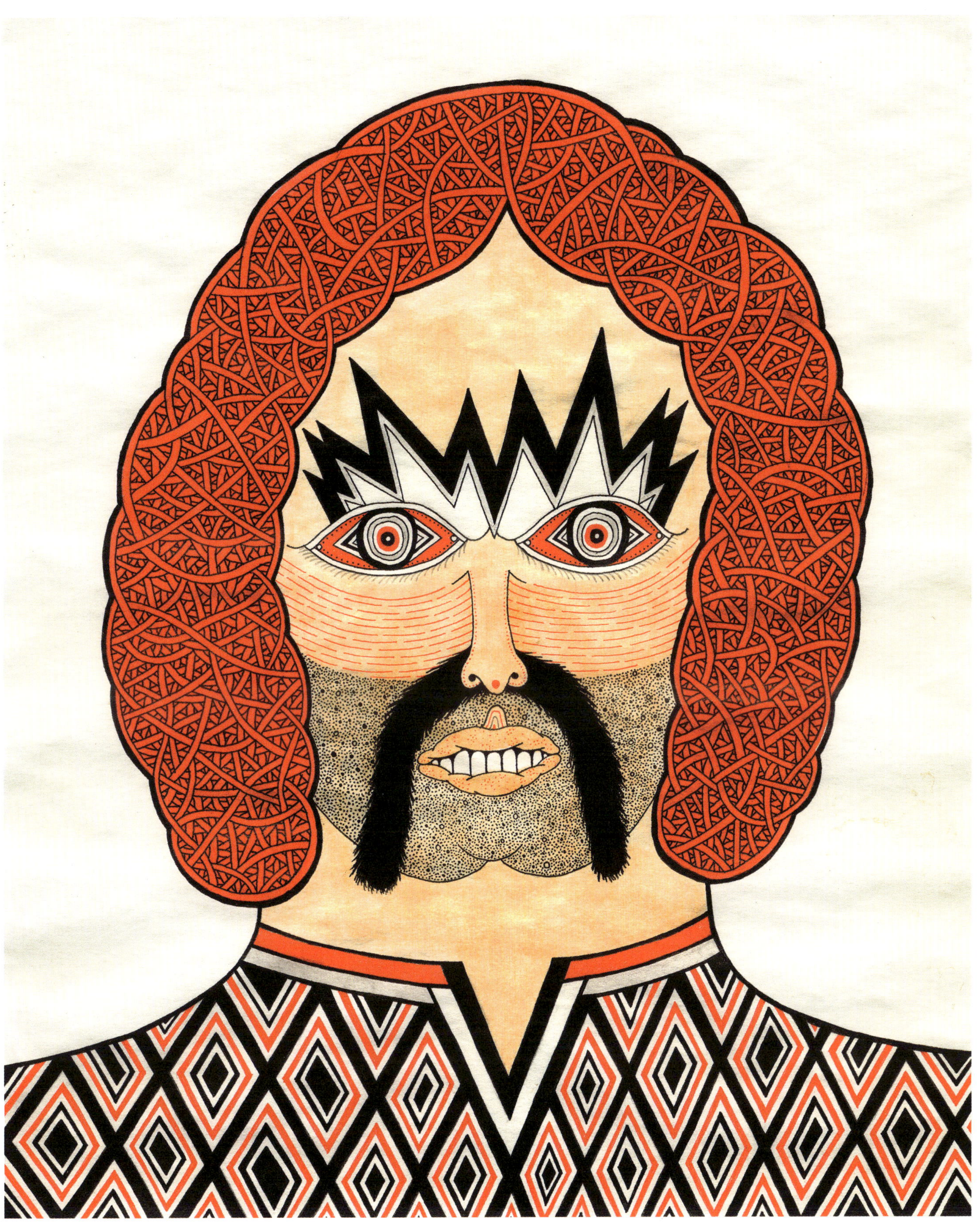

You Are Forgiven

30

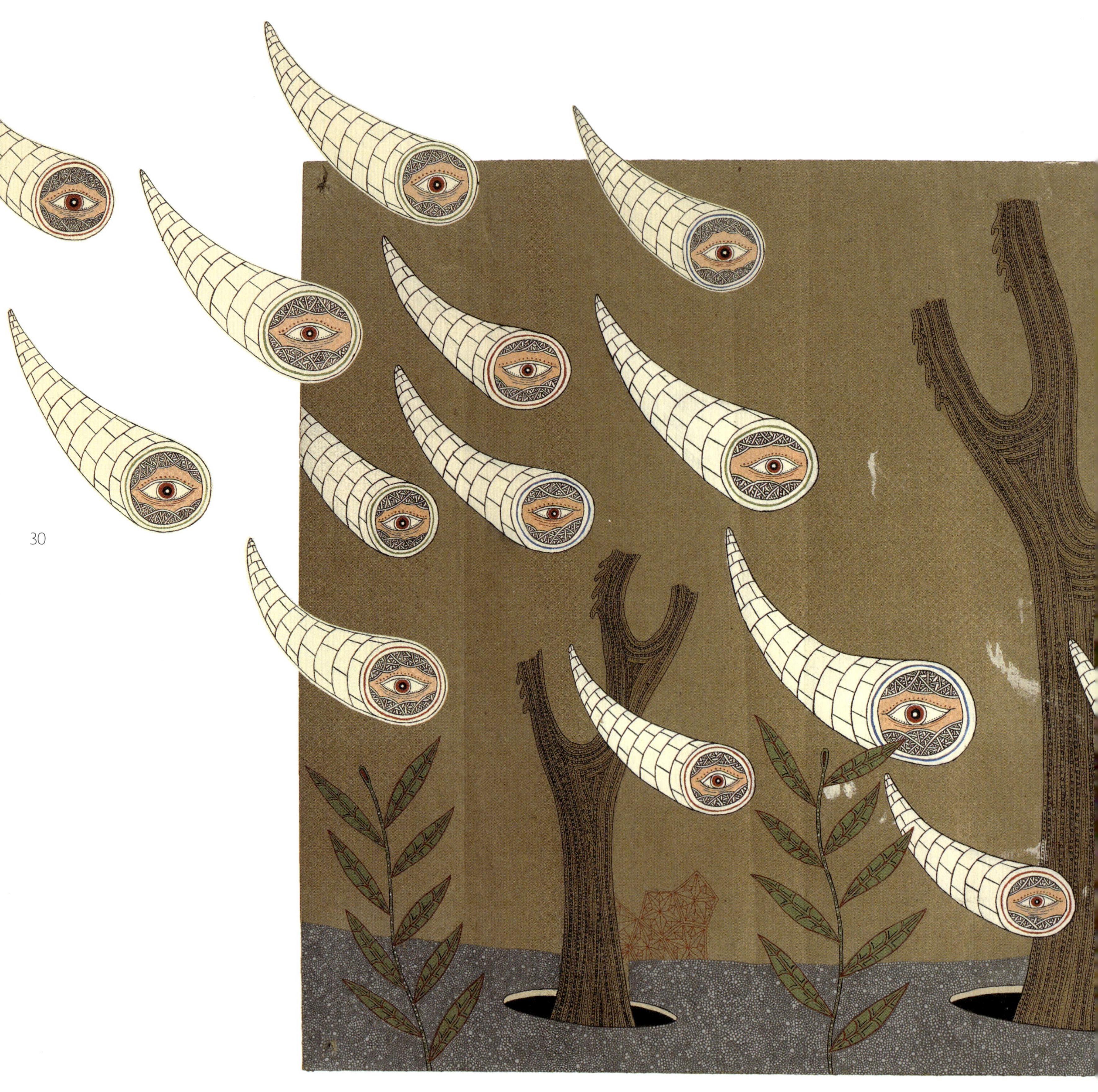

Matt Leines

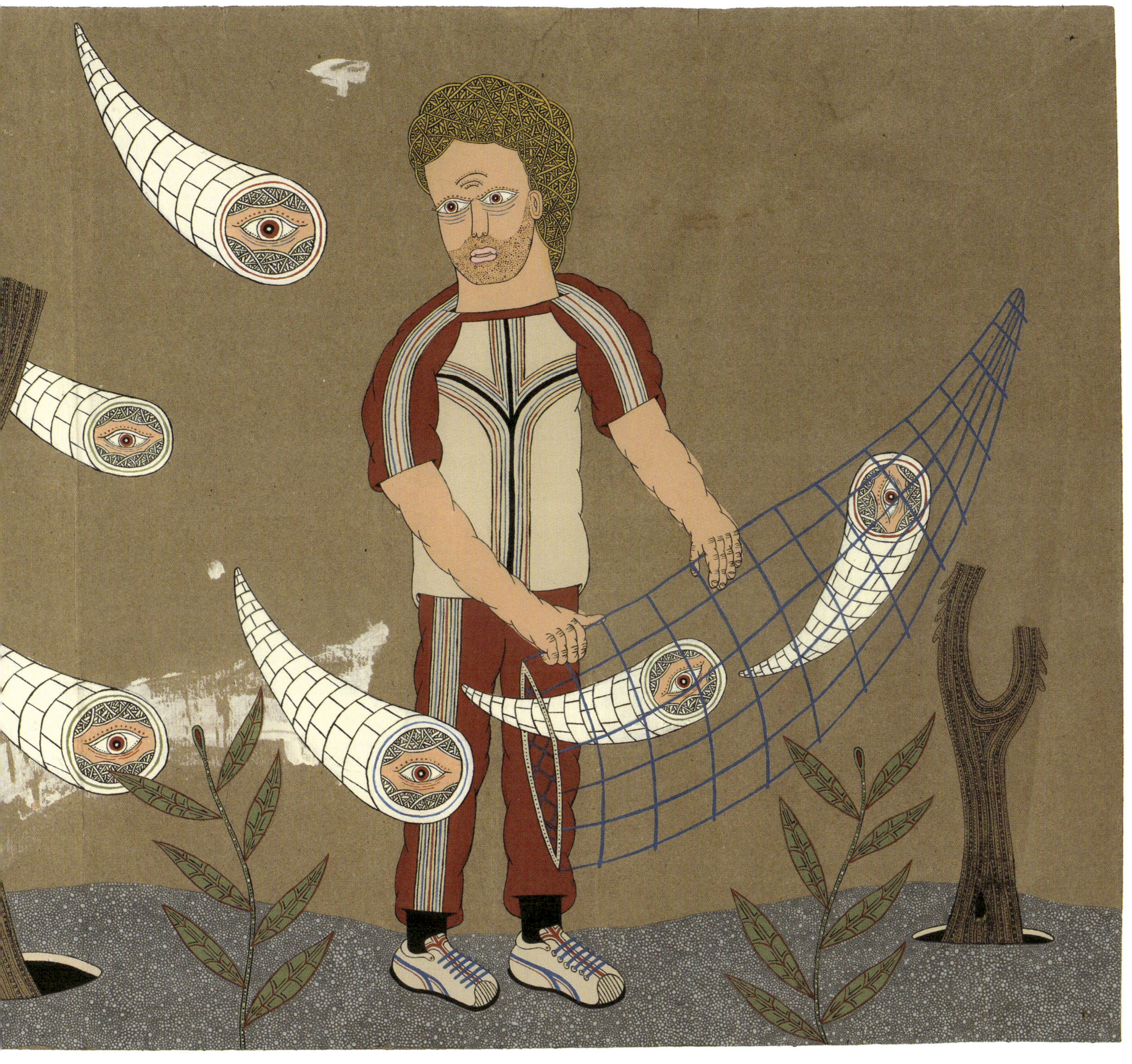

You Are Forgiven

Matt Leines

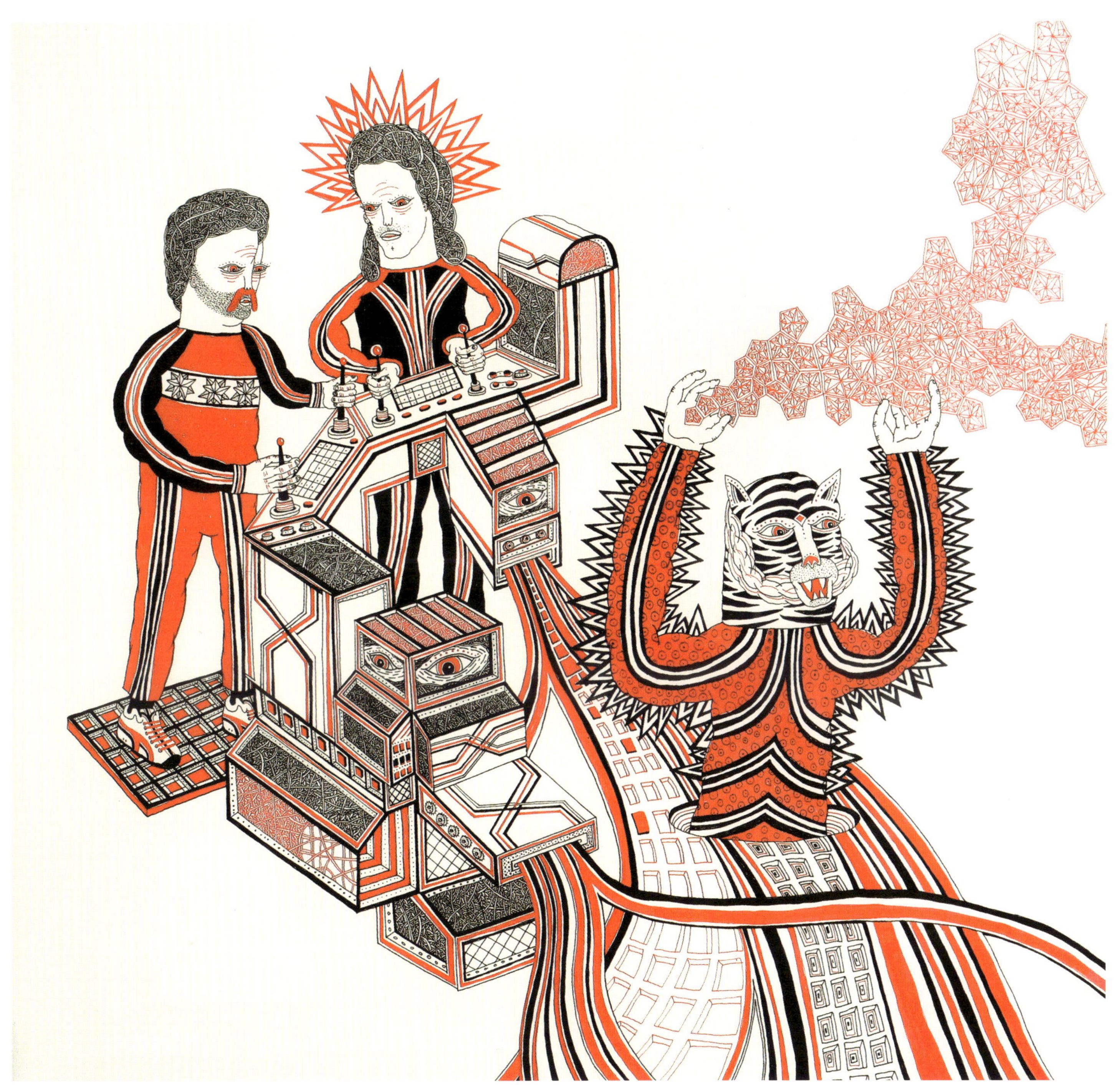

You Are Forgiven

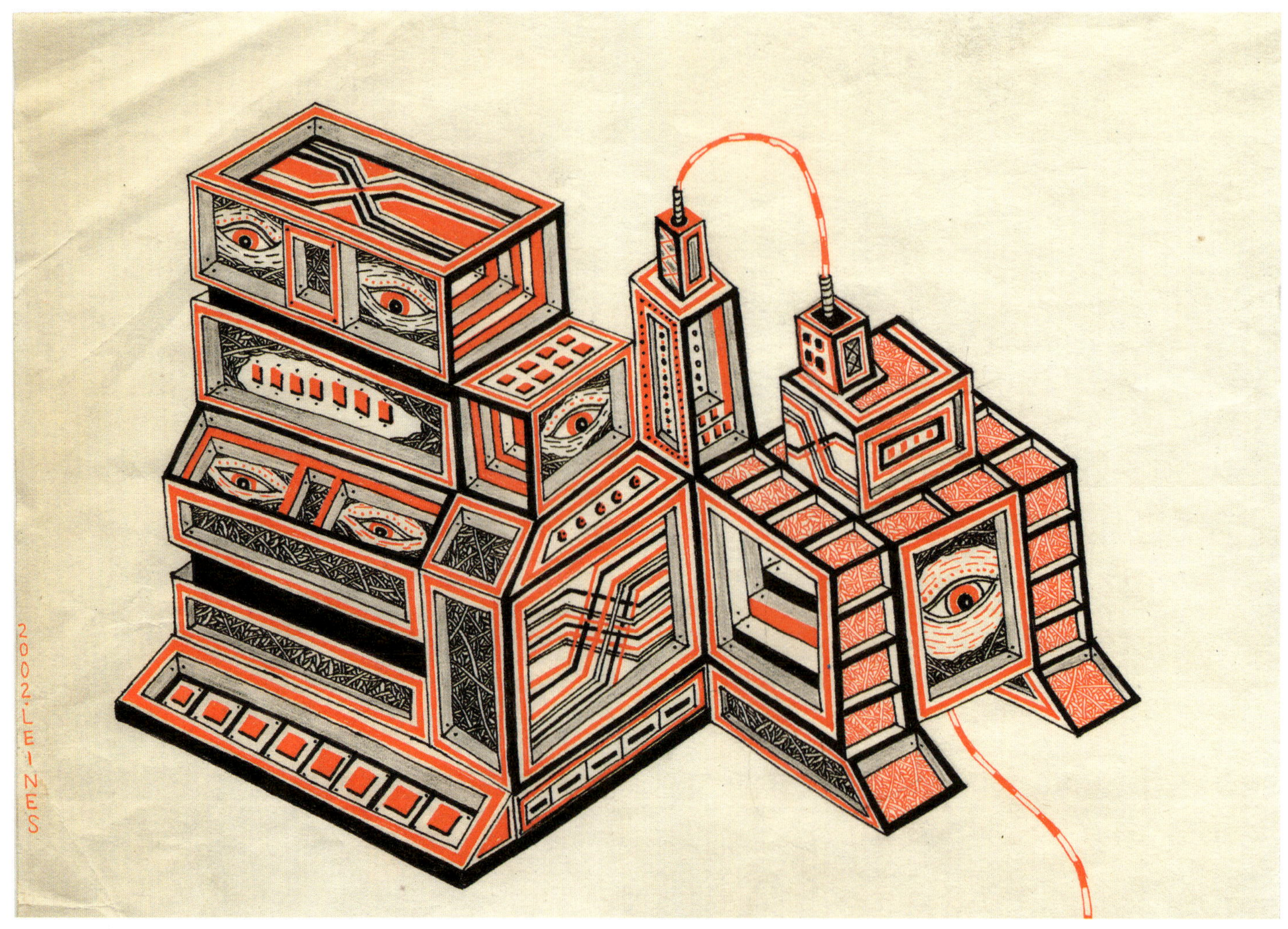

Matt Leines

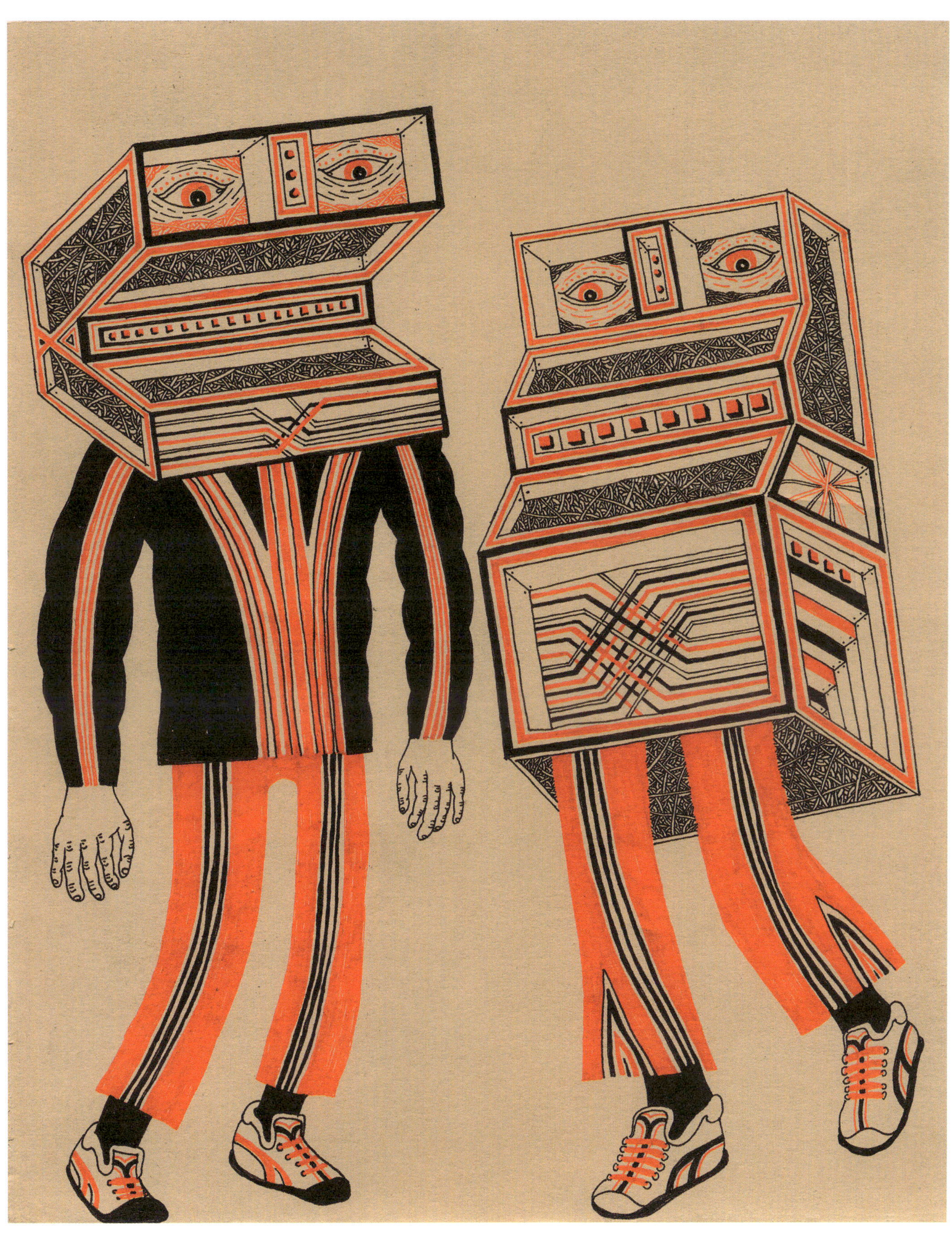

You Are Forgiven

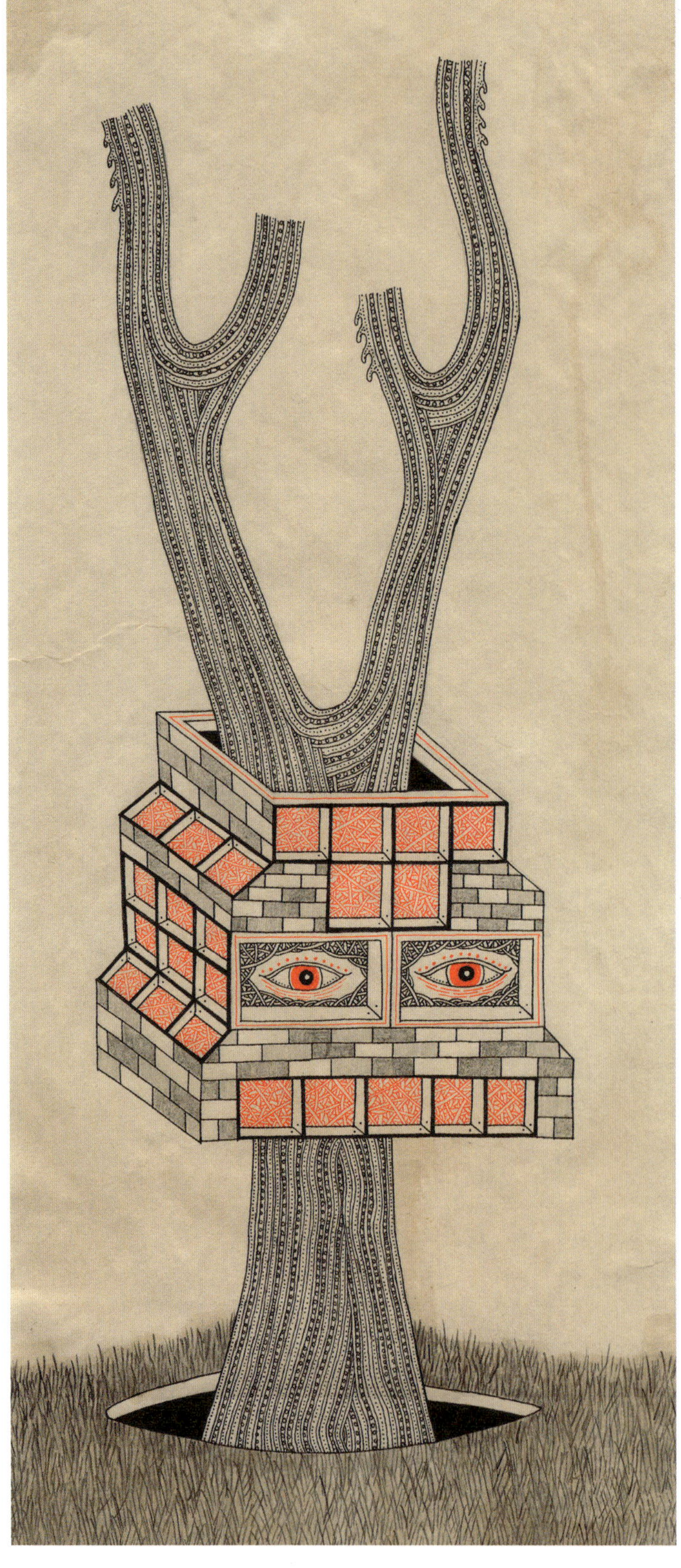

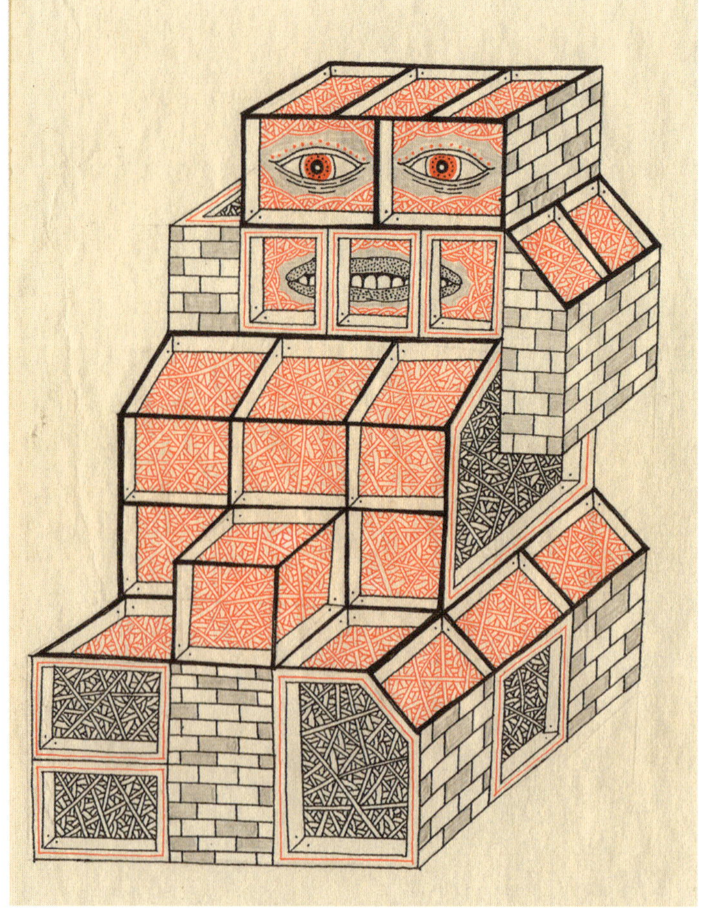

Matt Leines

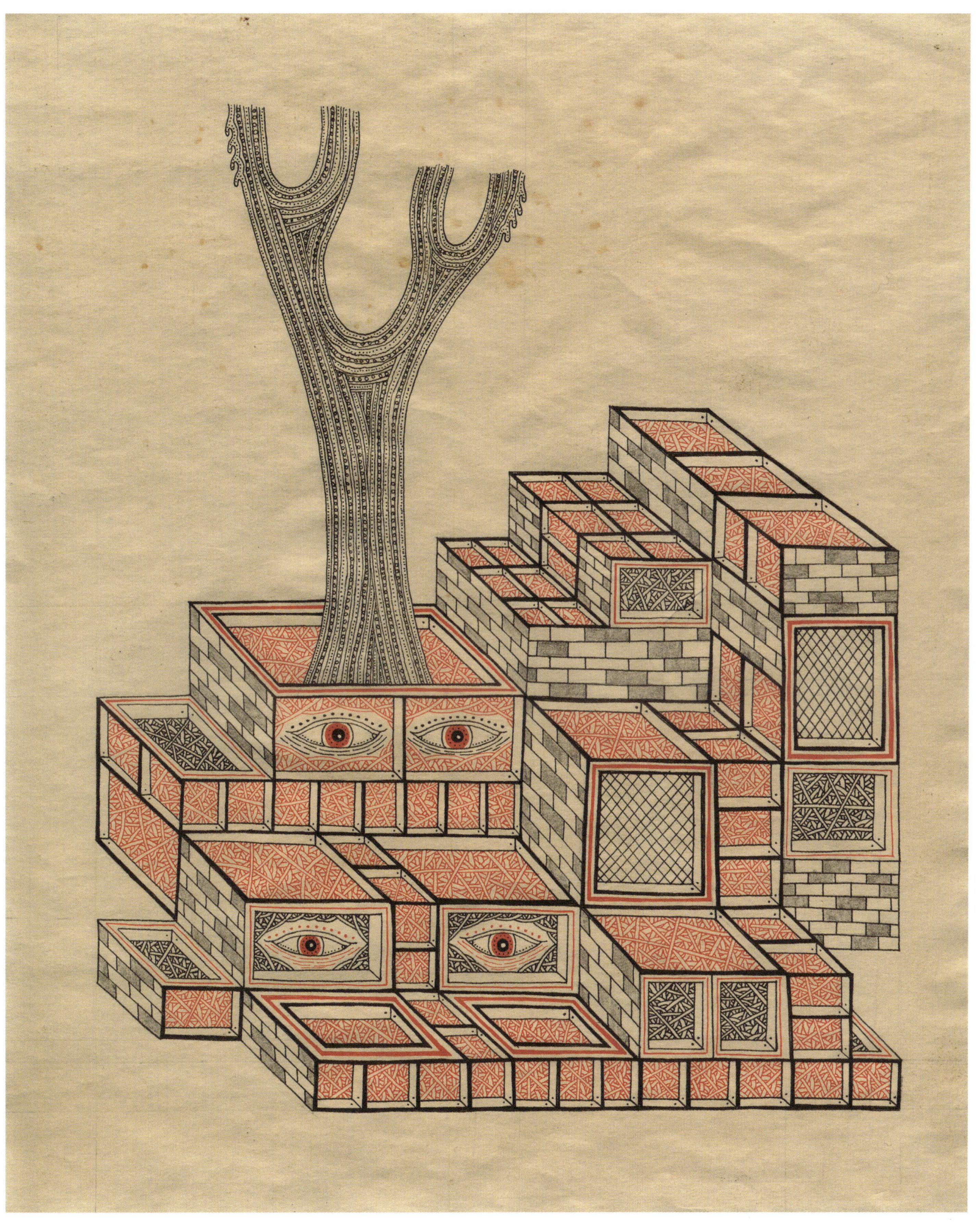

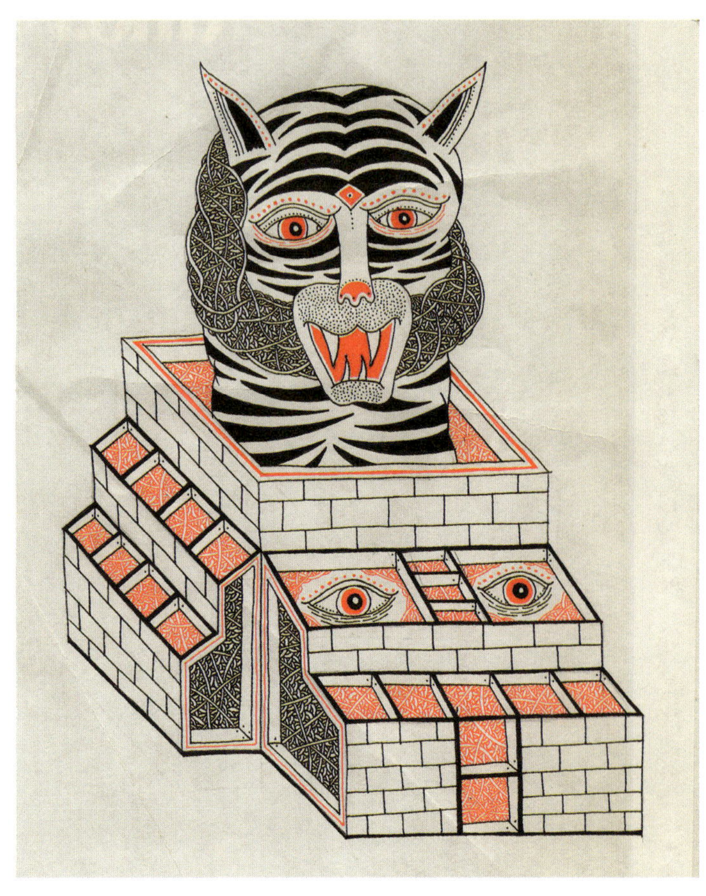
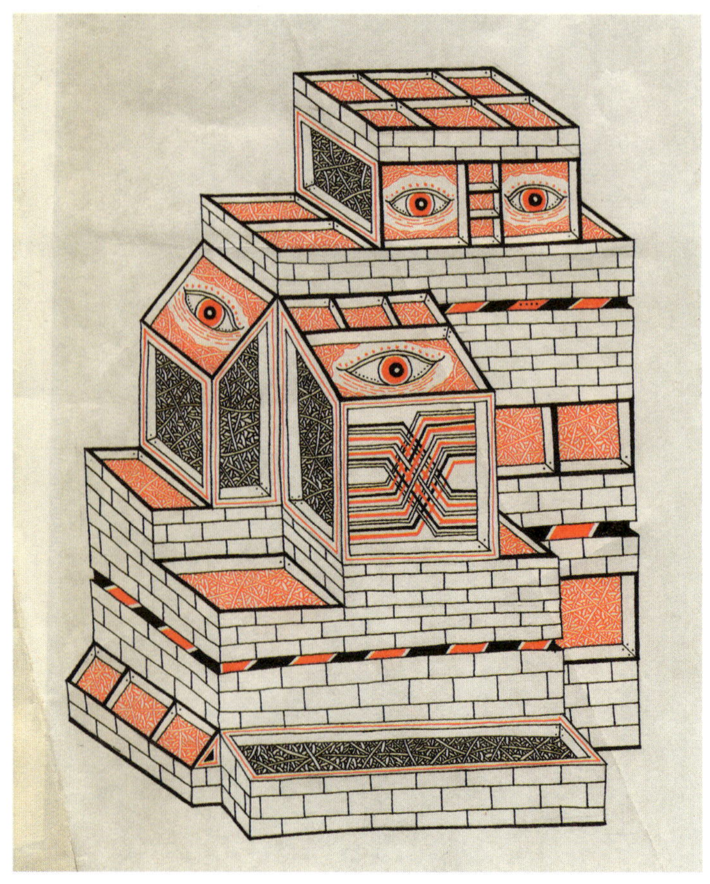
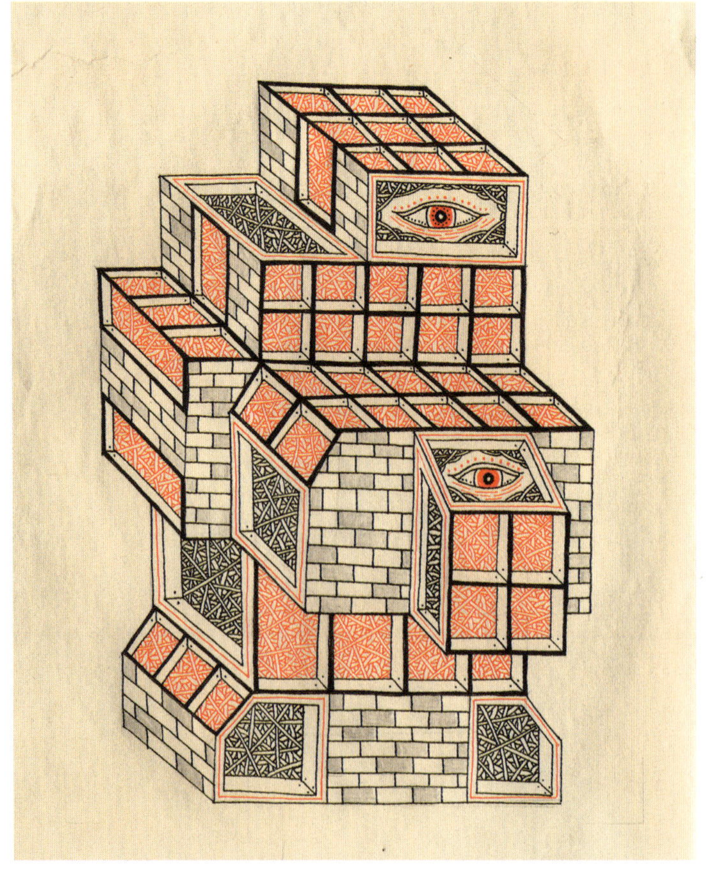
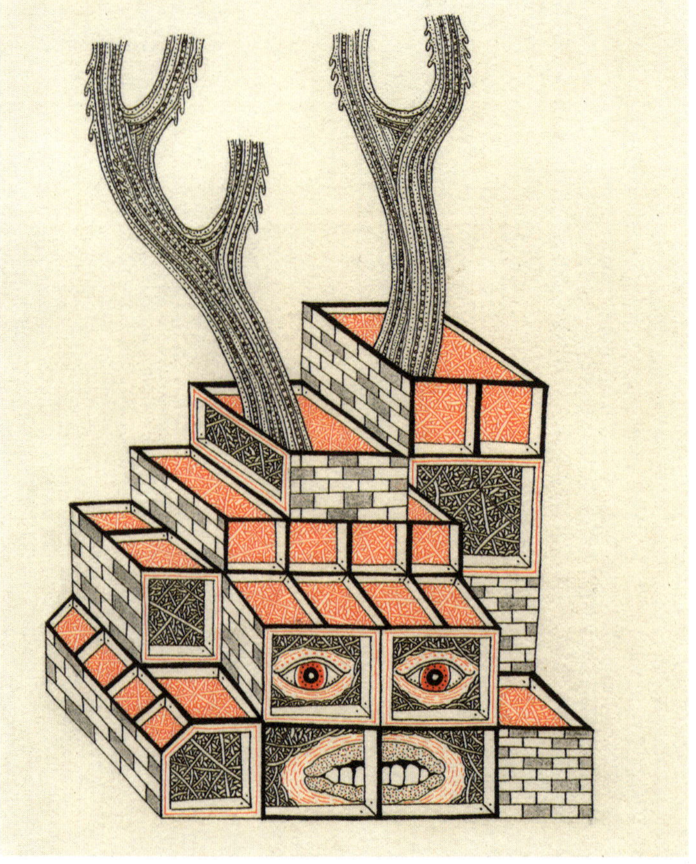

Matt Leines

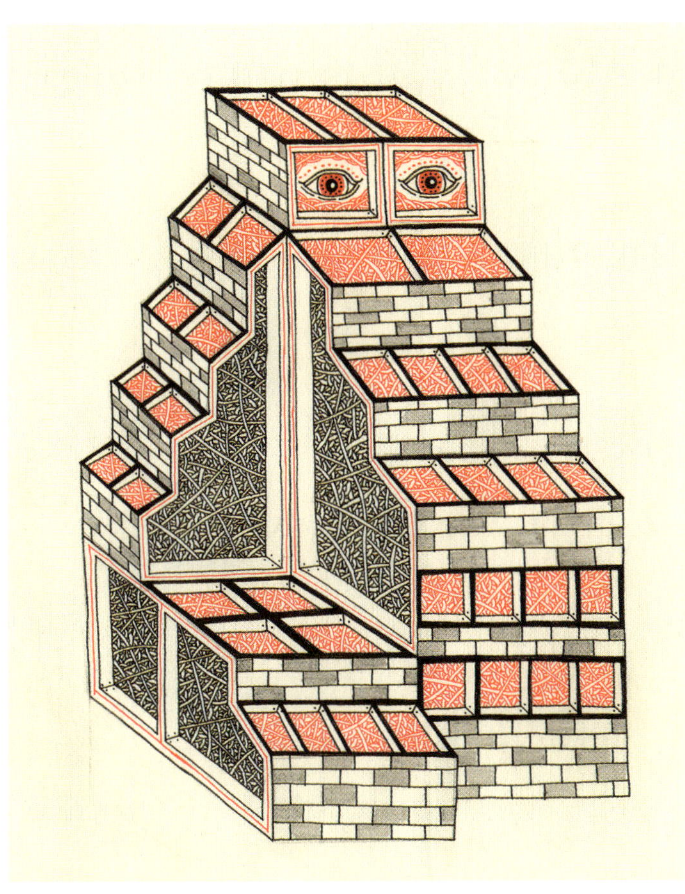
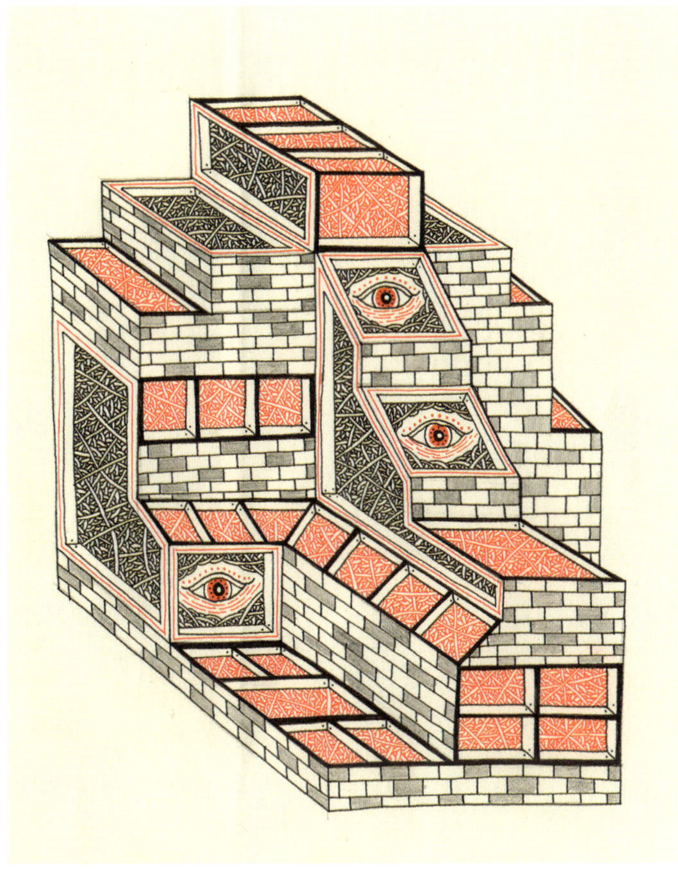
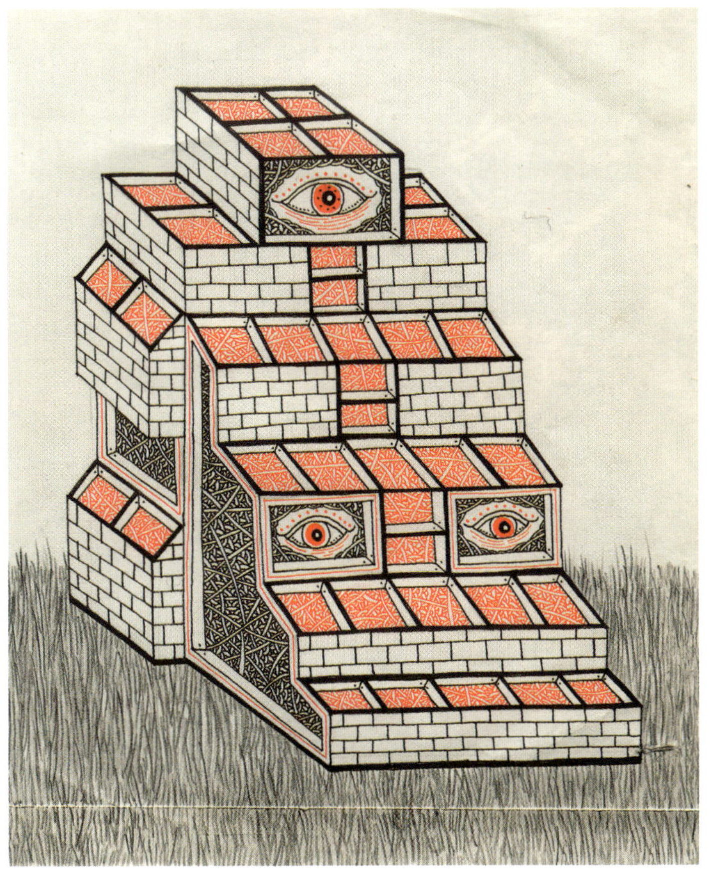
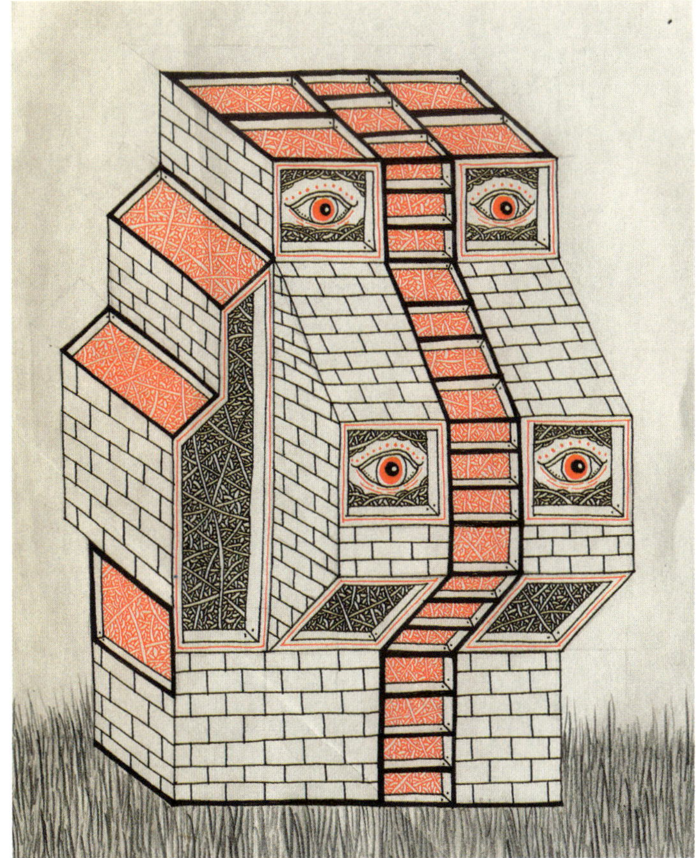

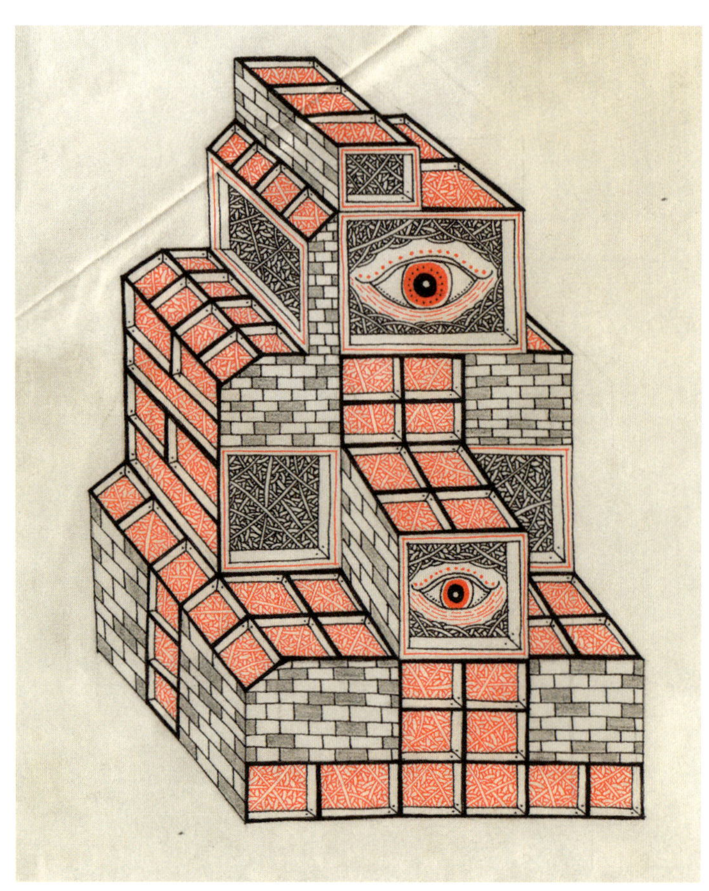
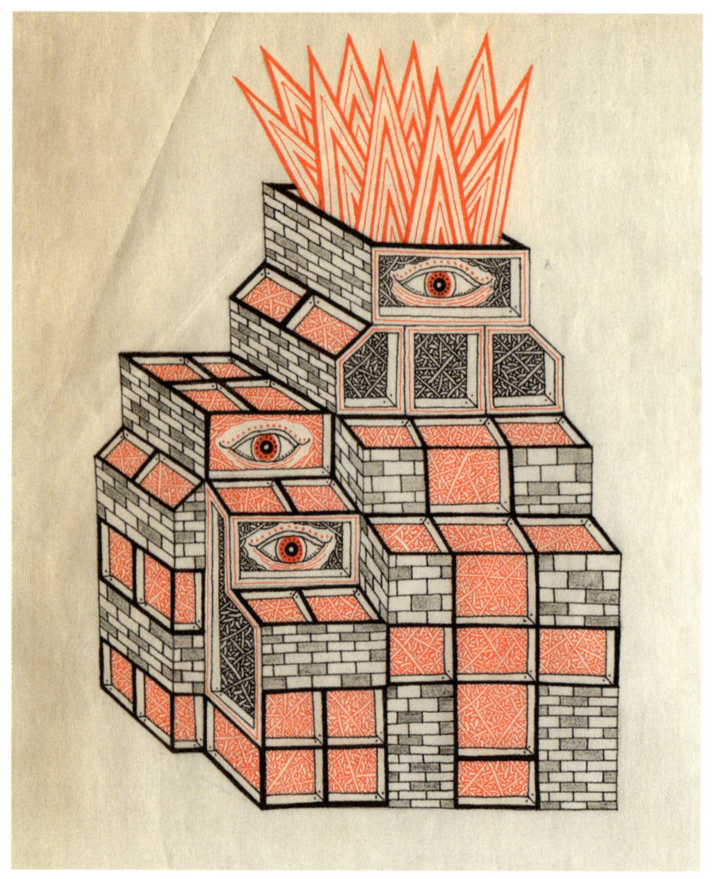
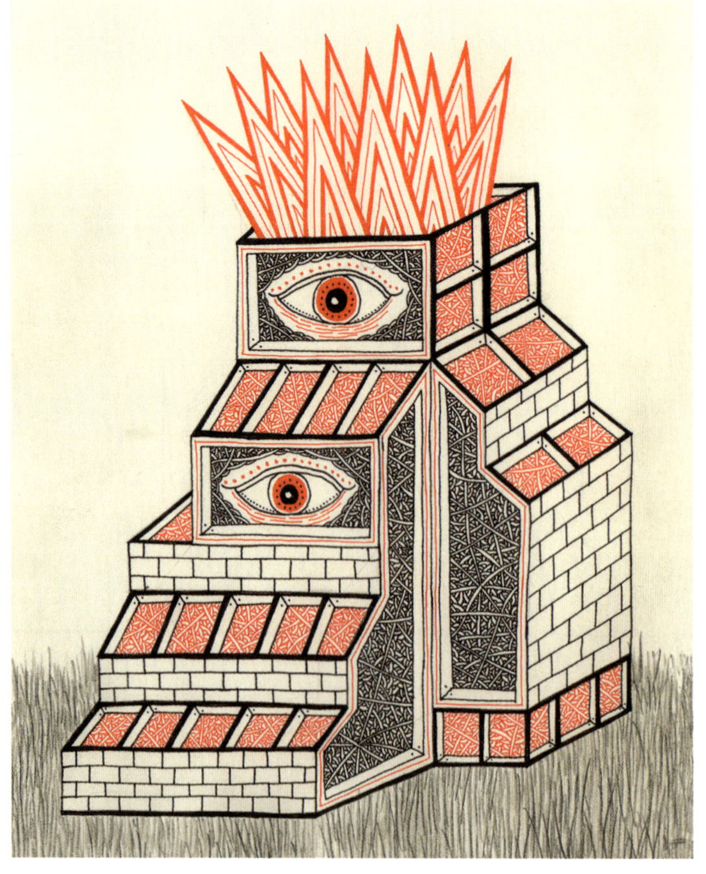
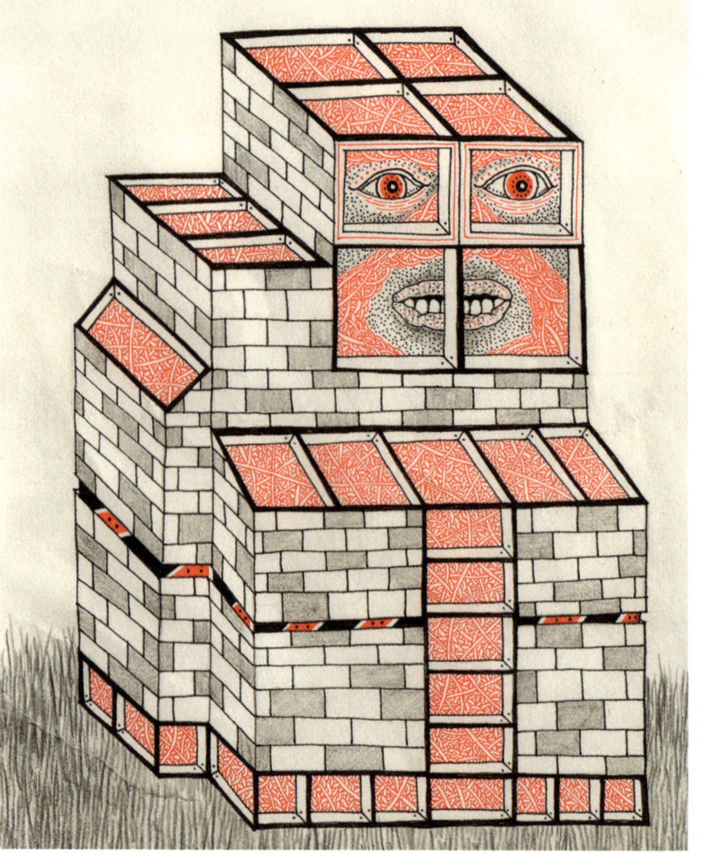

Matt Leines

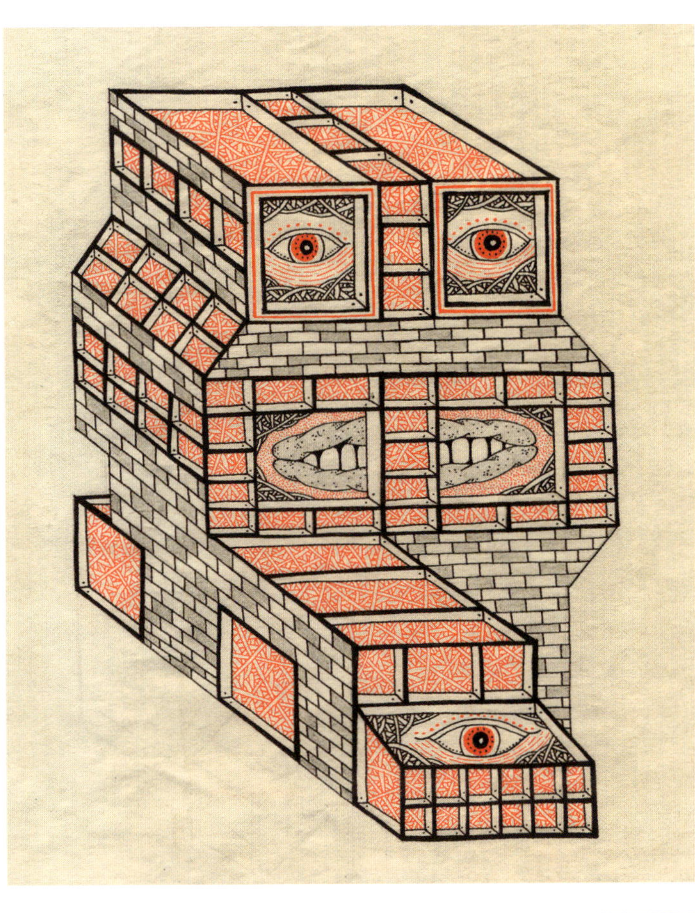

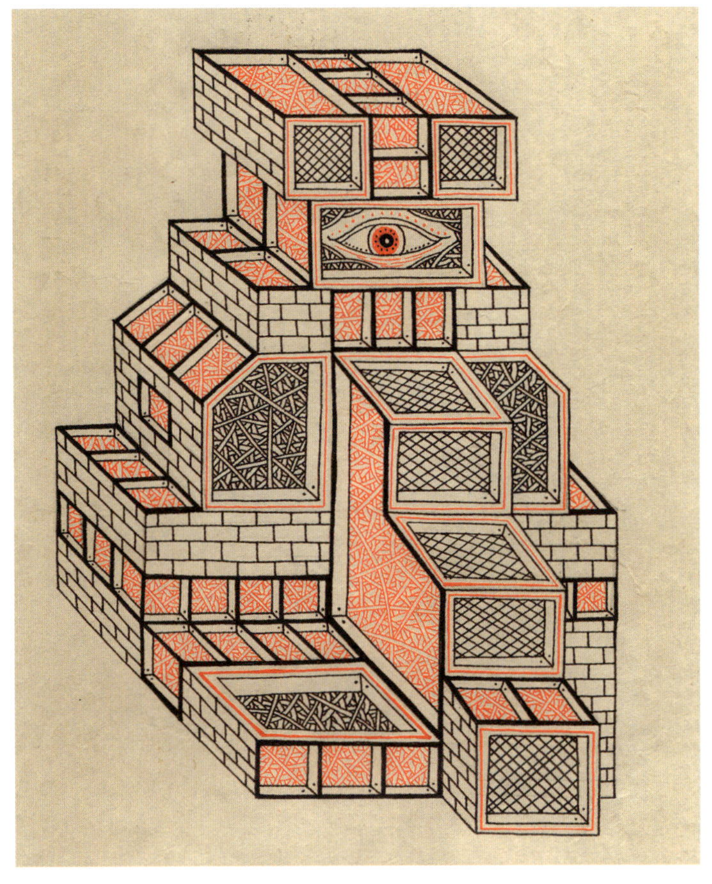

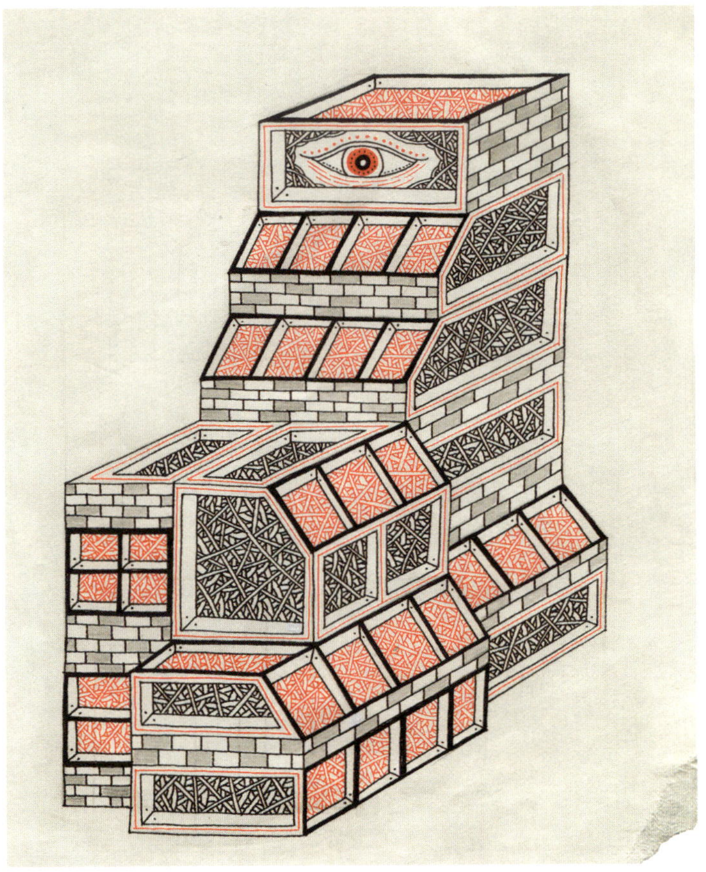

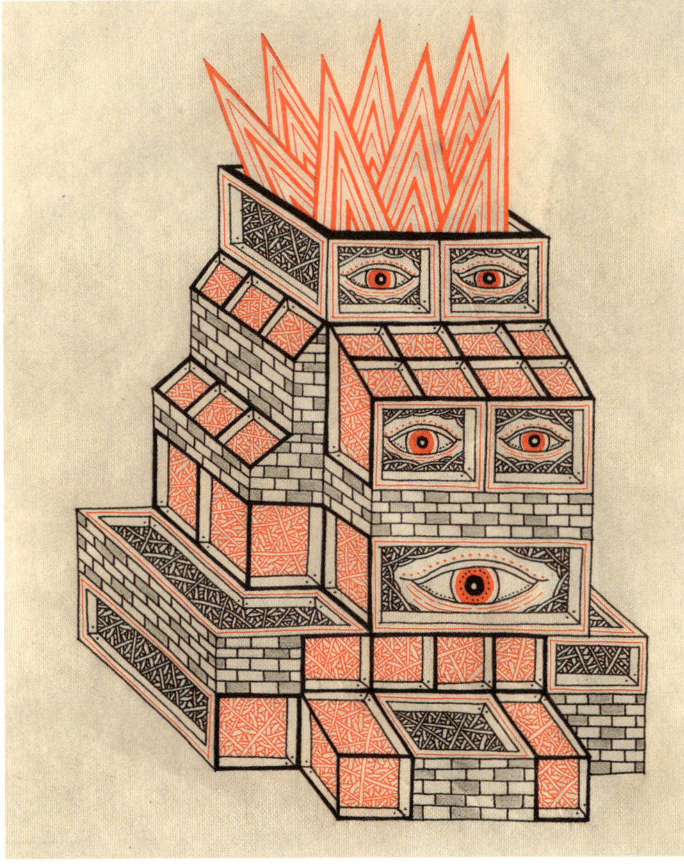

You Are Forgiven

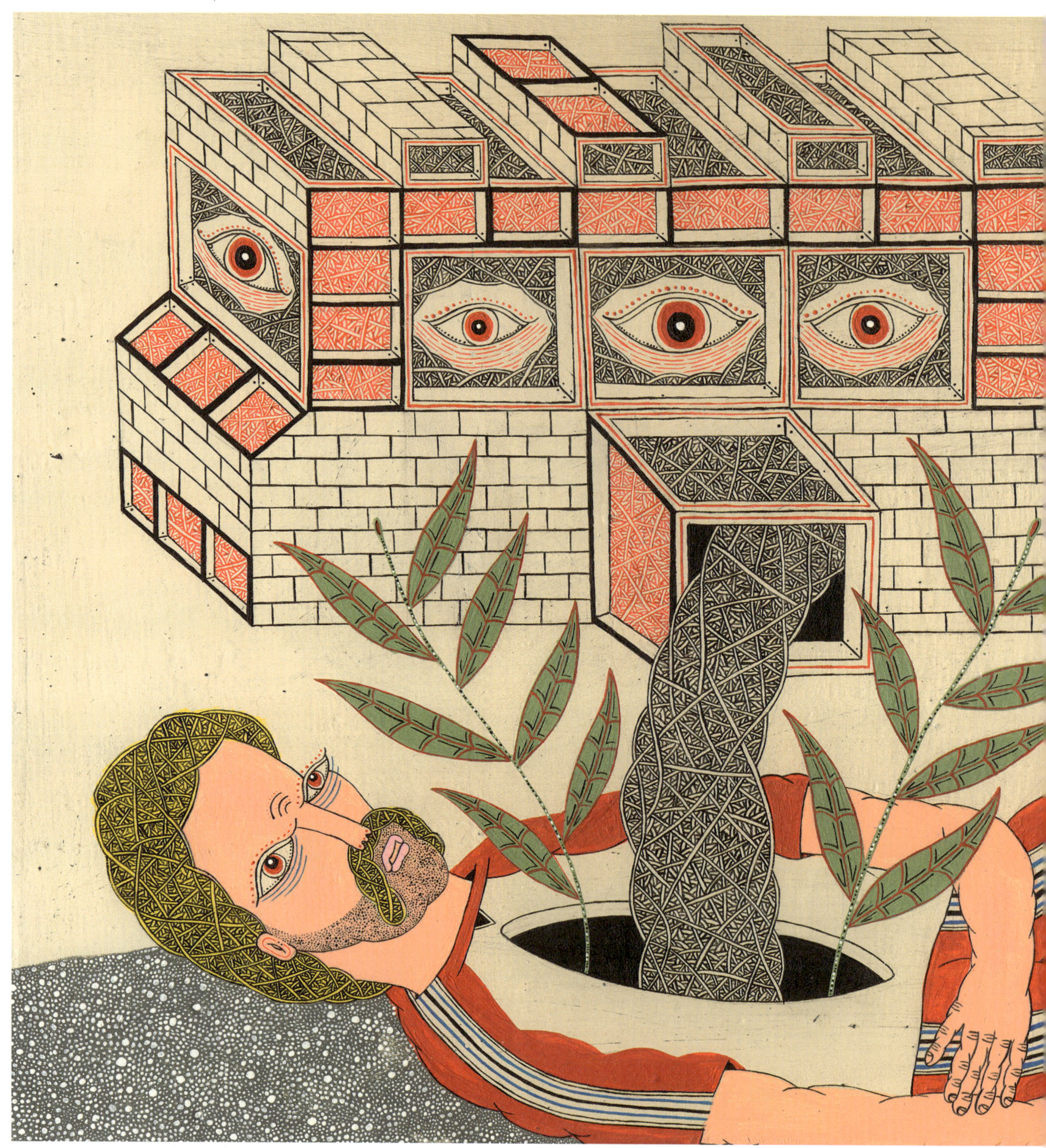

Matt Leines

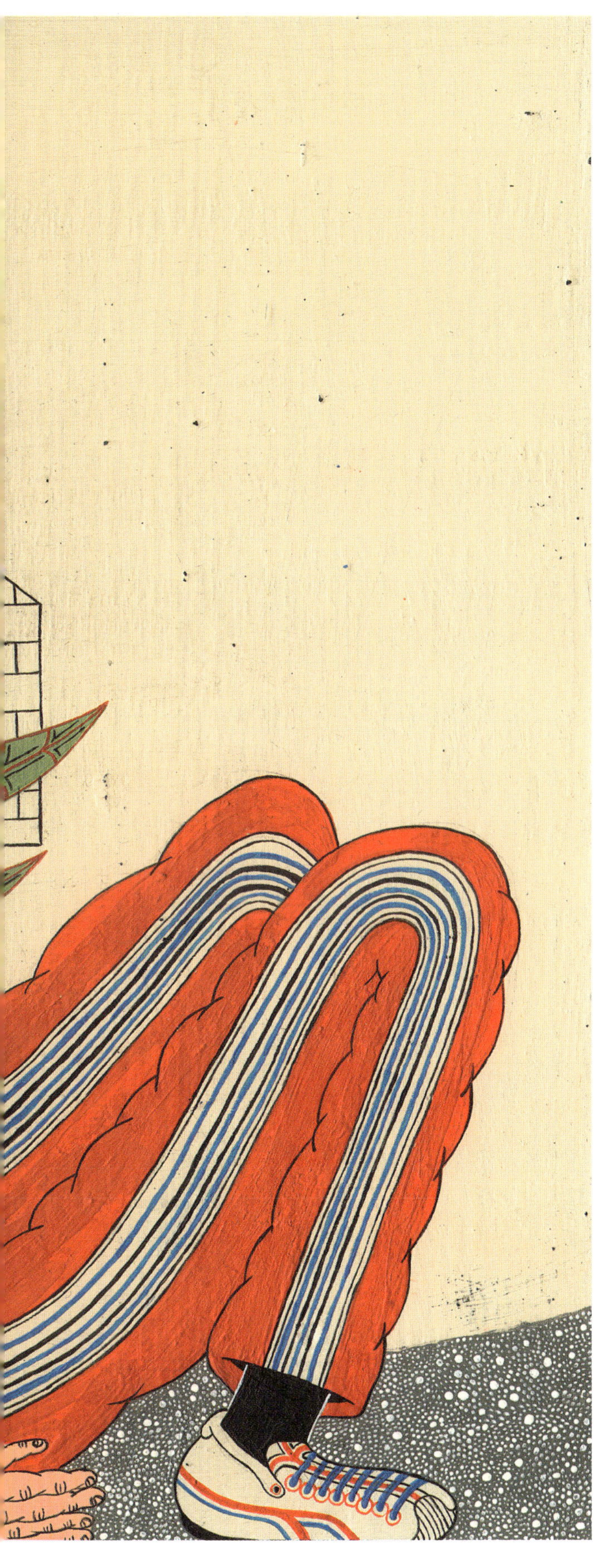

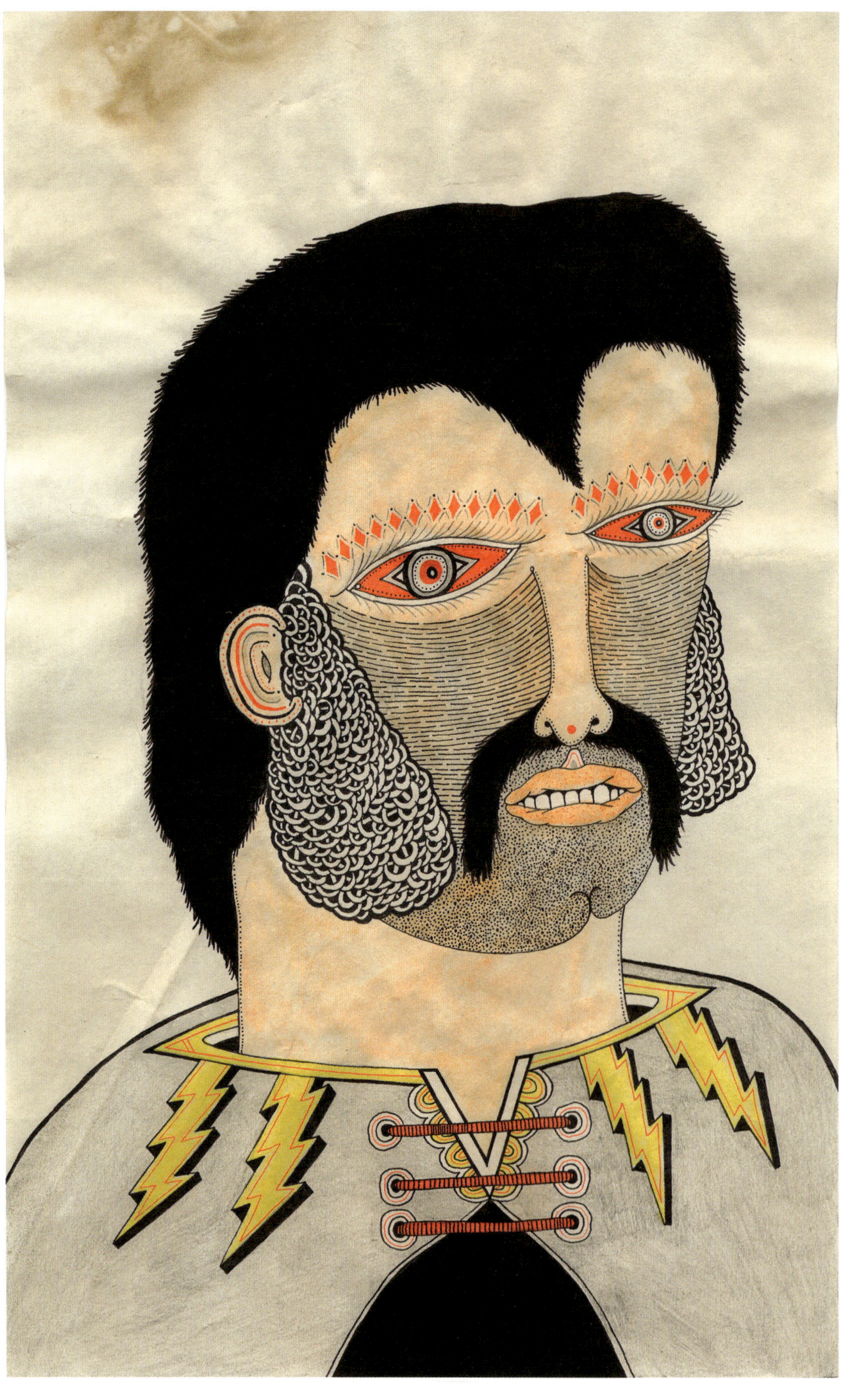

44

Matt Leines

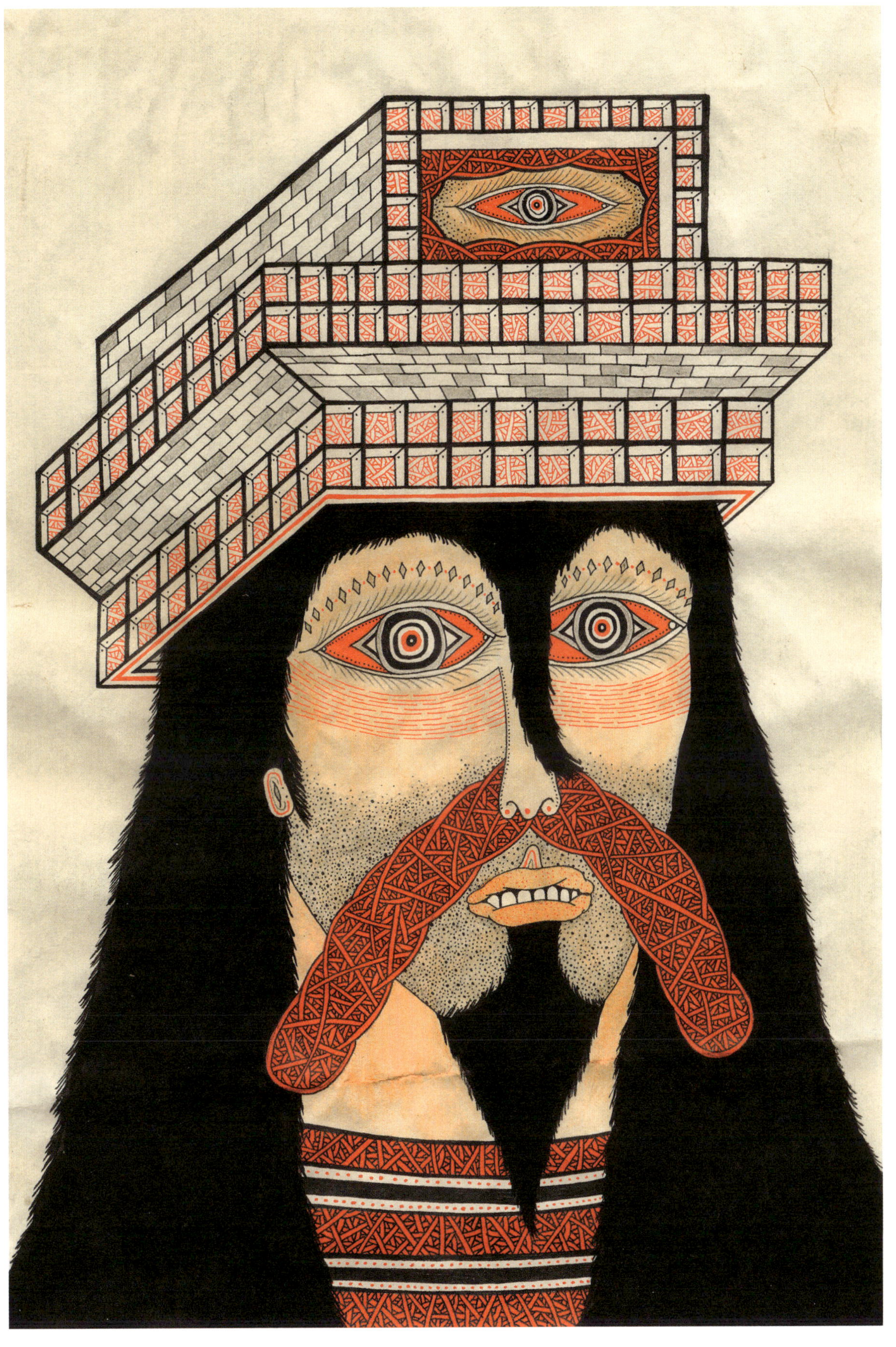

You Are Forgiven

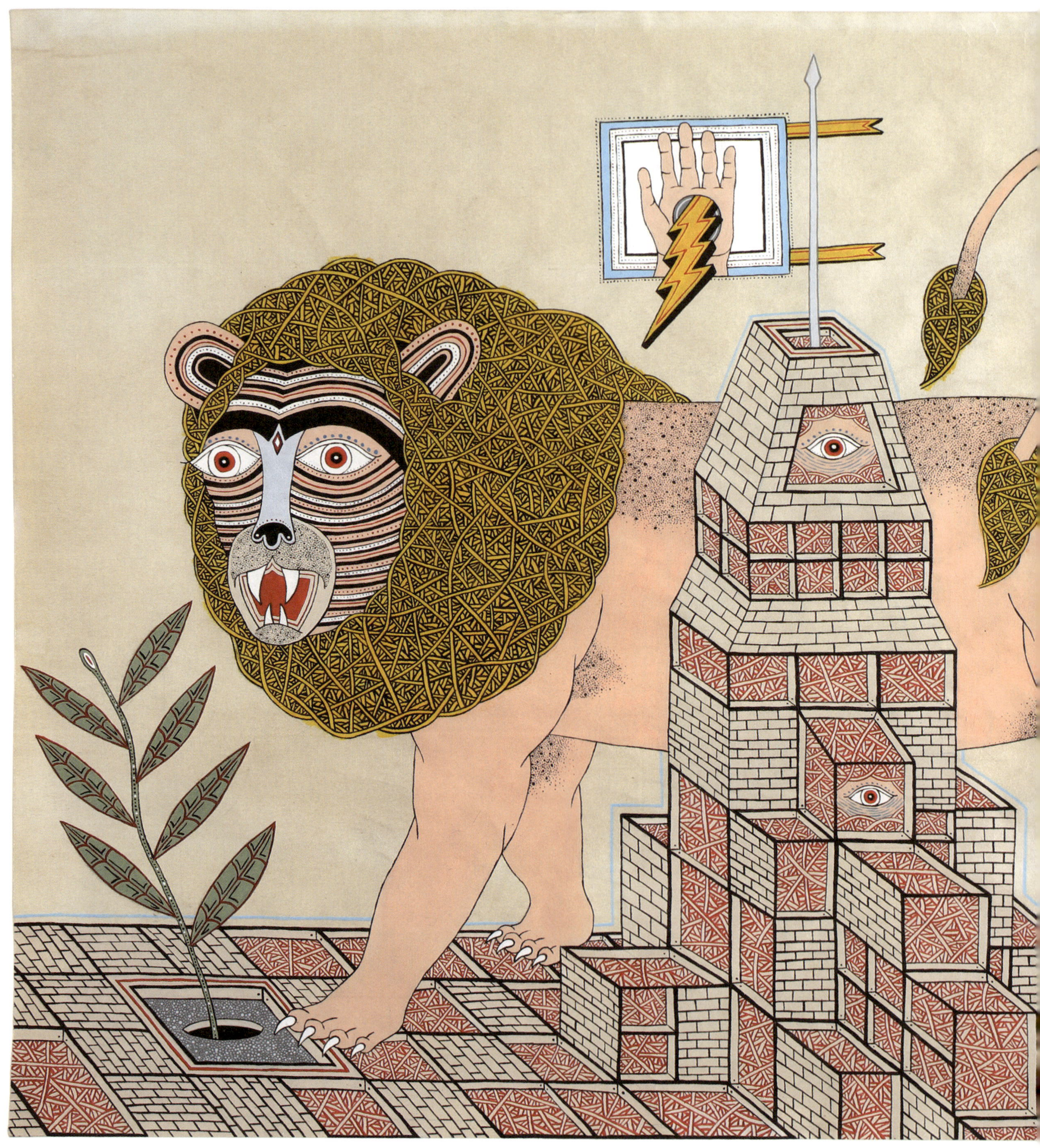

Matt Leines

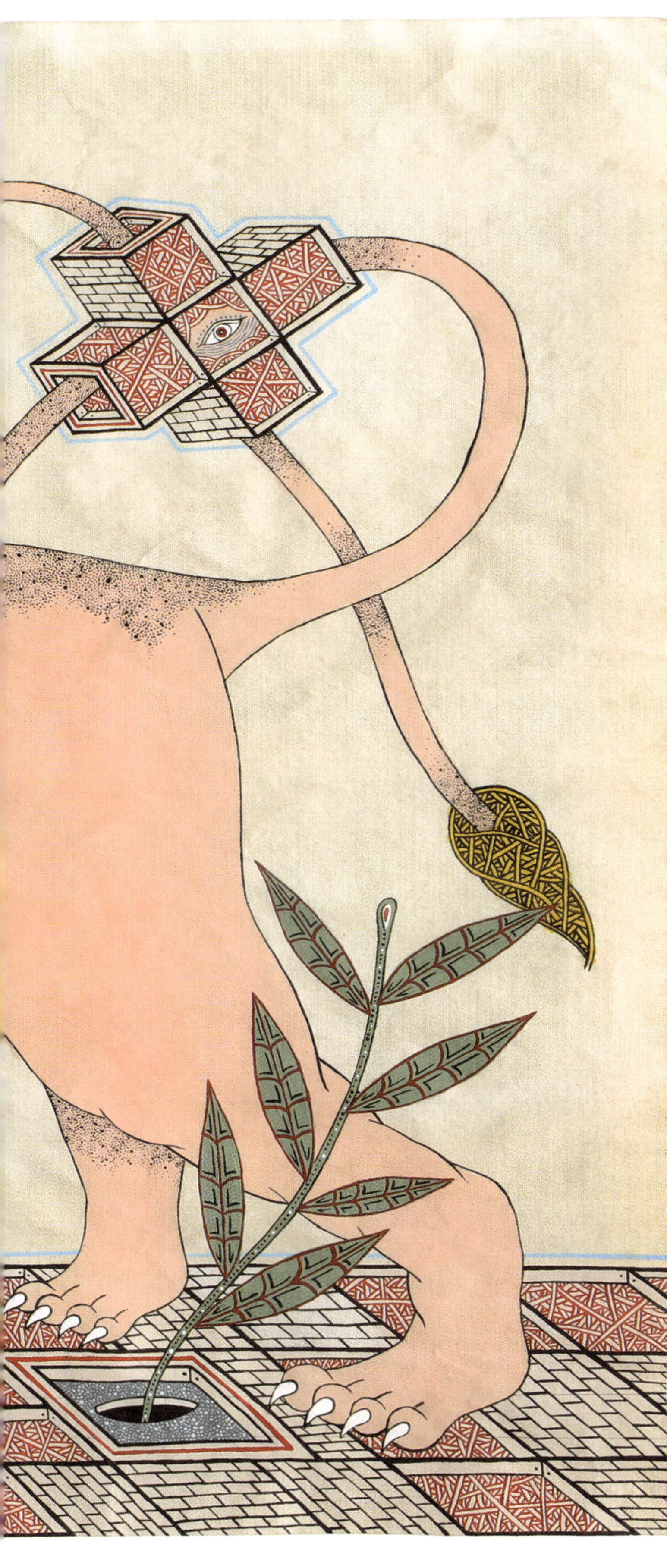

47

You Are Forgiven

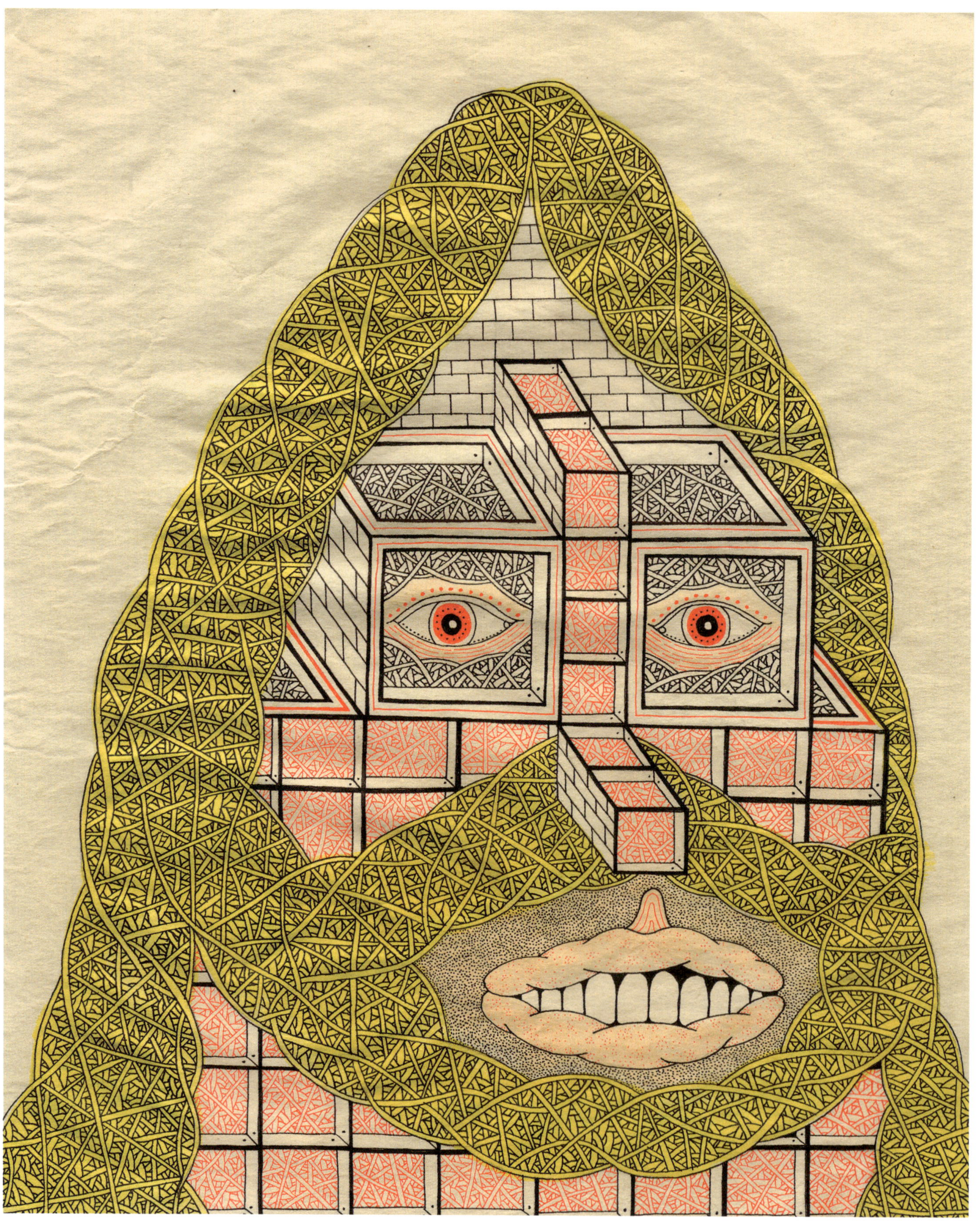

Matt Leines

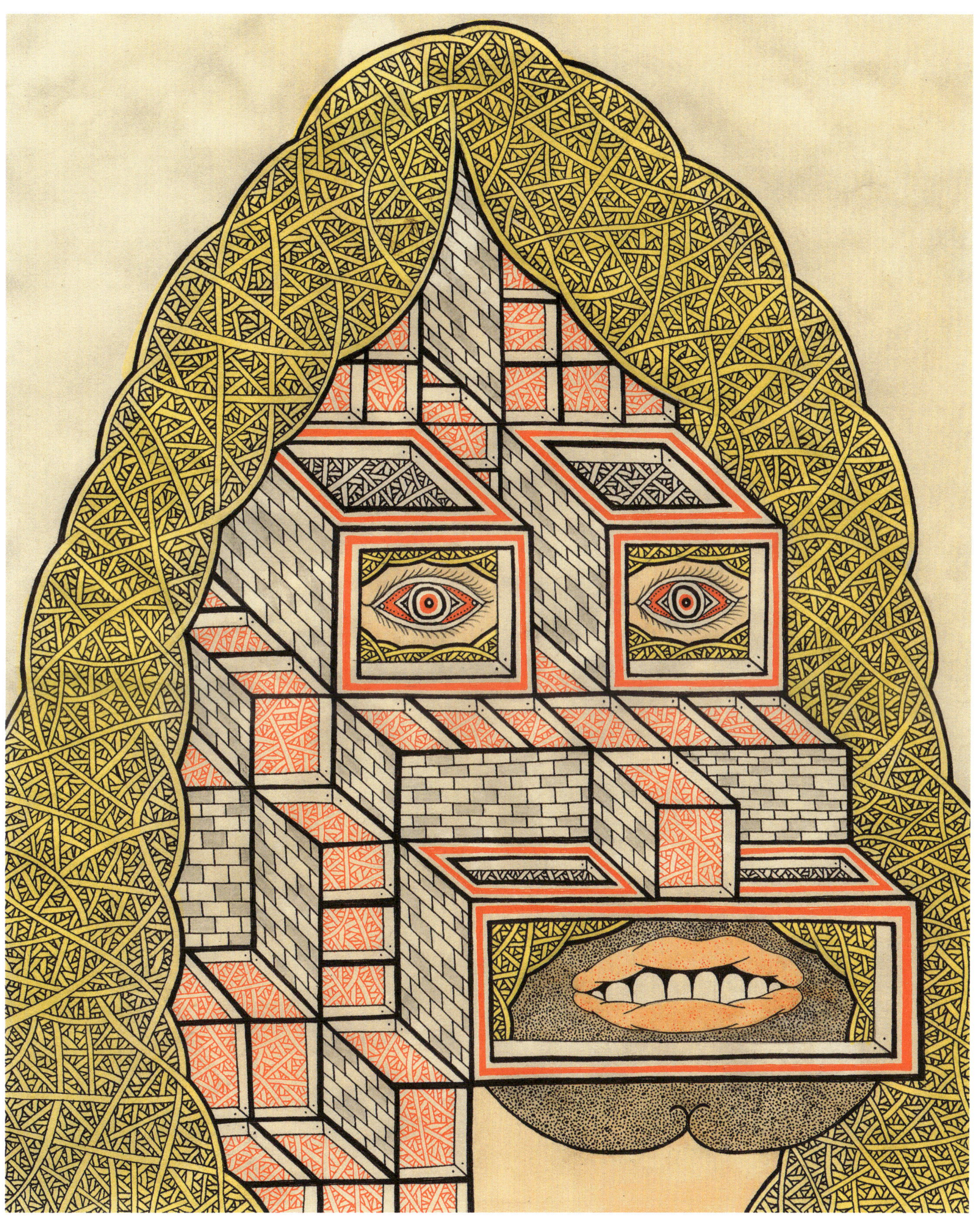

You Are Forgiven

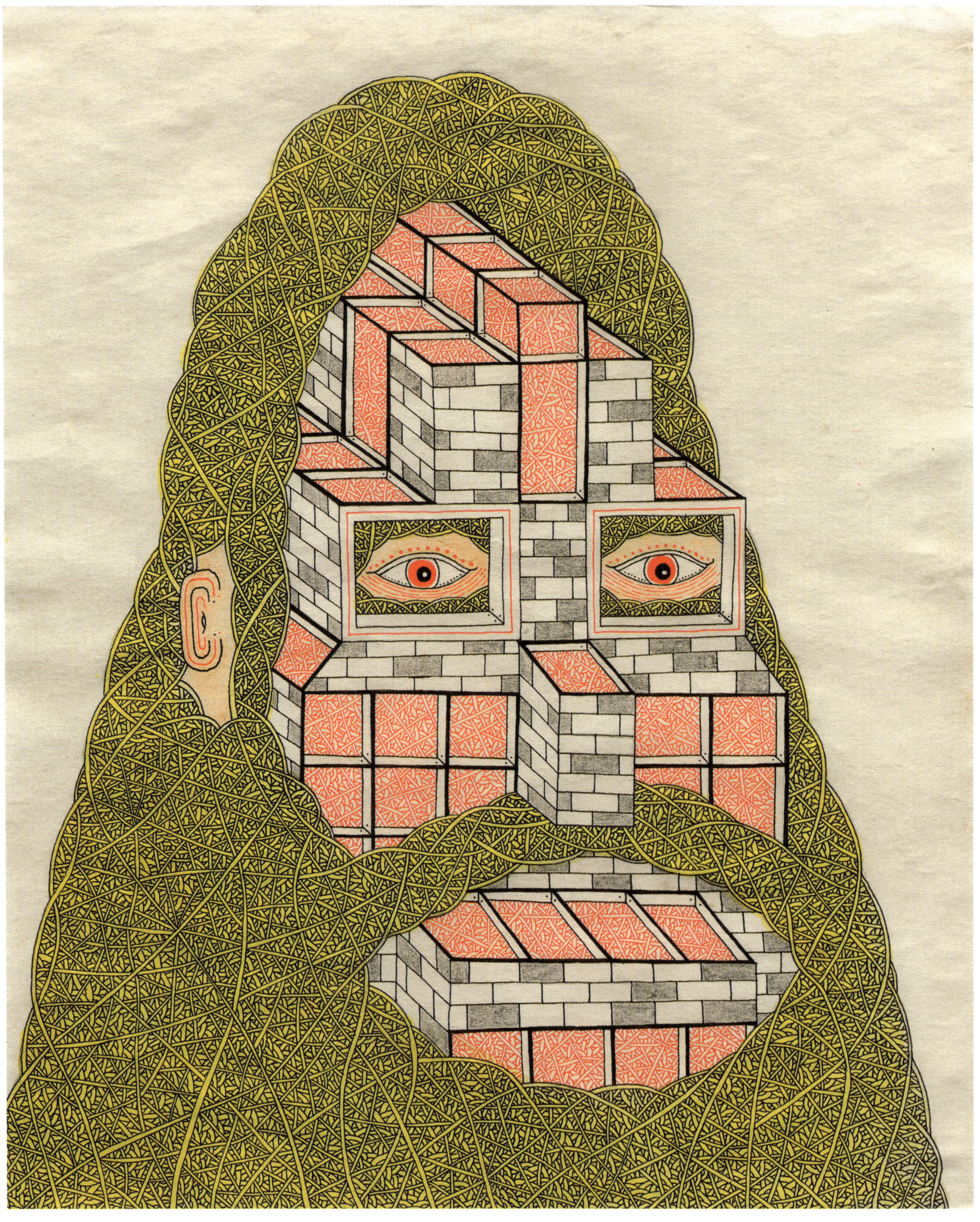

Matt Leines

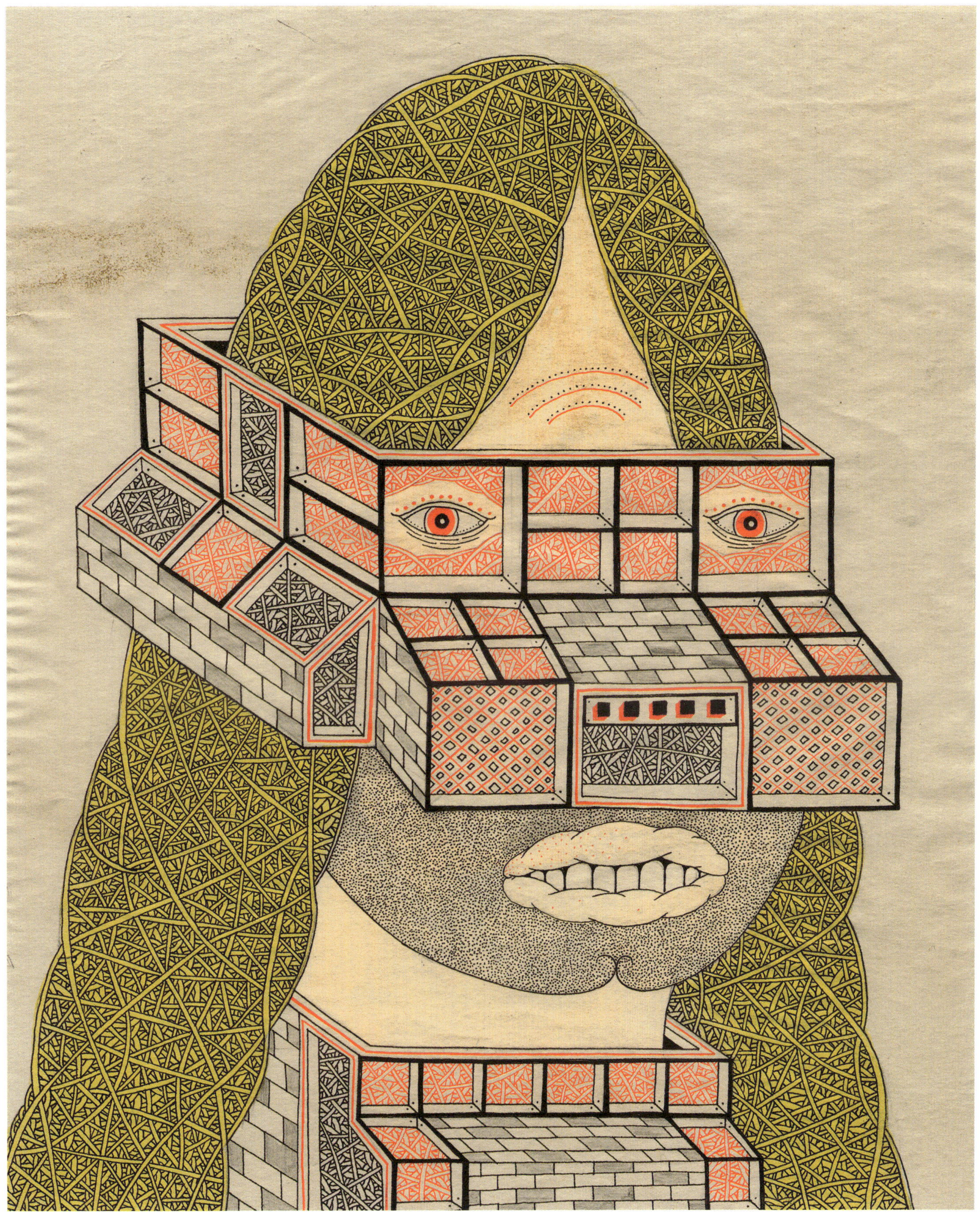

You Are Forgiven

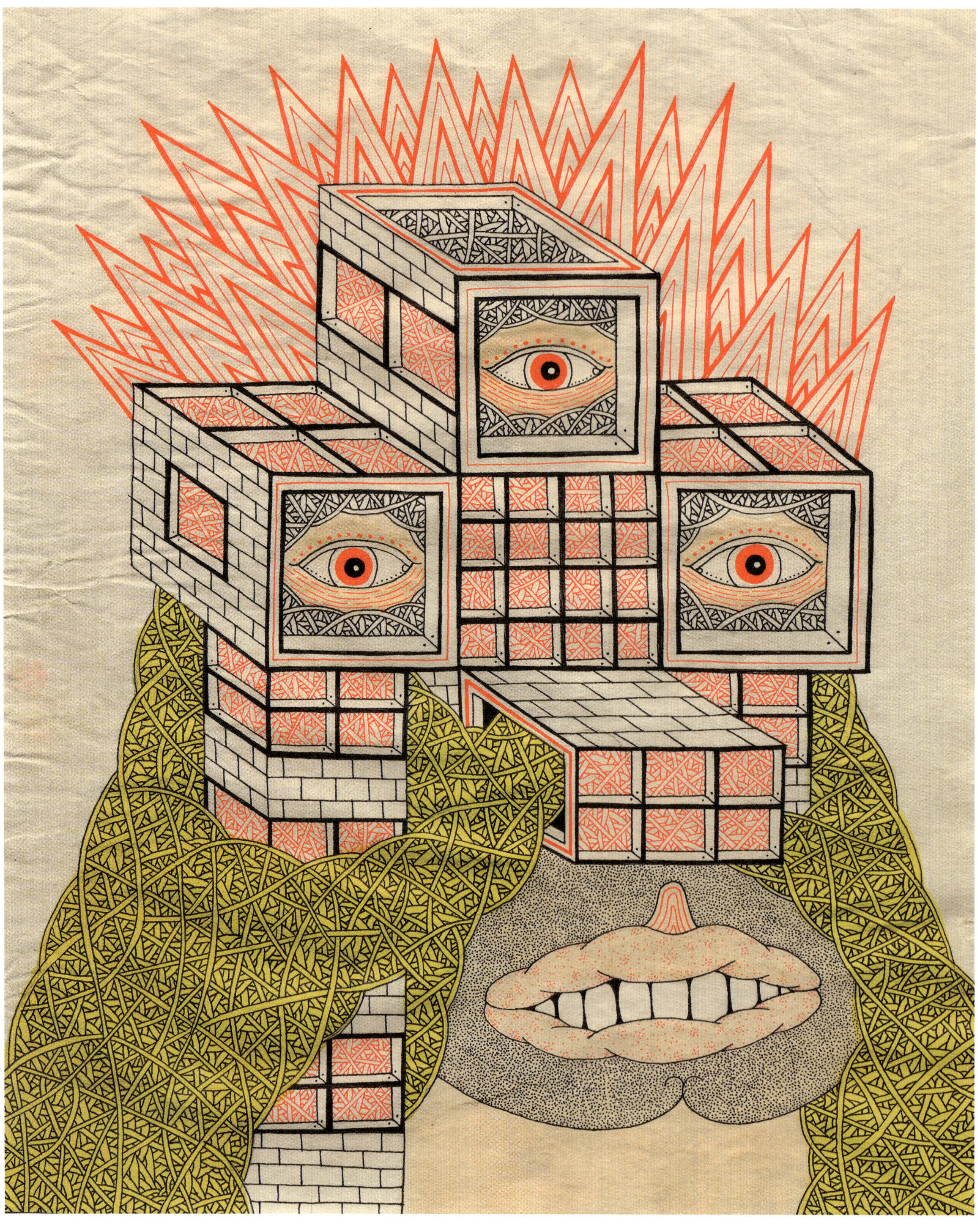

Matt Leines

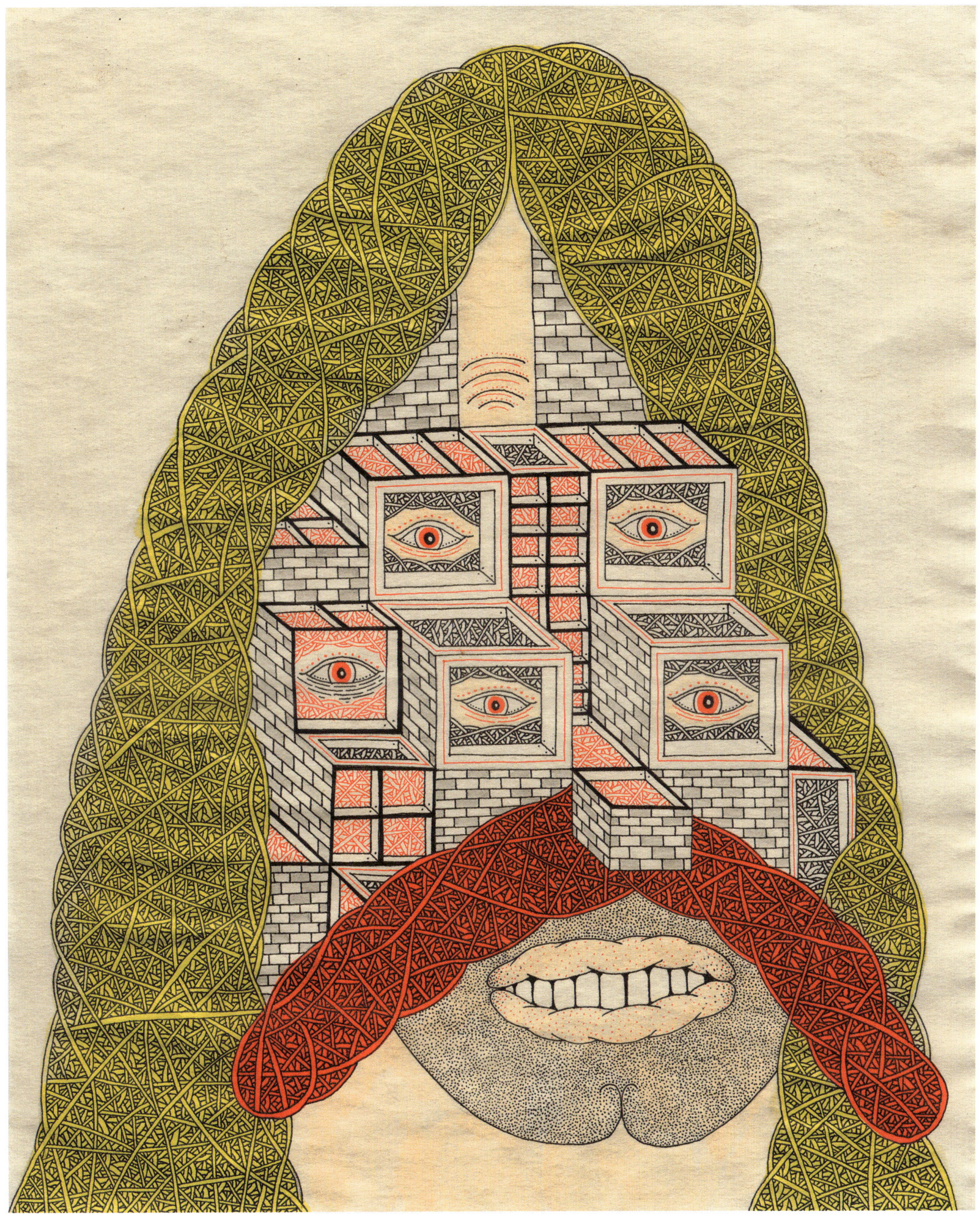

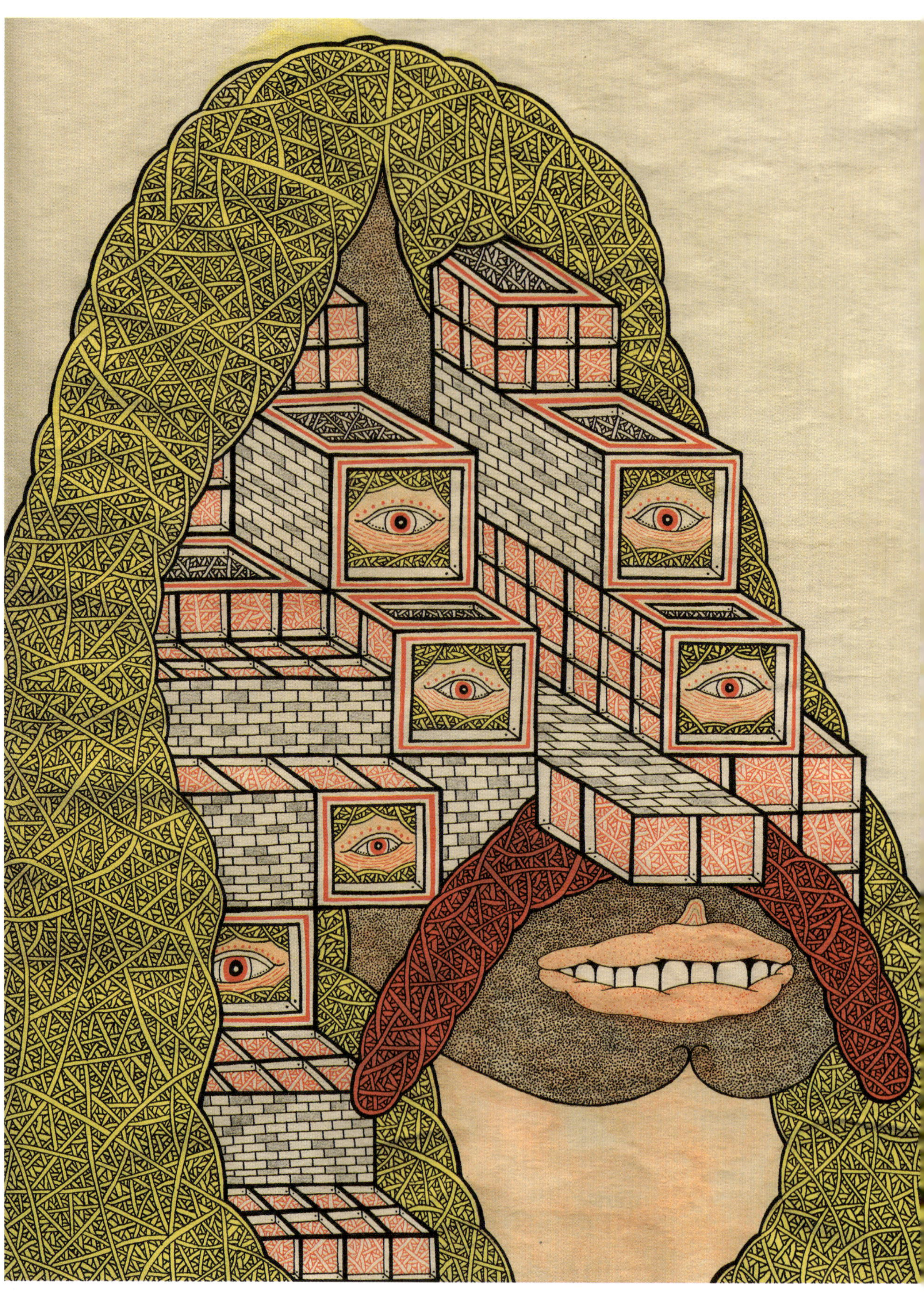

Matt Leines

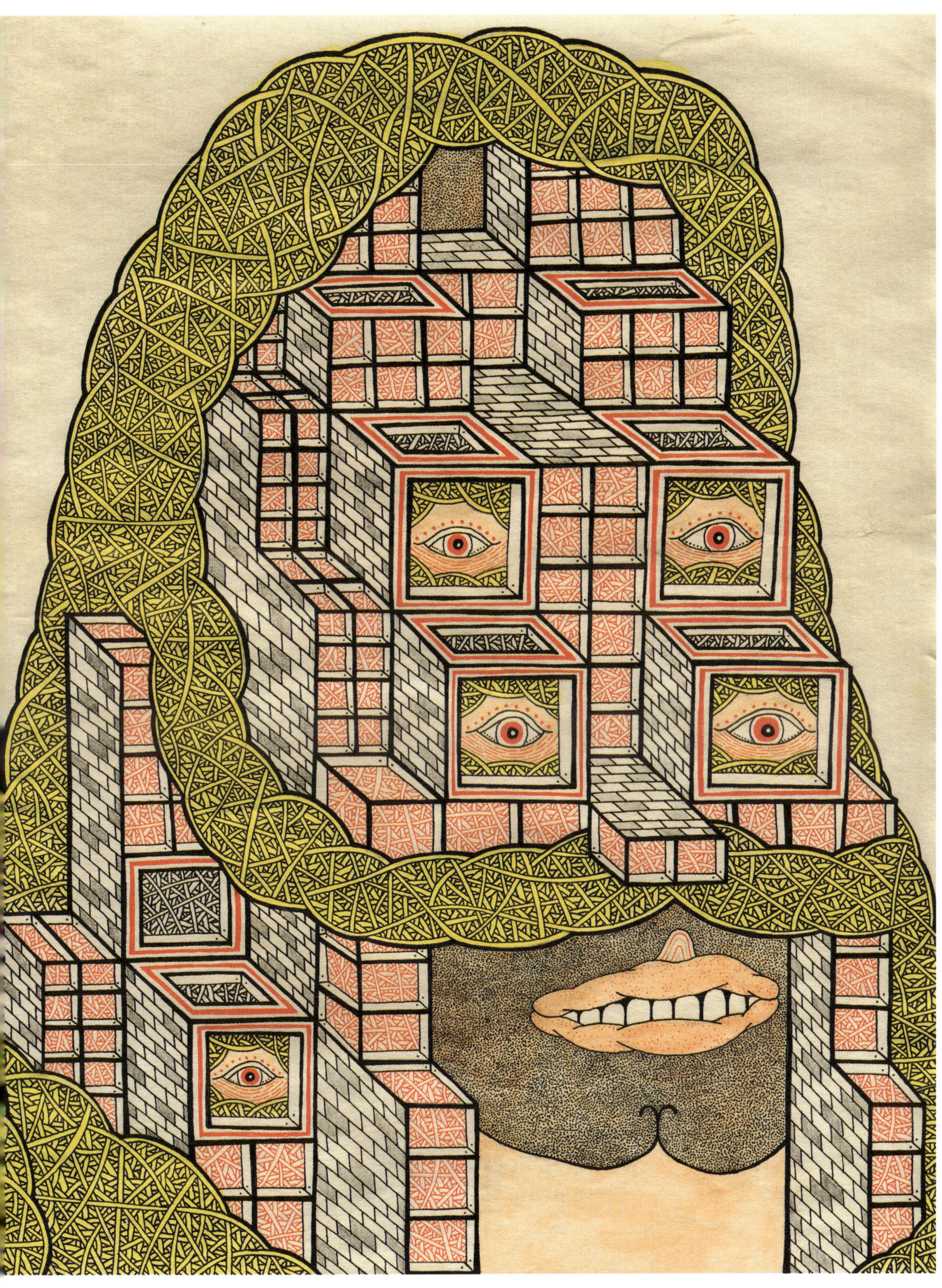

You Are Forgiven

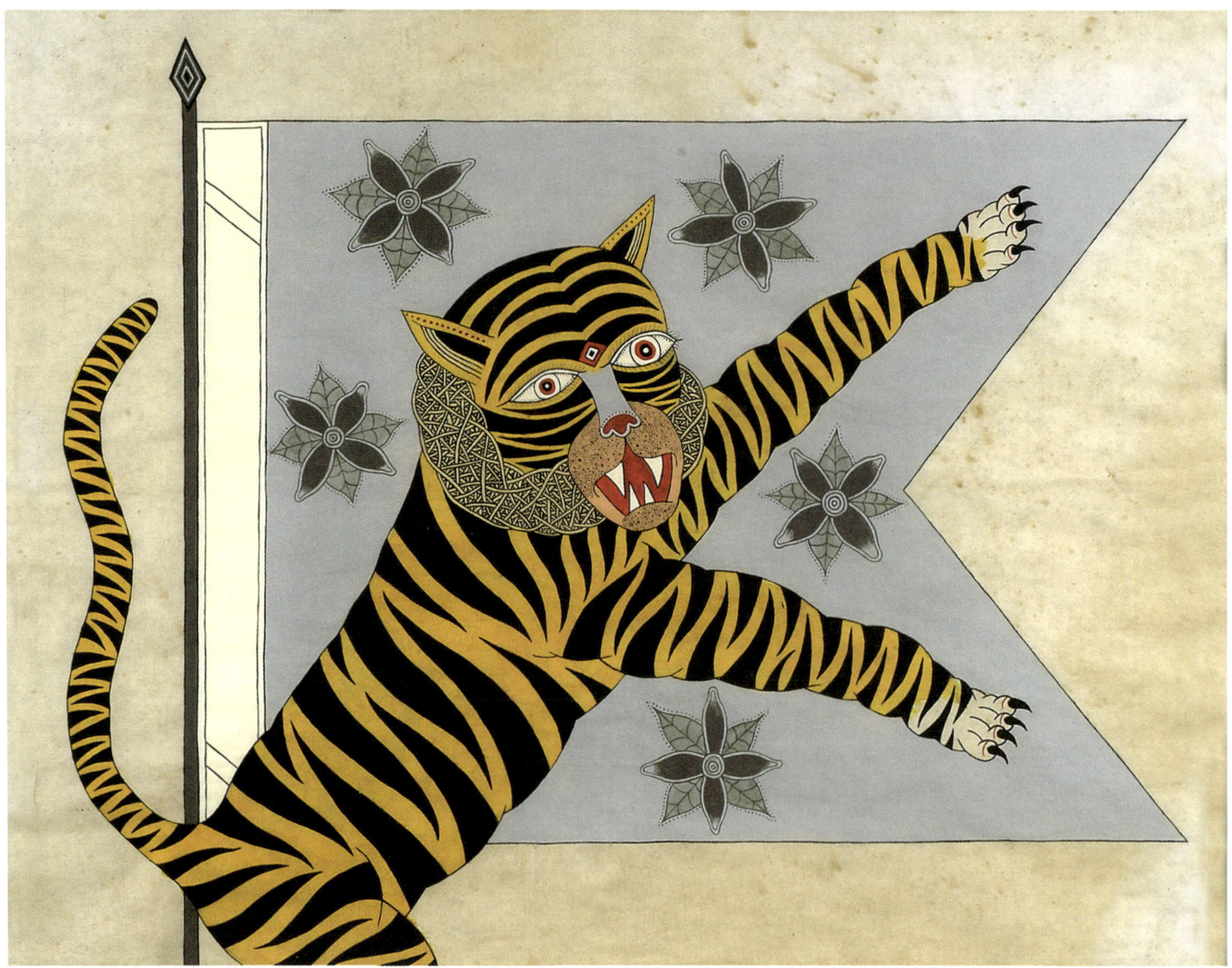

56

Matt Leines

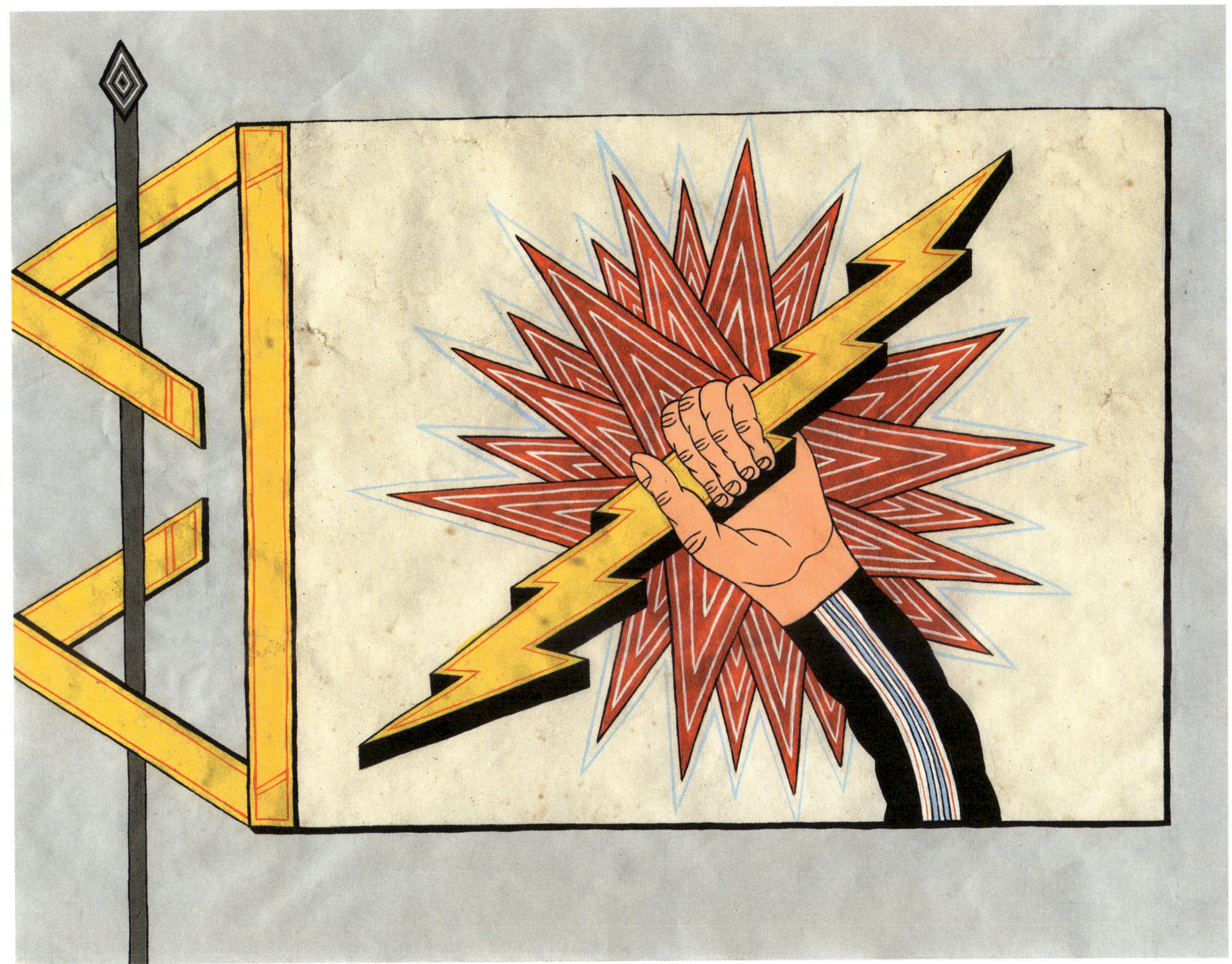

Matt Leines

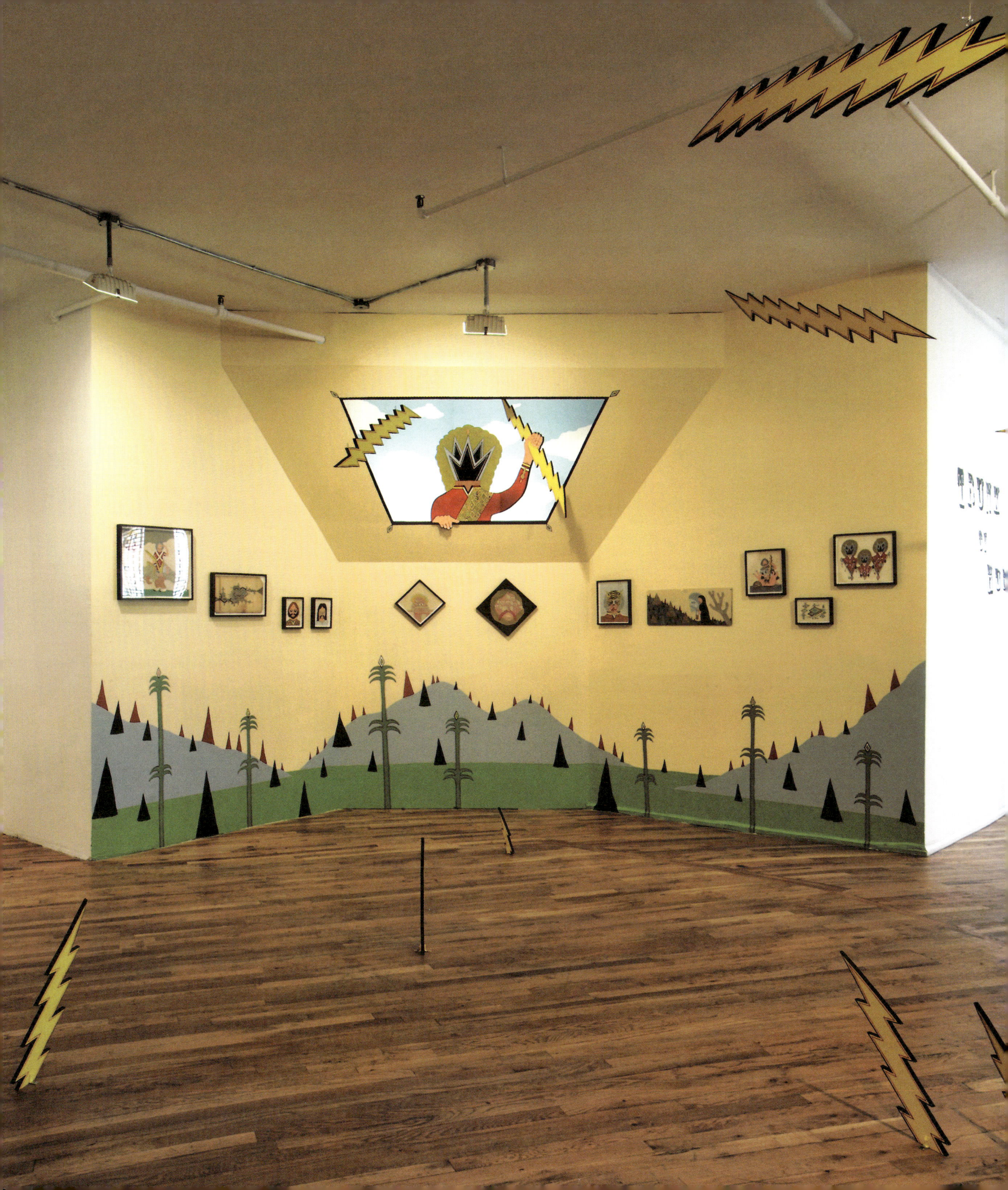

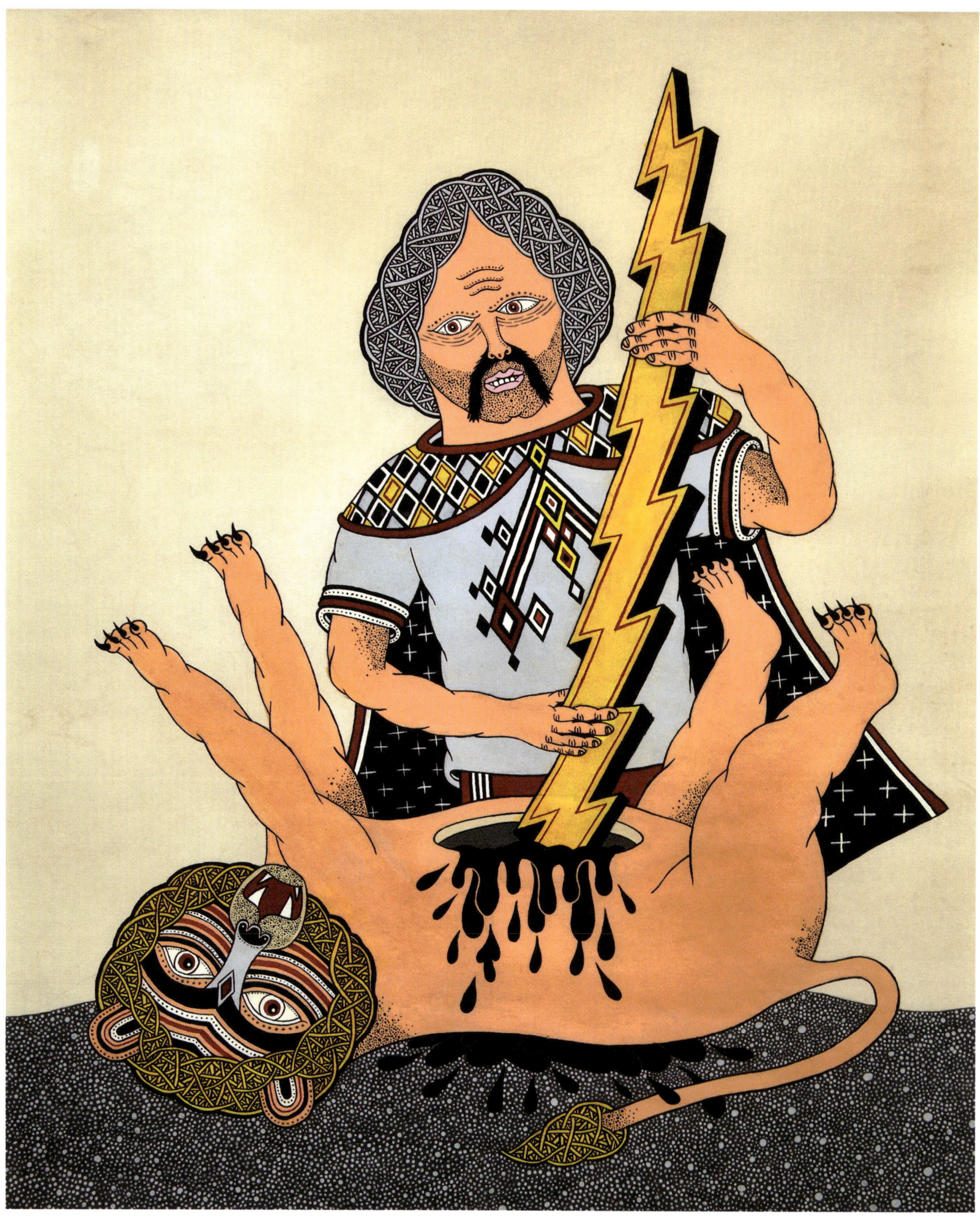

Matt Leines

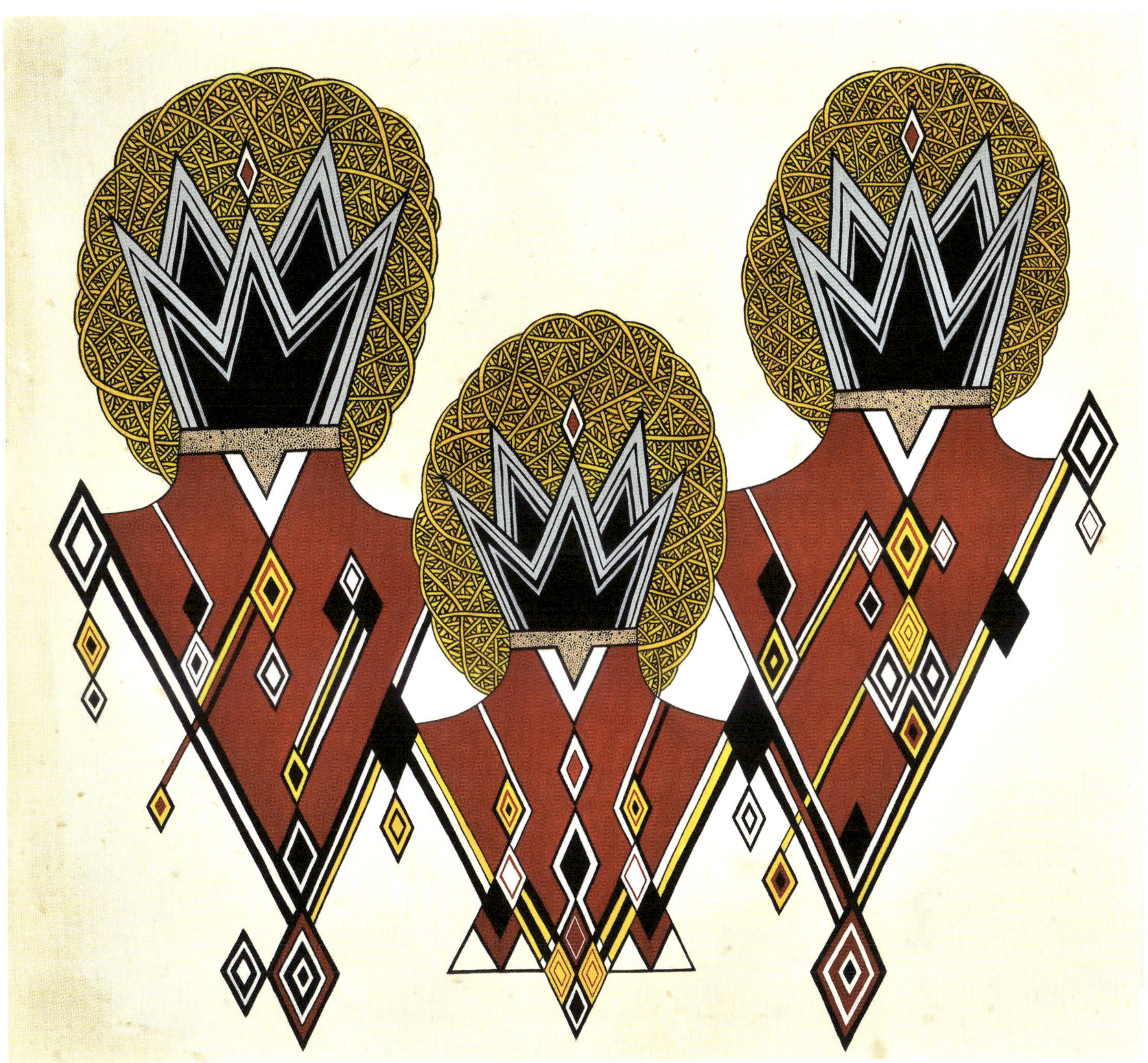

You Are Forgiven

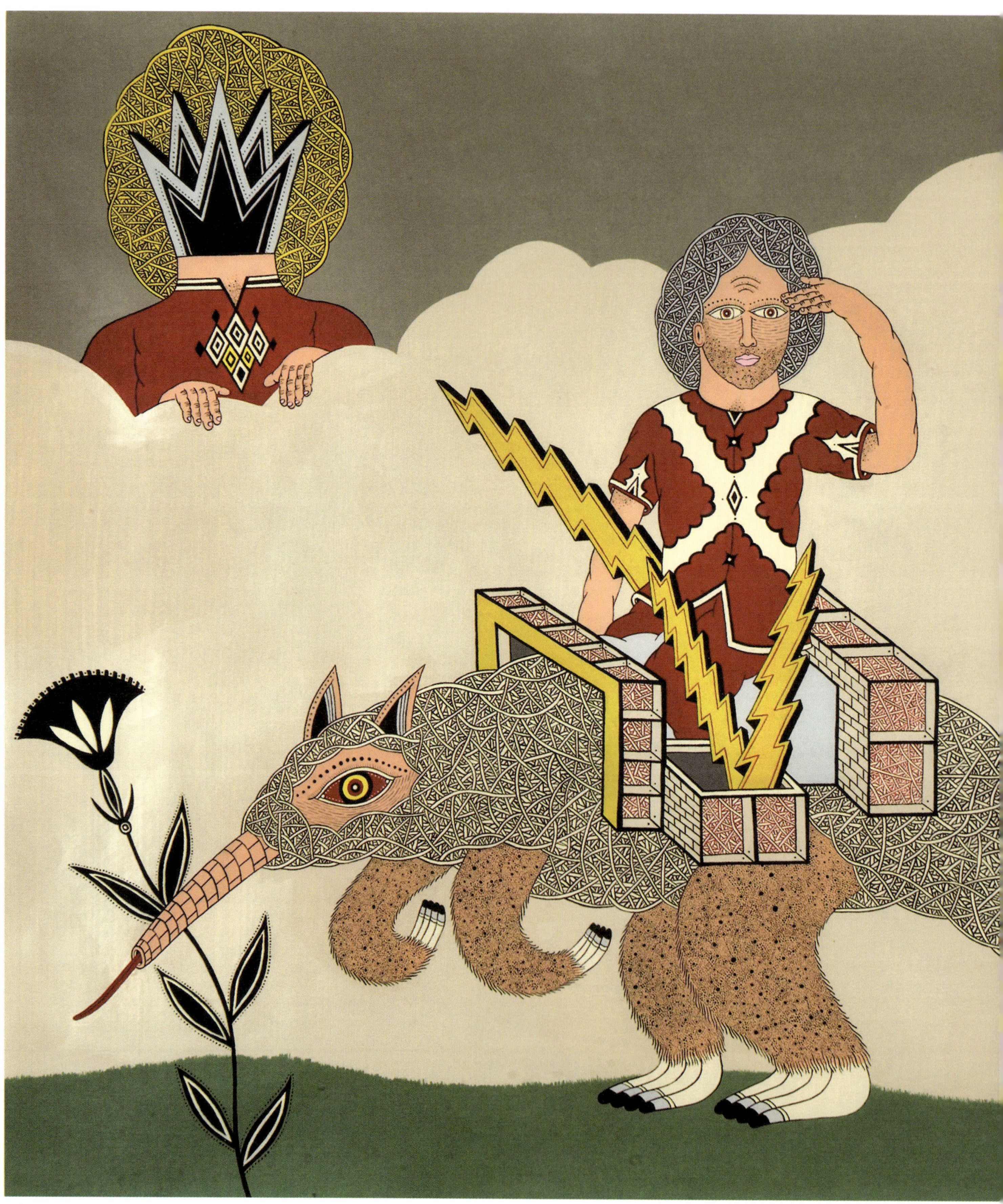

Matt Leines

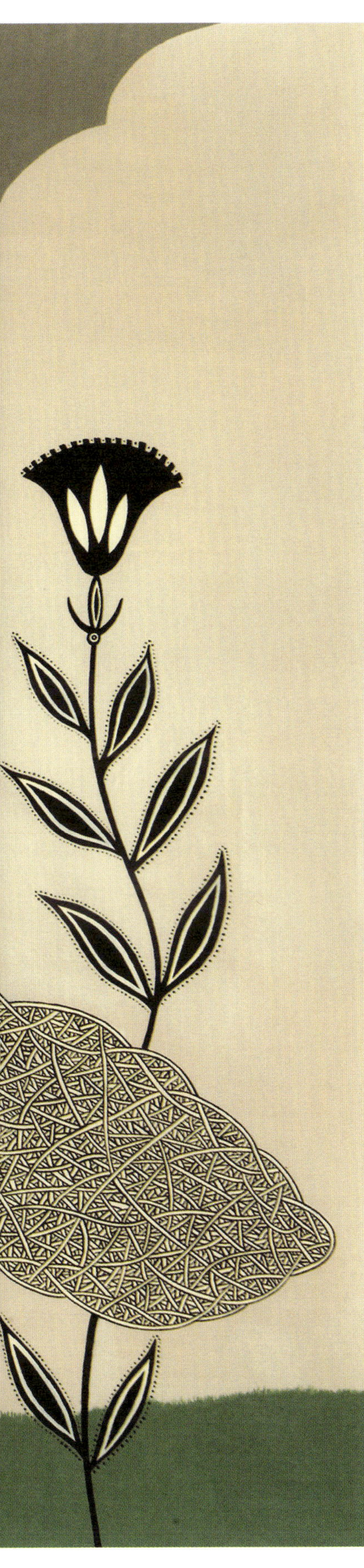

You Are Forgiven

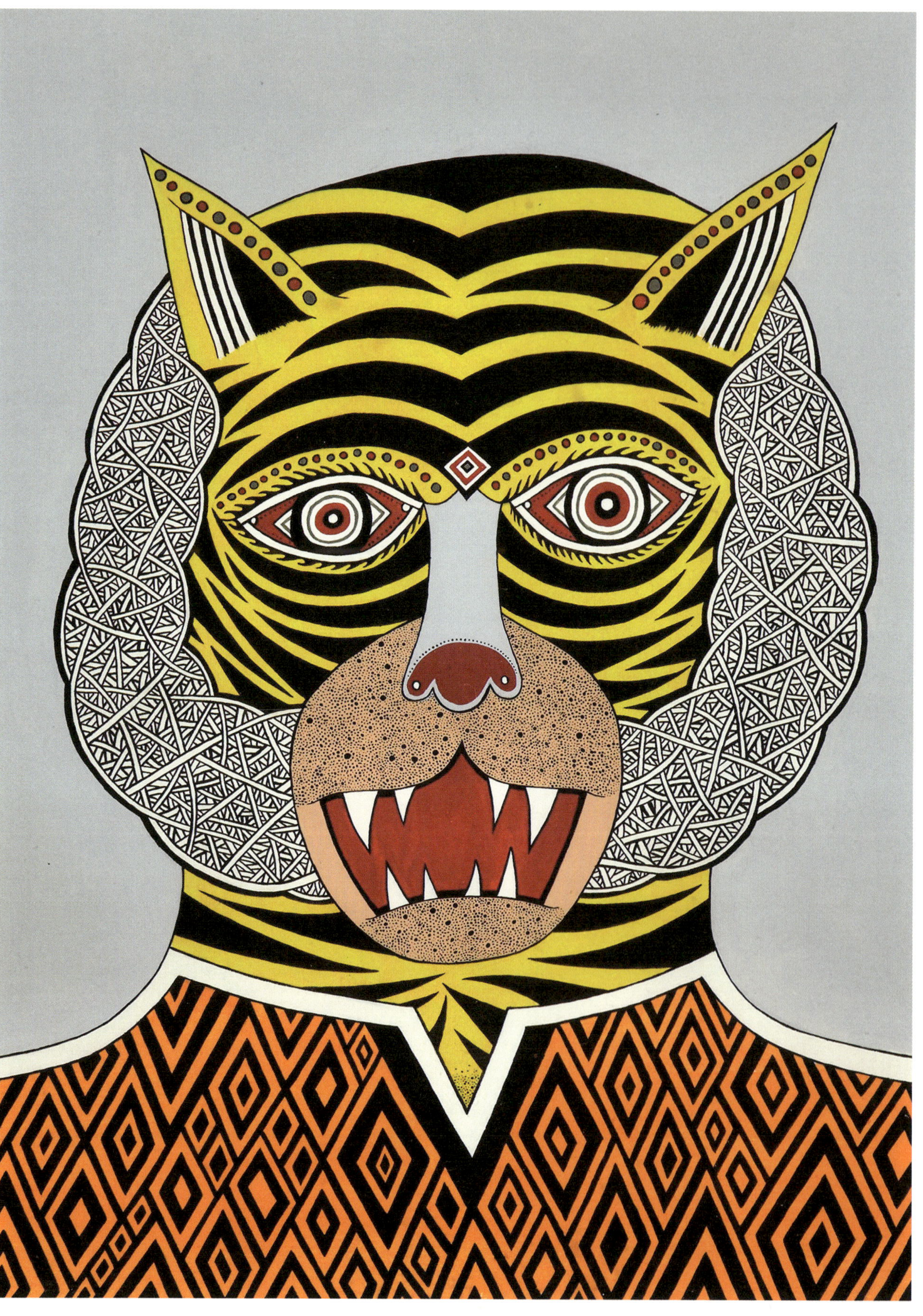

Matt Leines

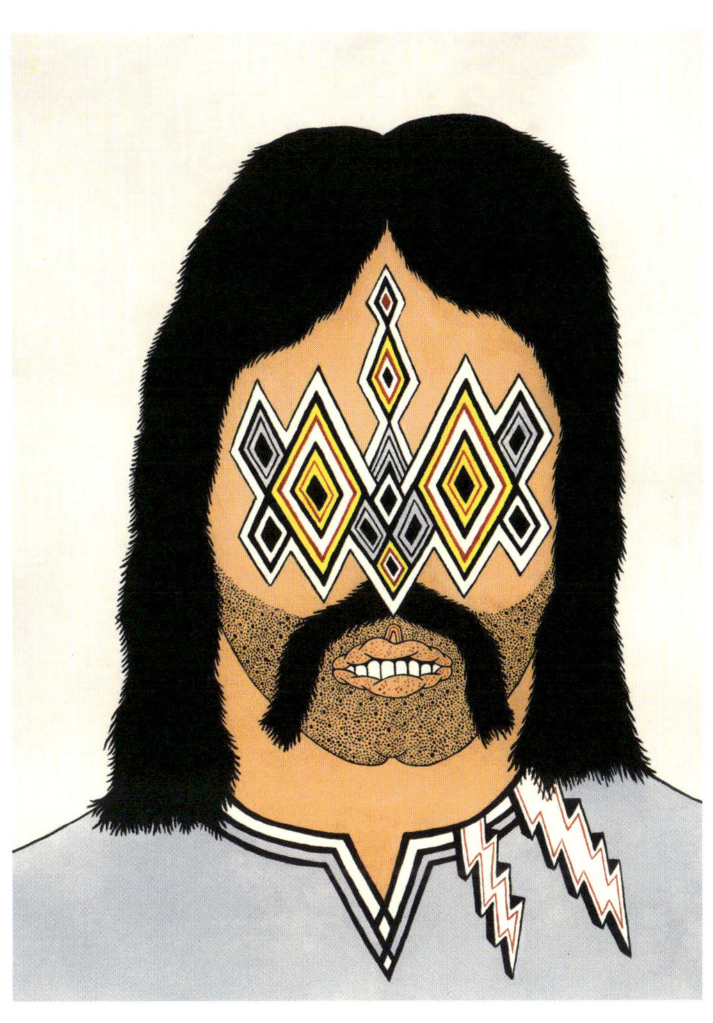

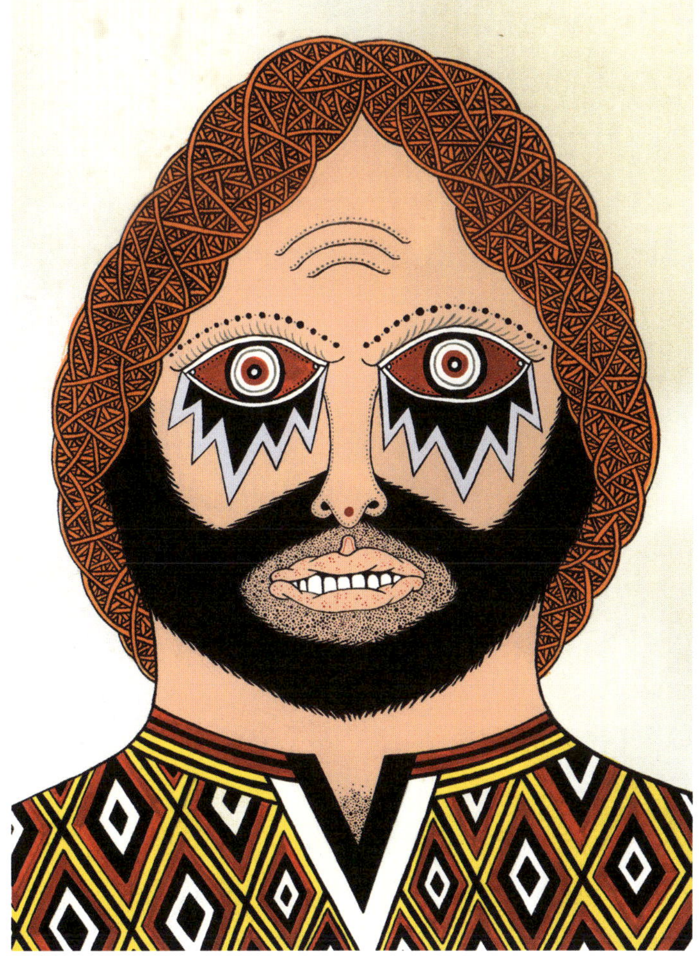

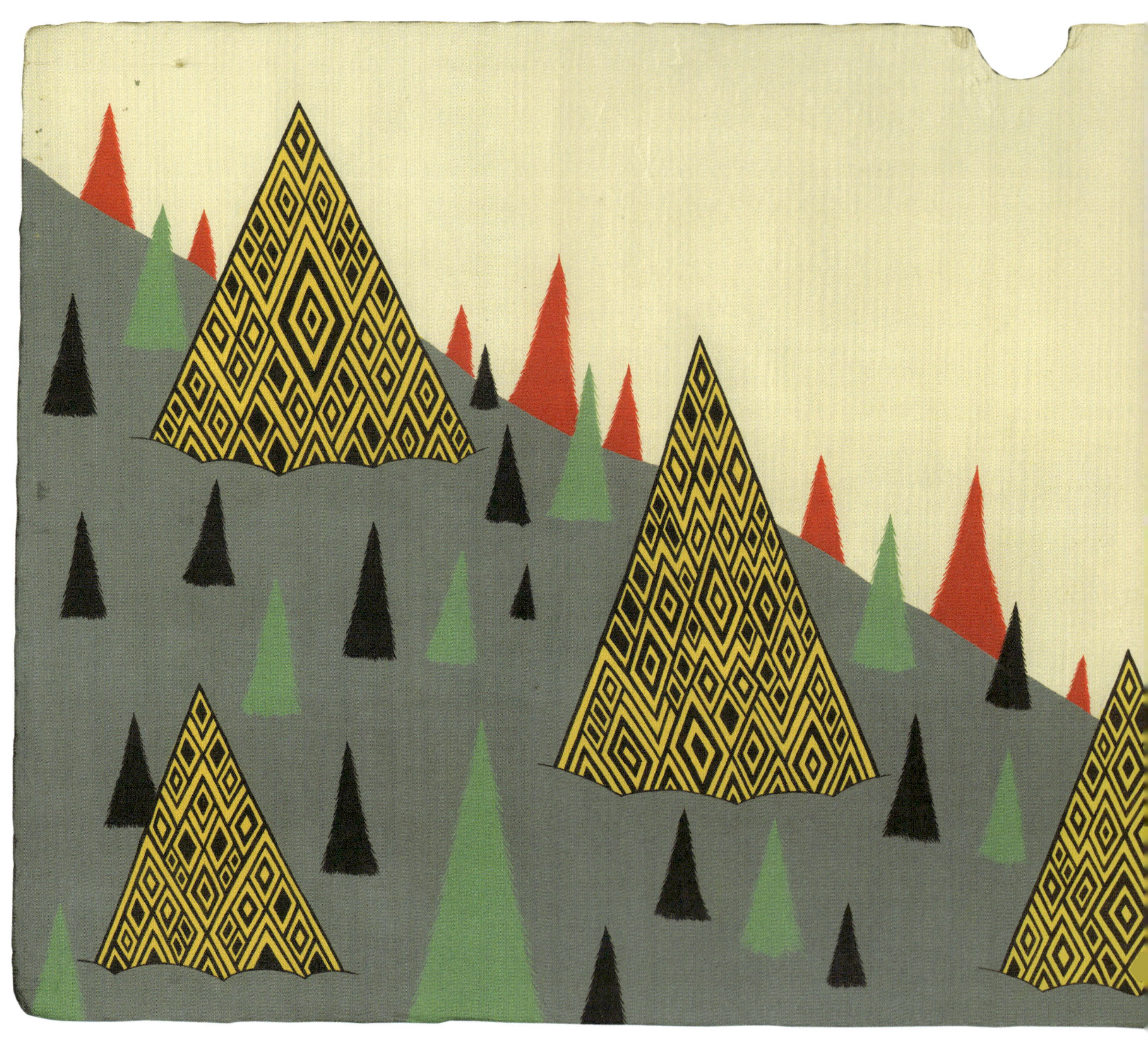

Matt Leines

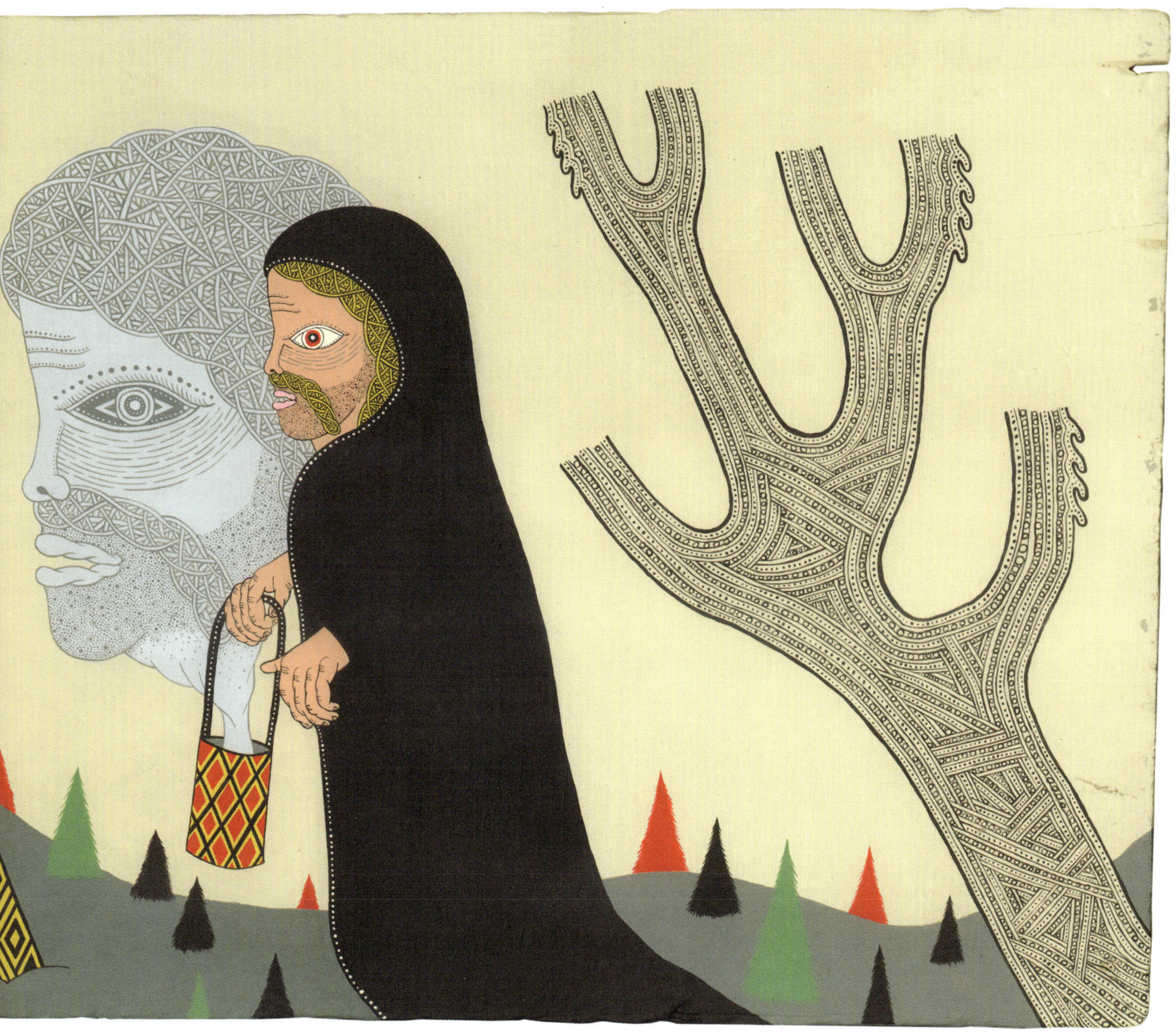

You Are Forgiven

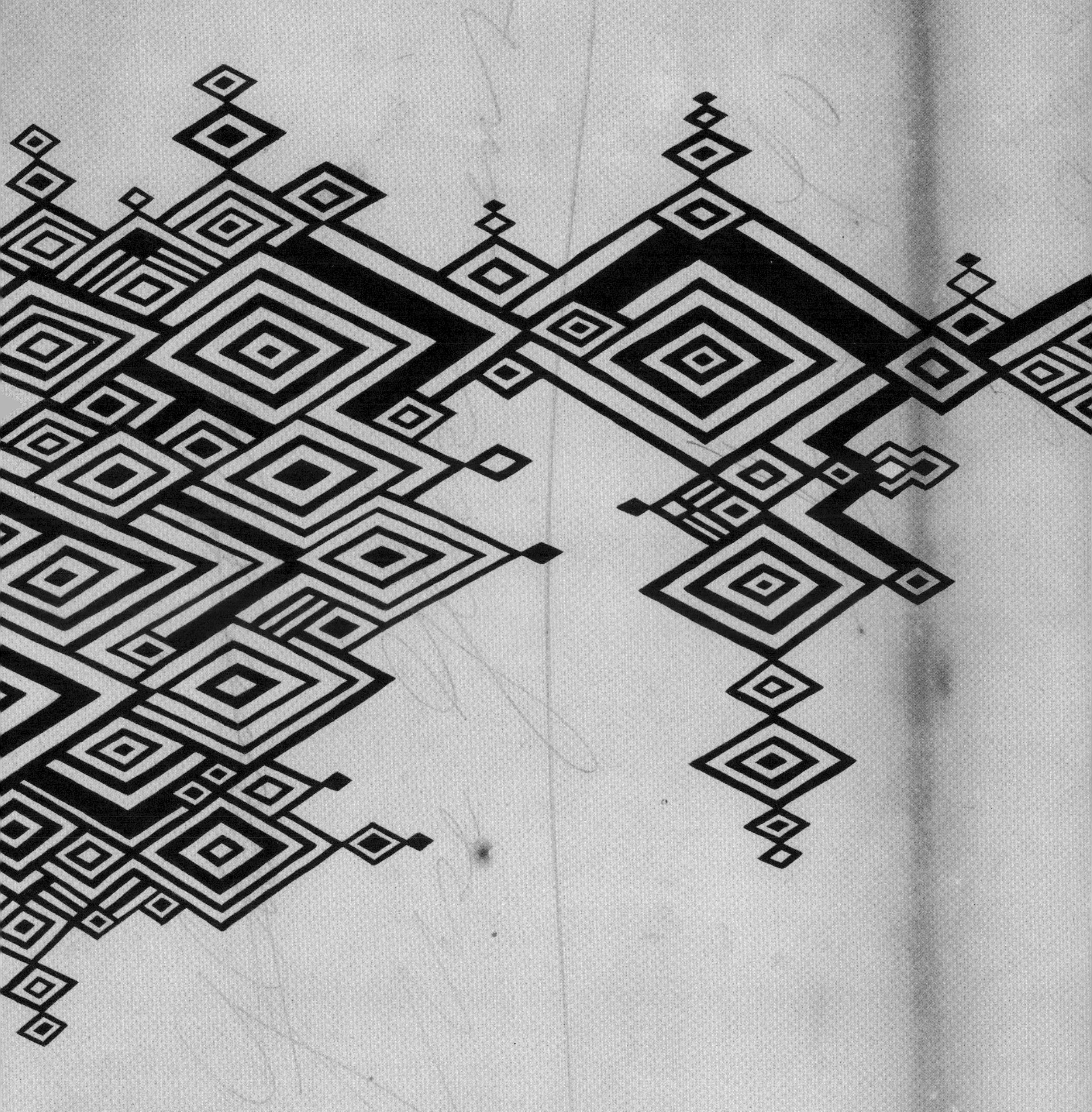

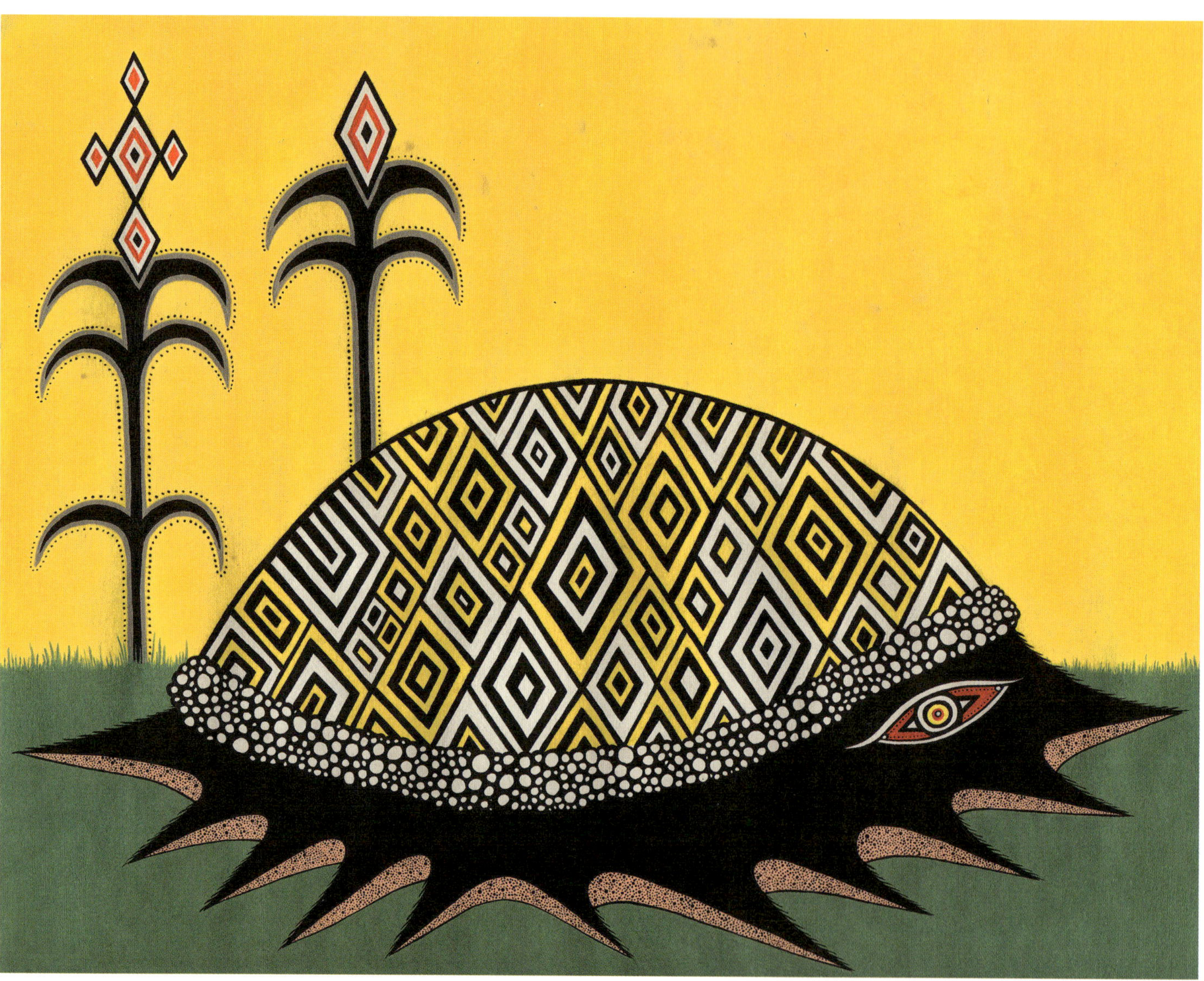

Matt Leines

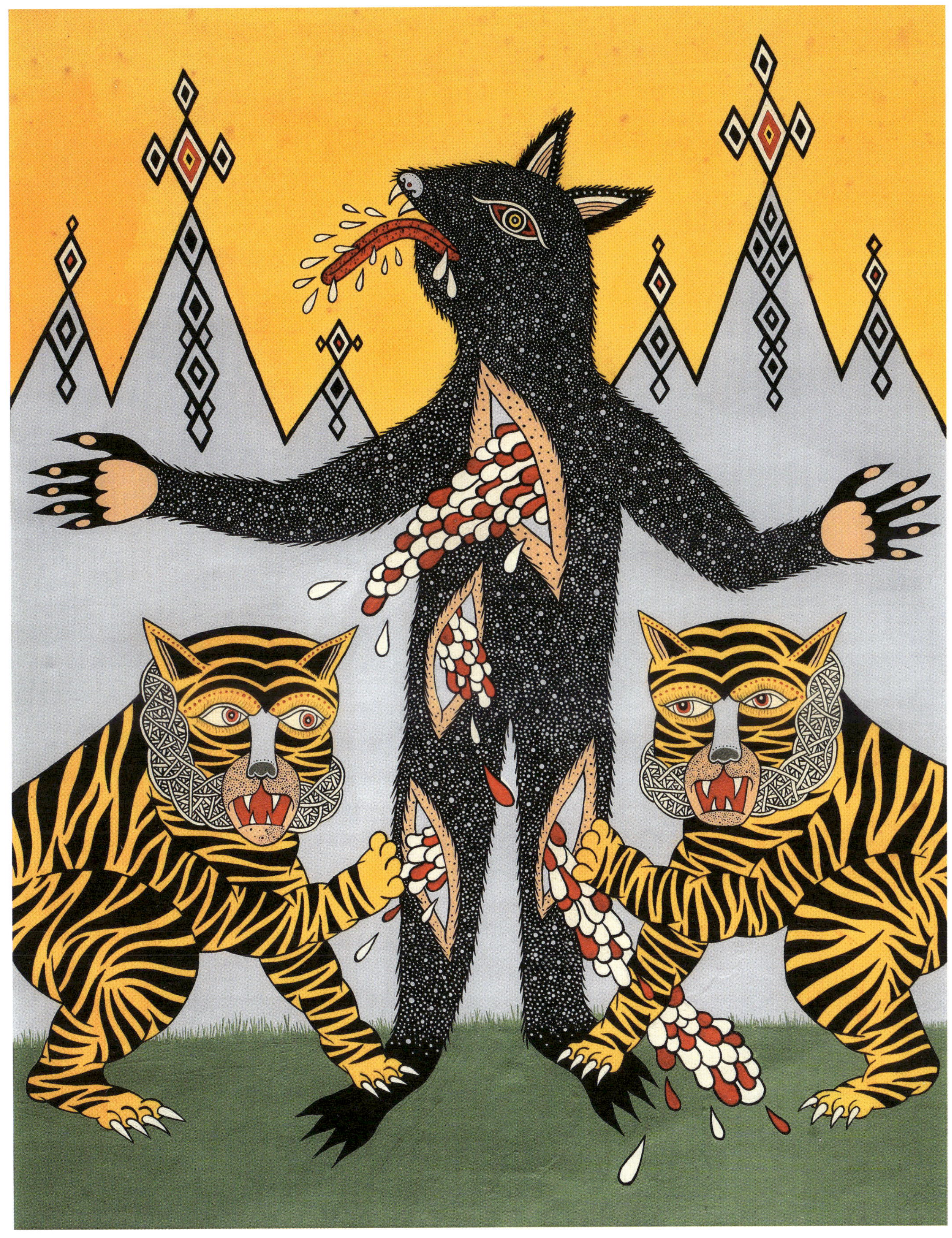

You Are Forgiven

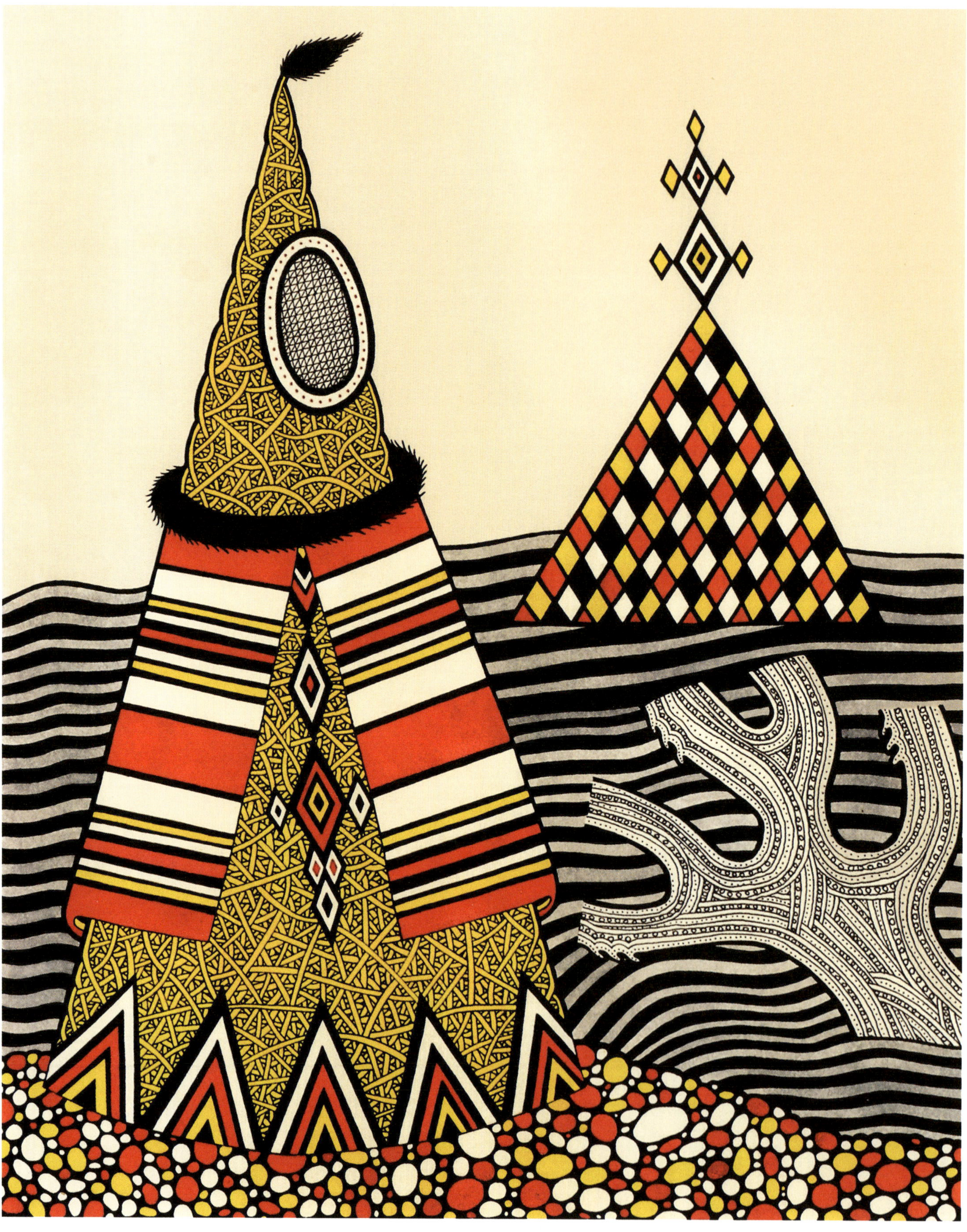

Matt Leines

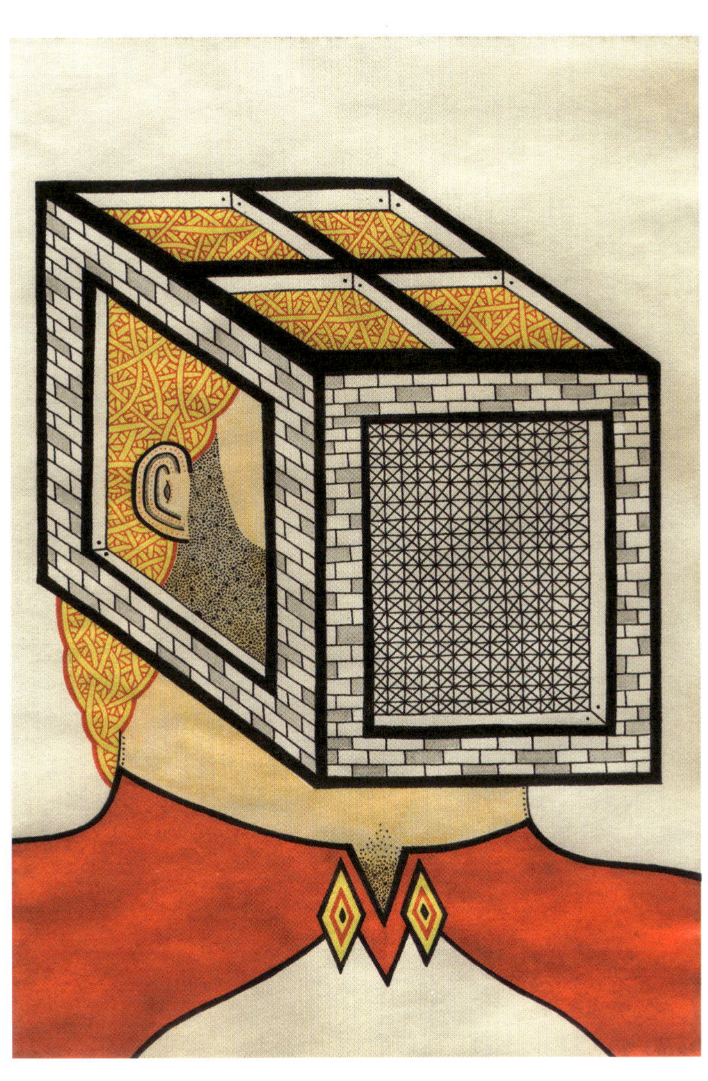

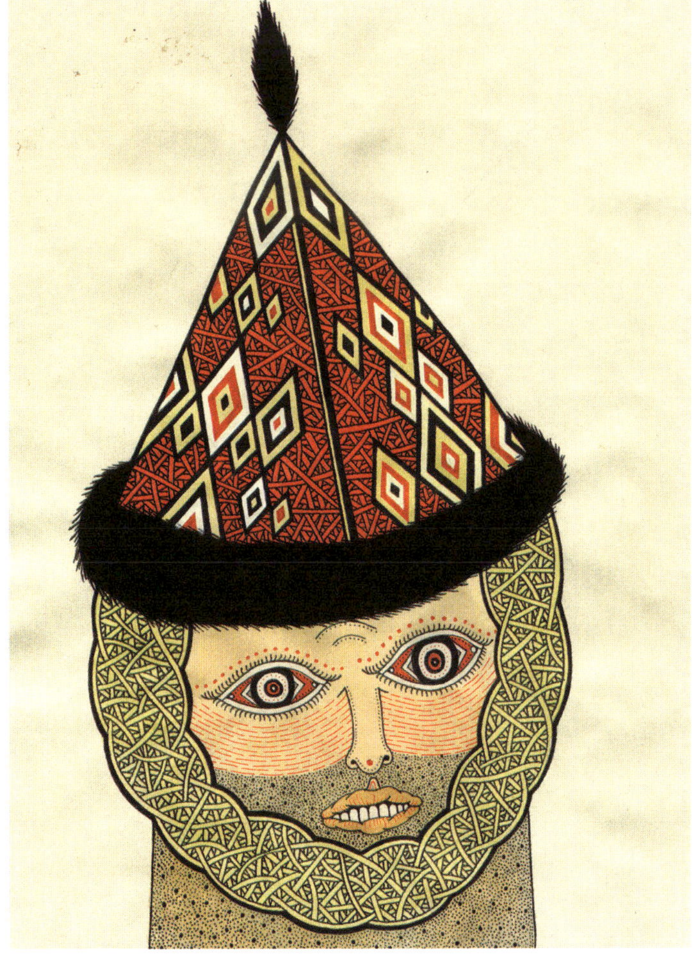

You Are Forgiven

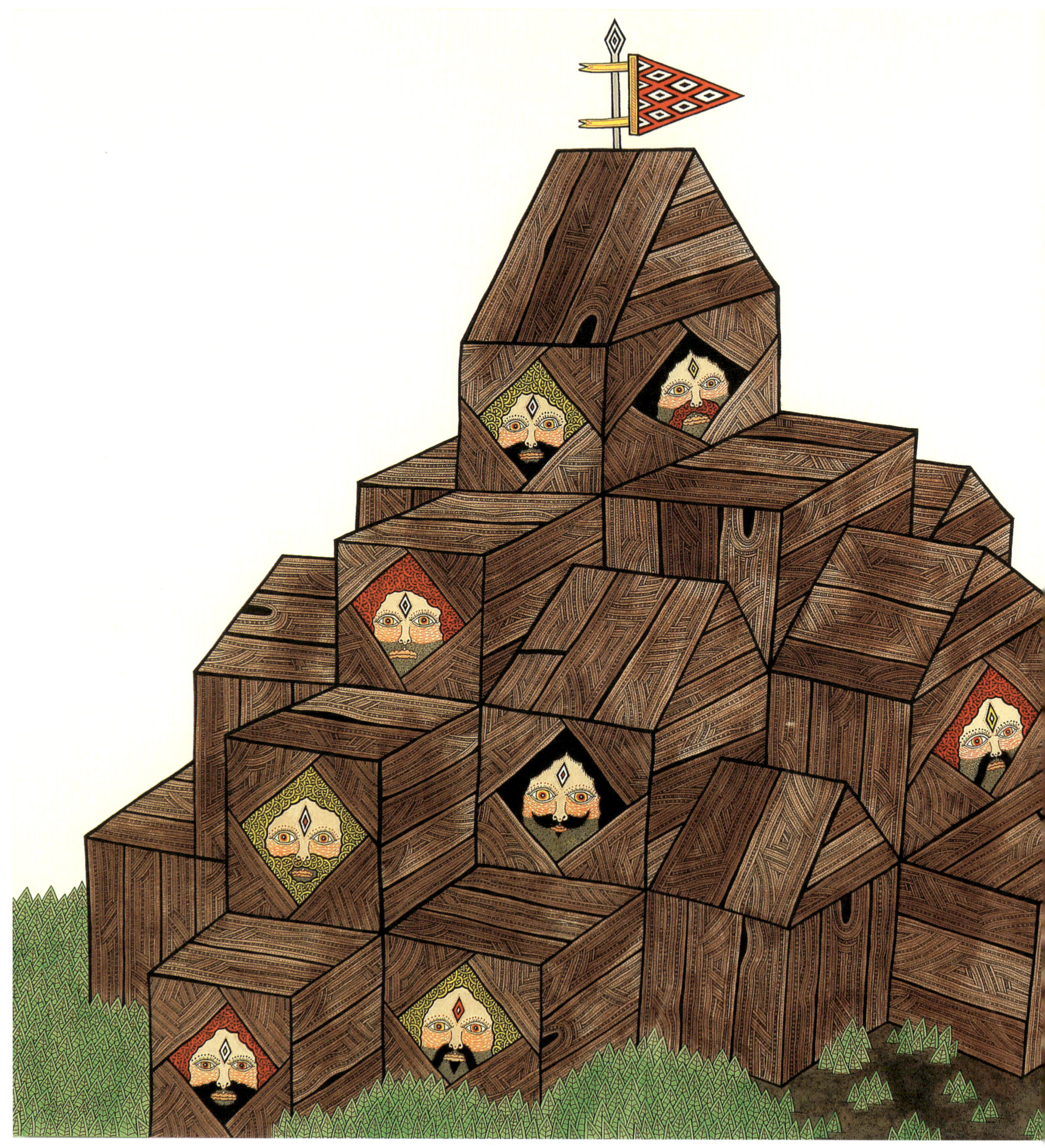

Matt Leines

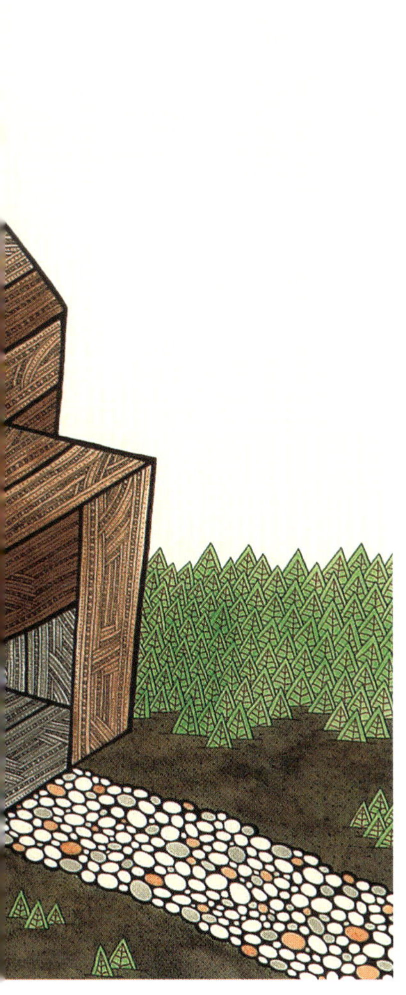

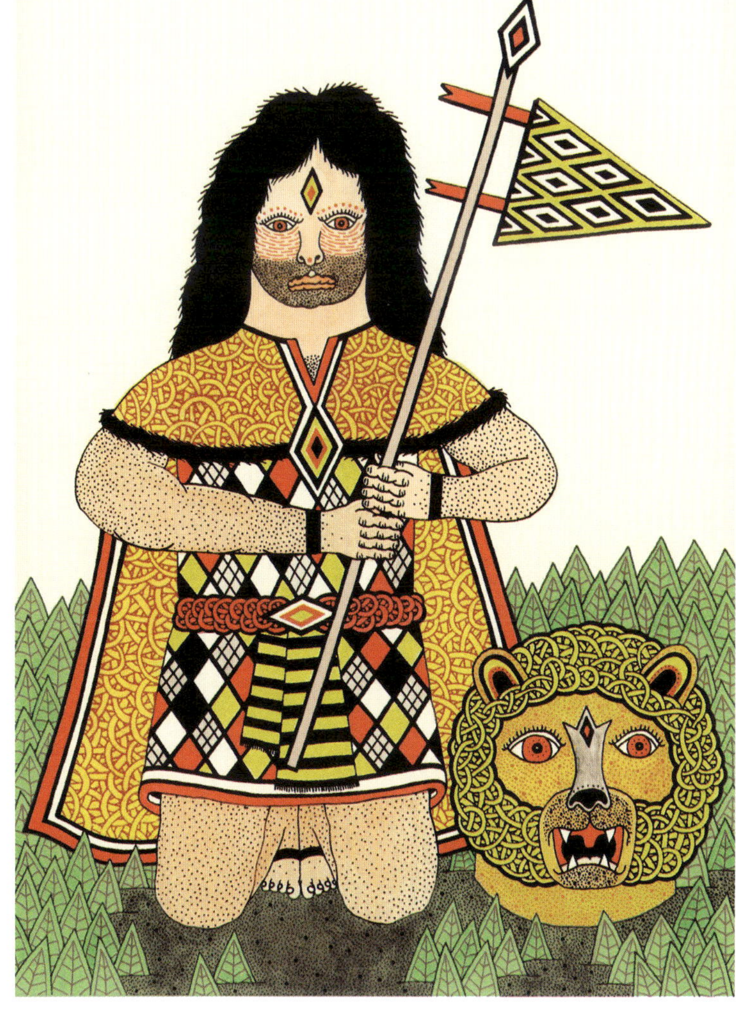

You Are Forgiven

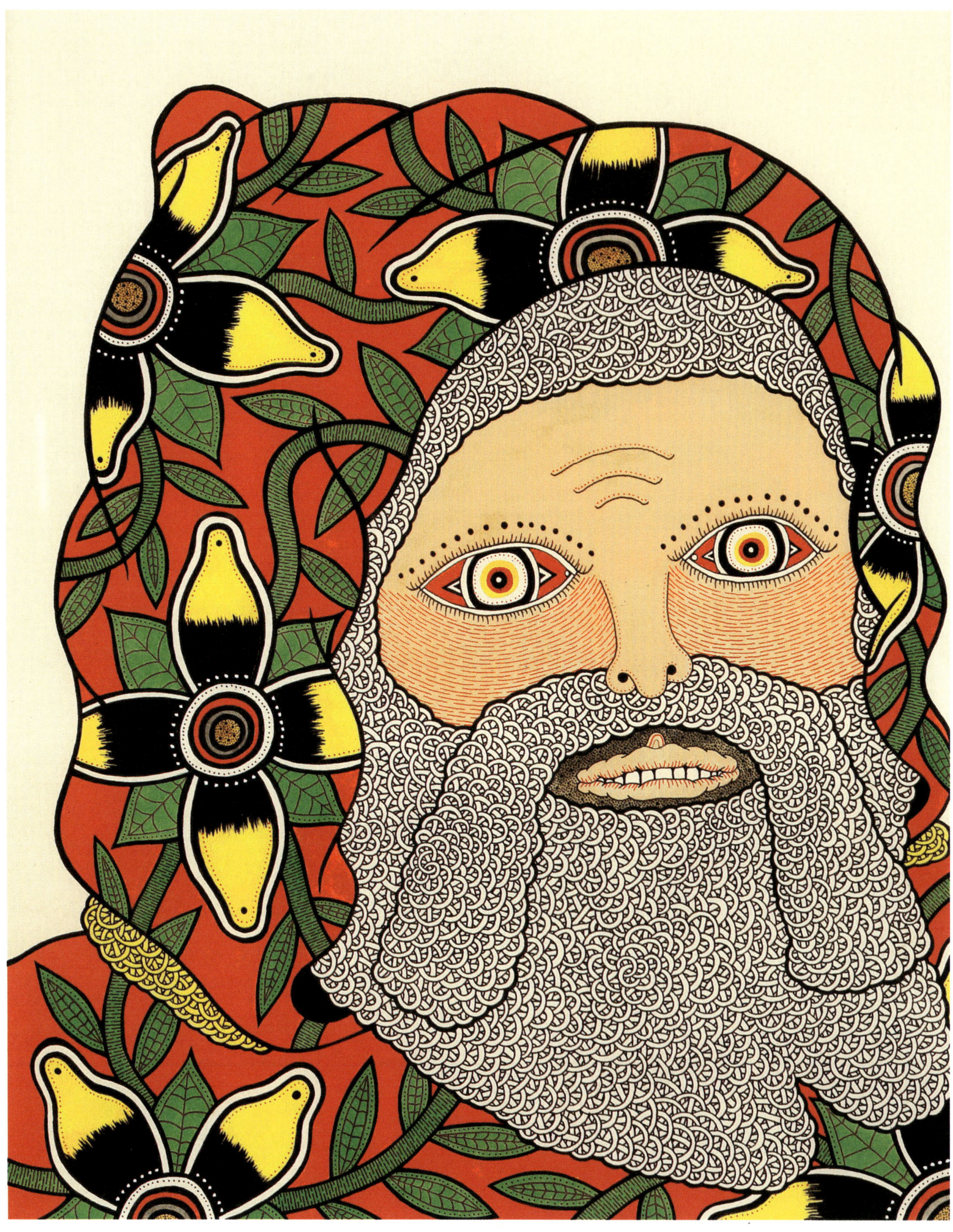

Matt Leines

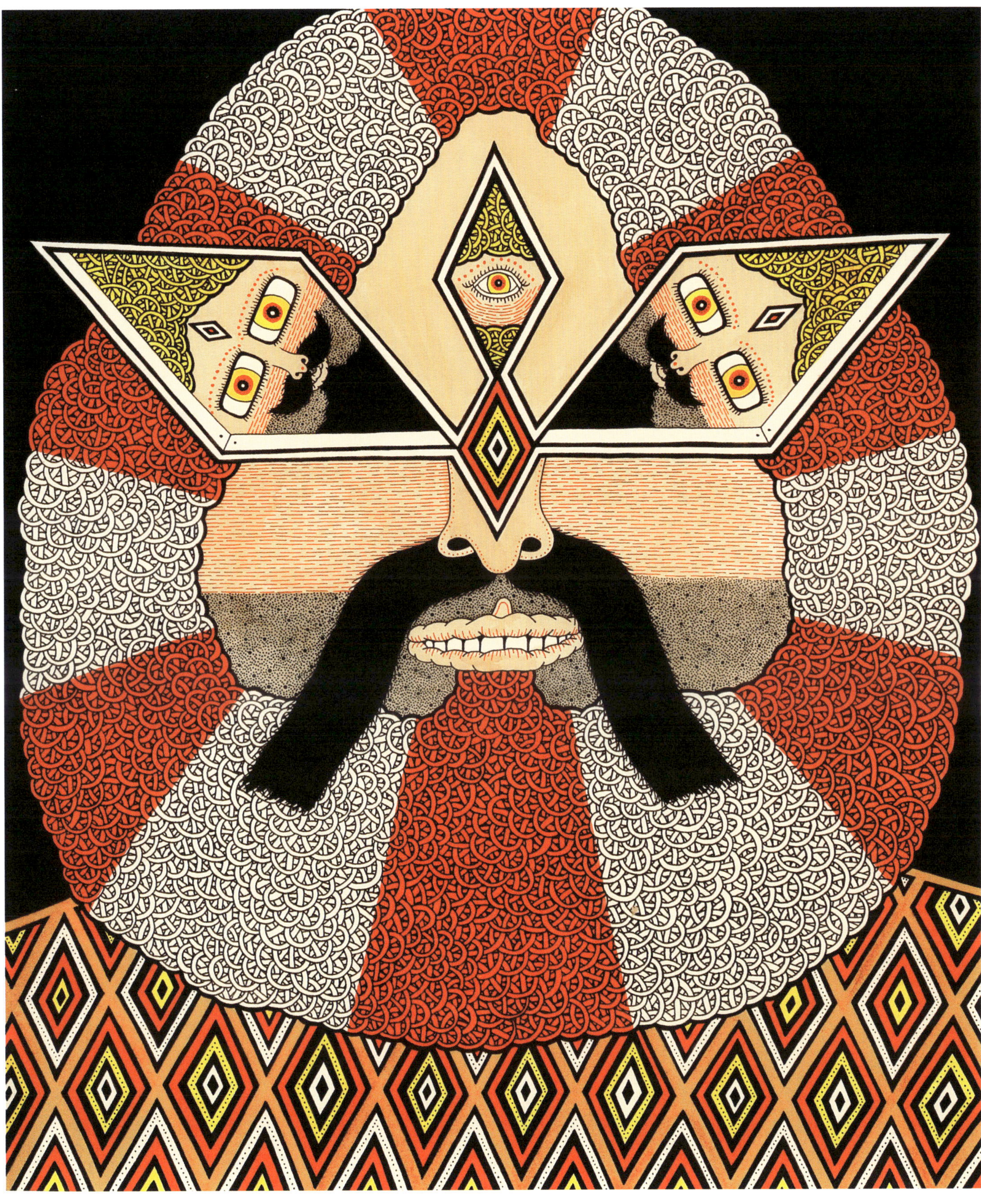

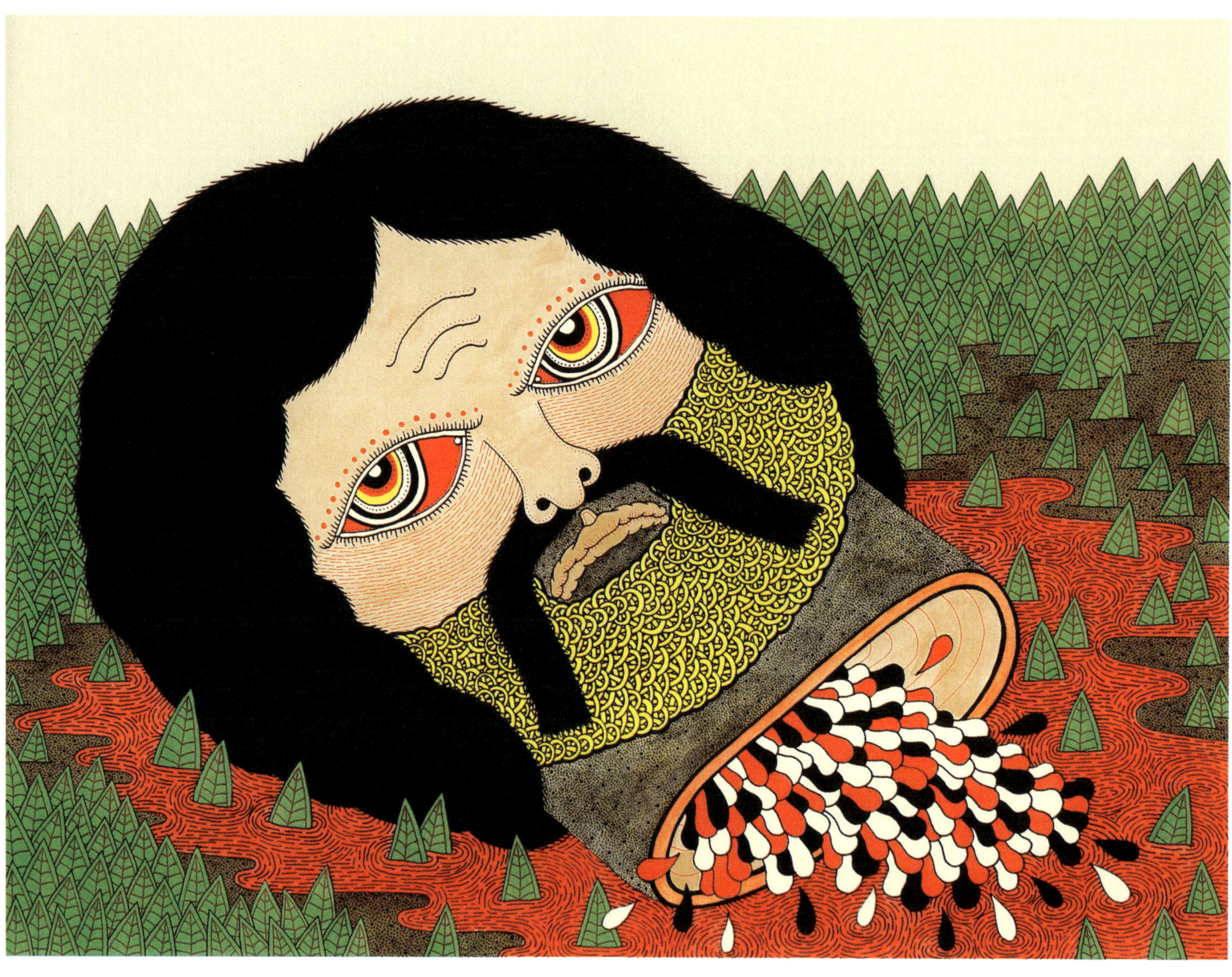

Matt Leines

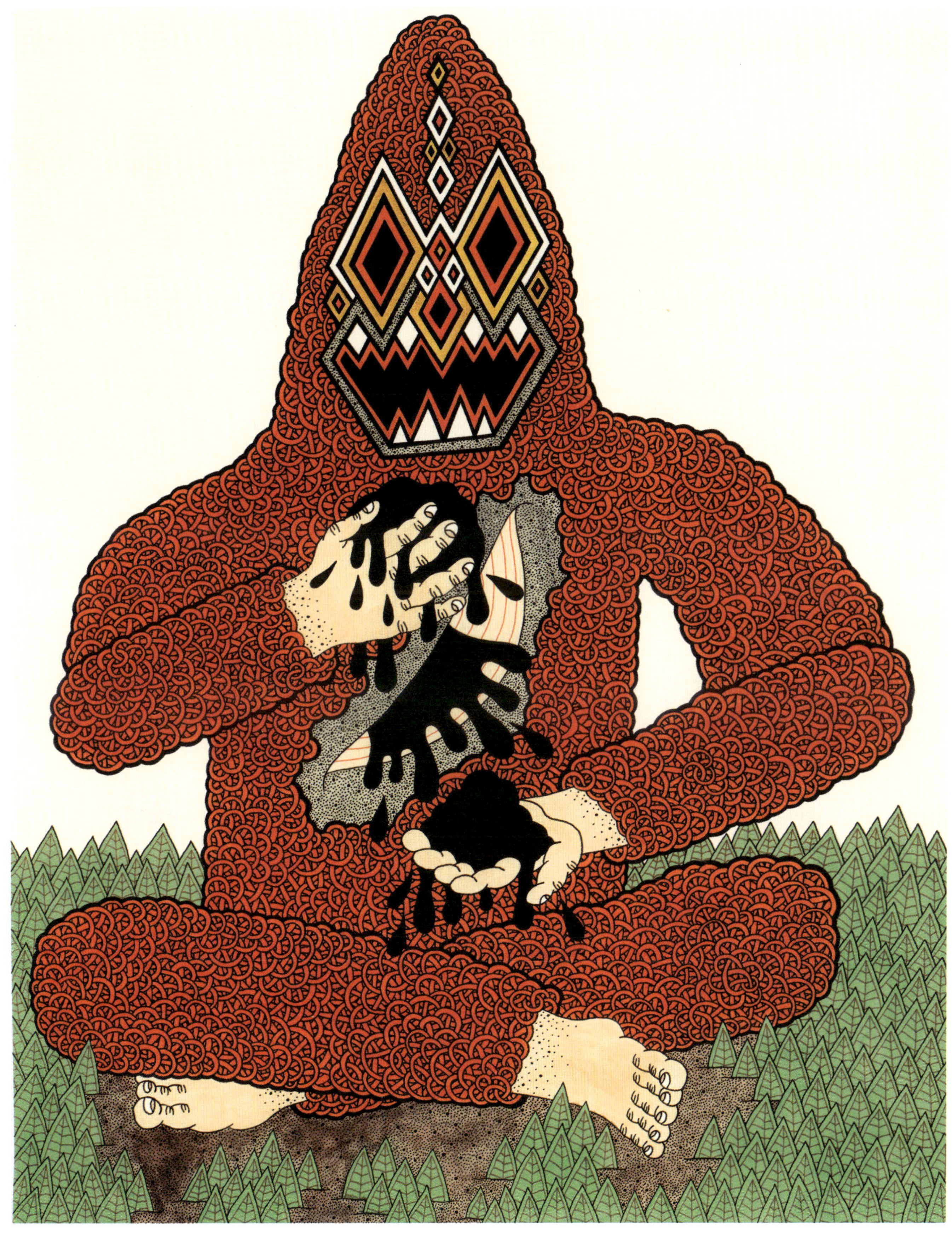

You Are Forgiven

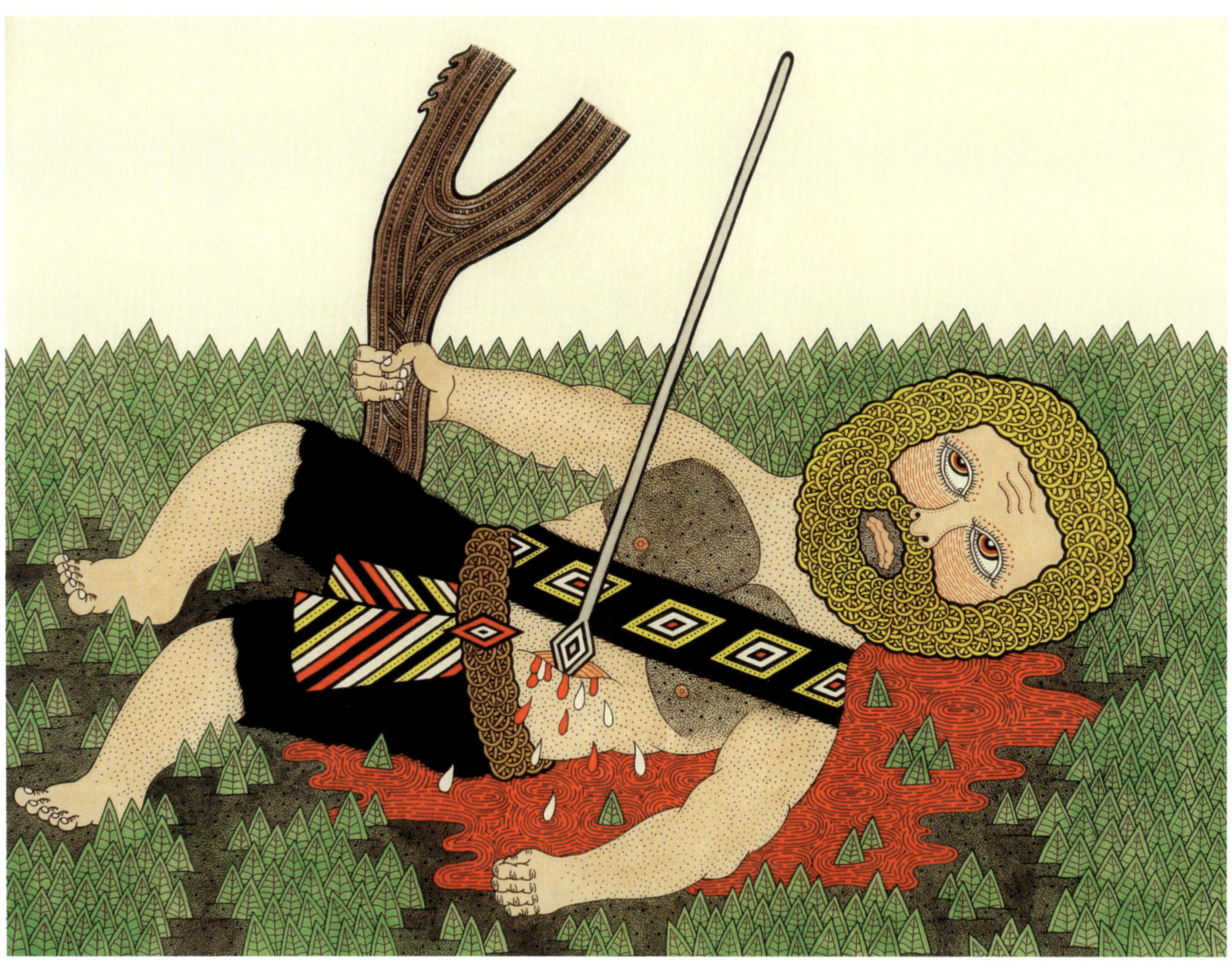

80

Matt Leines

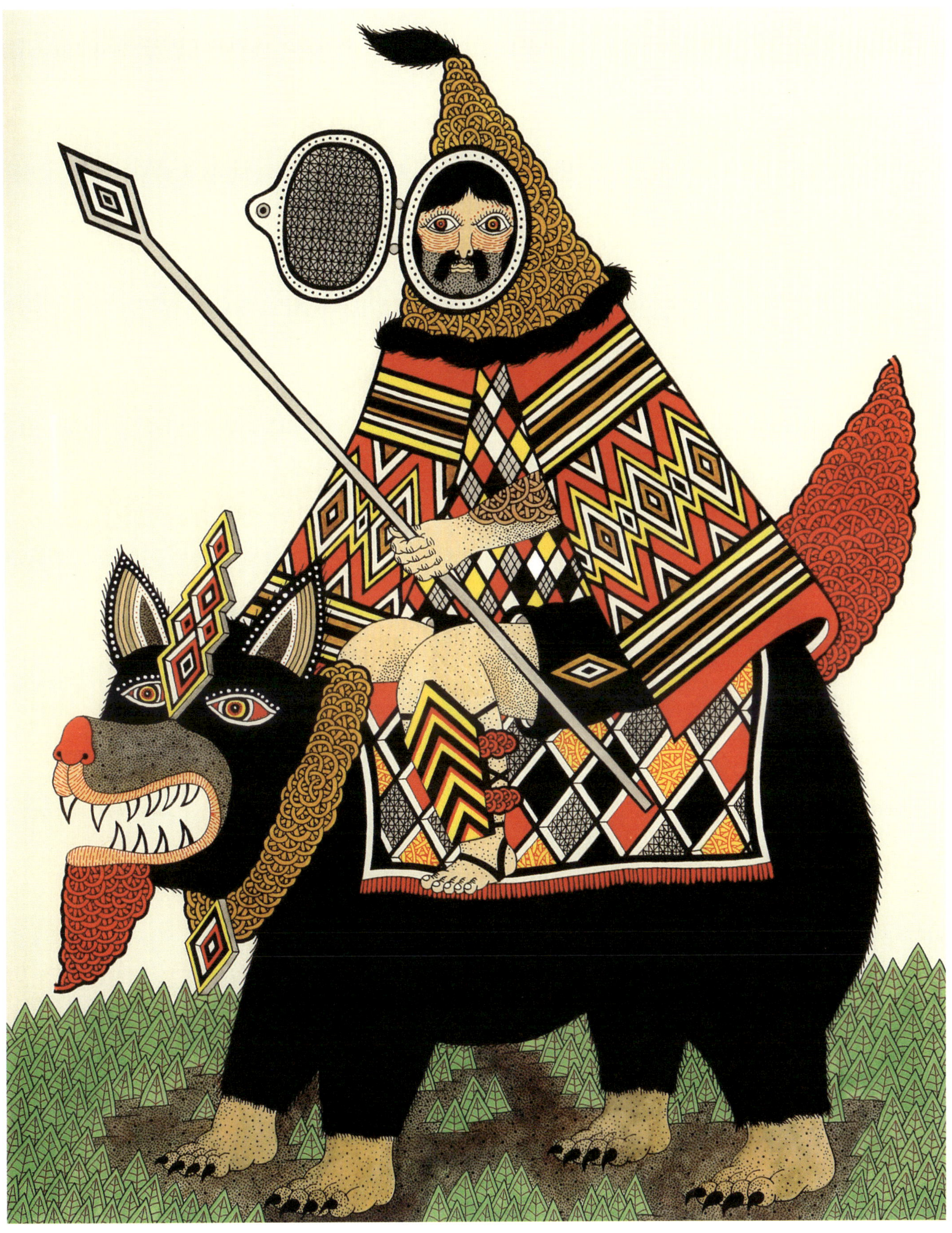

You Are Forgiven

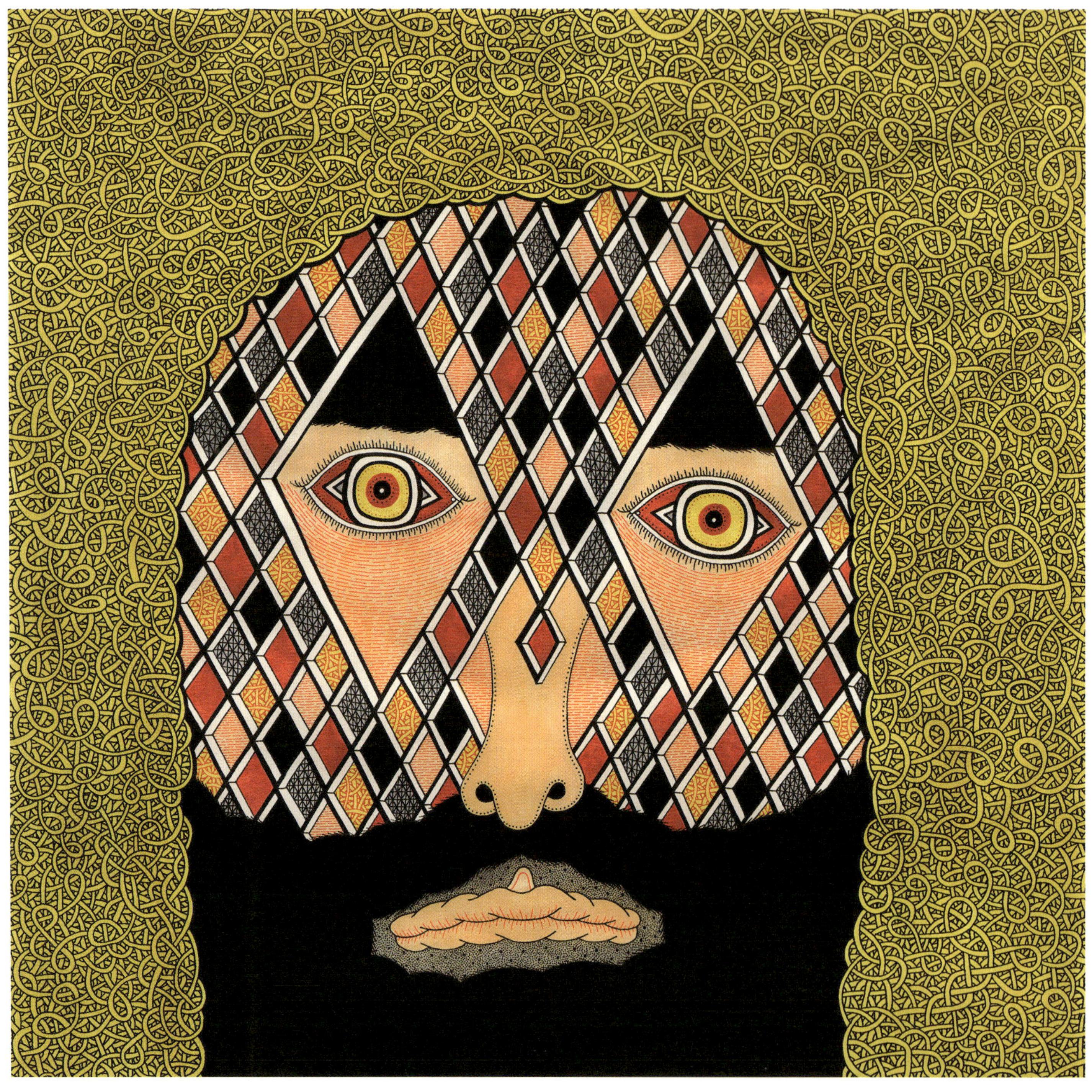

Matt Leines

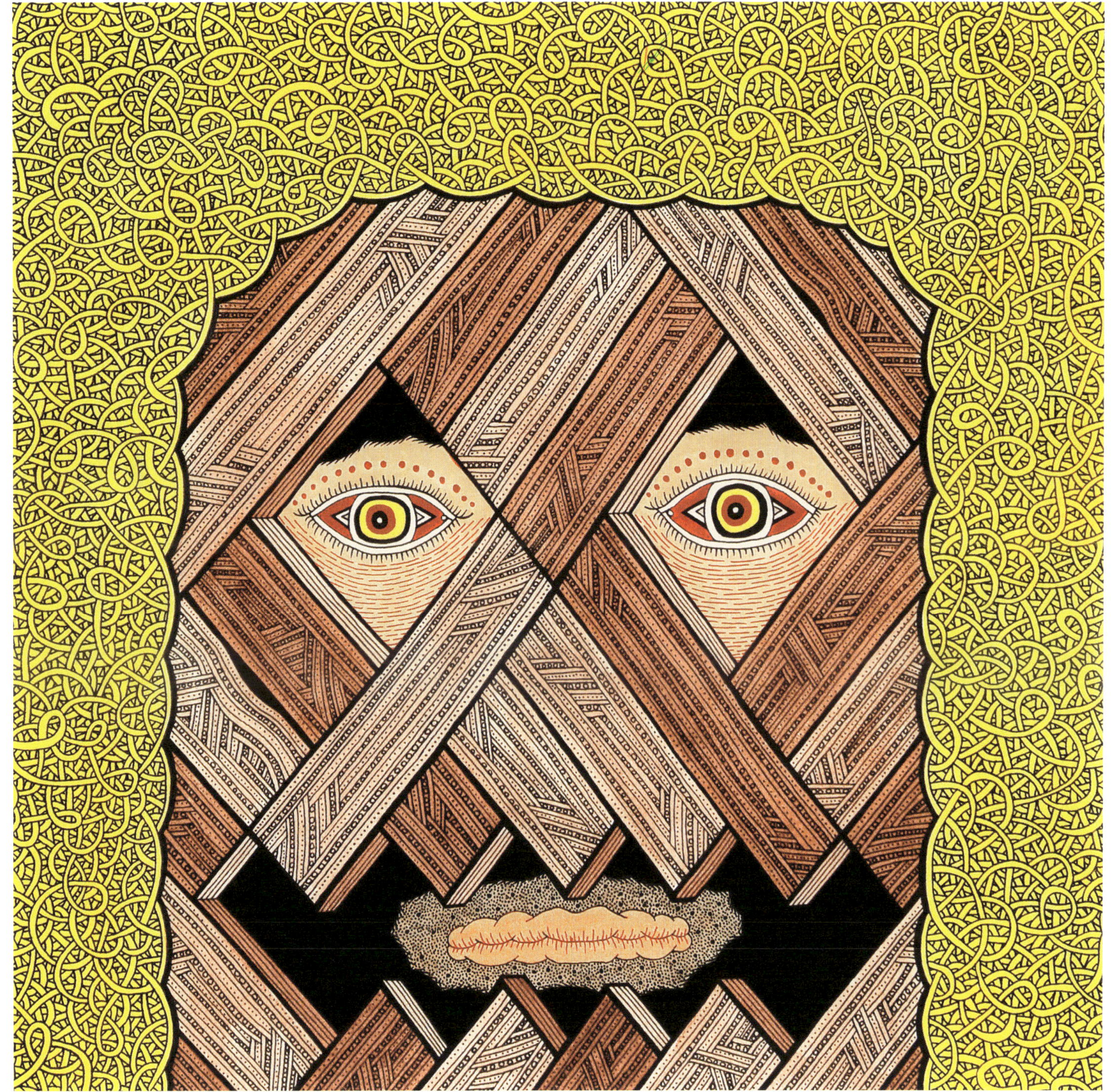

You Are Forgiven

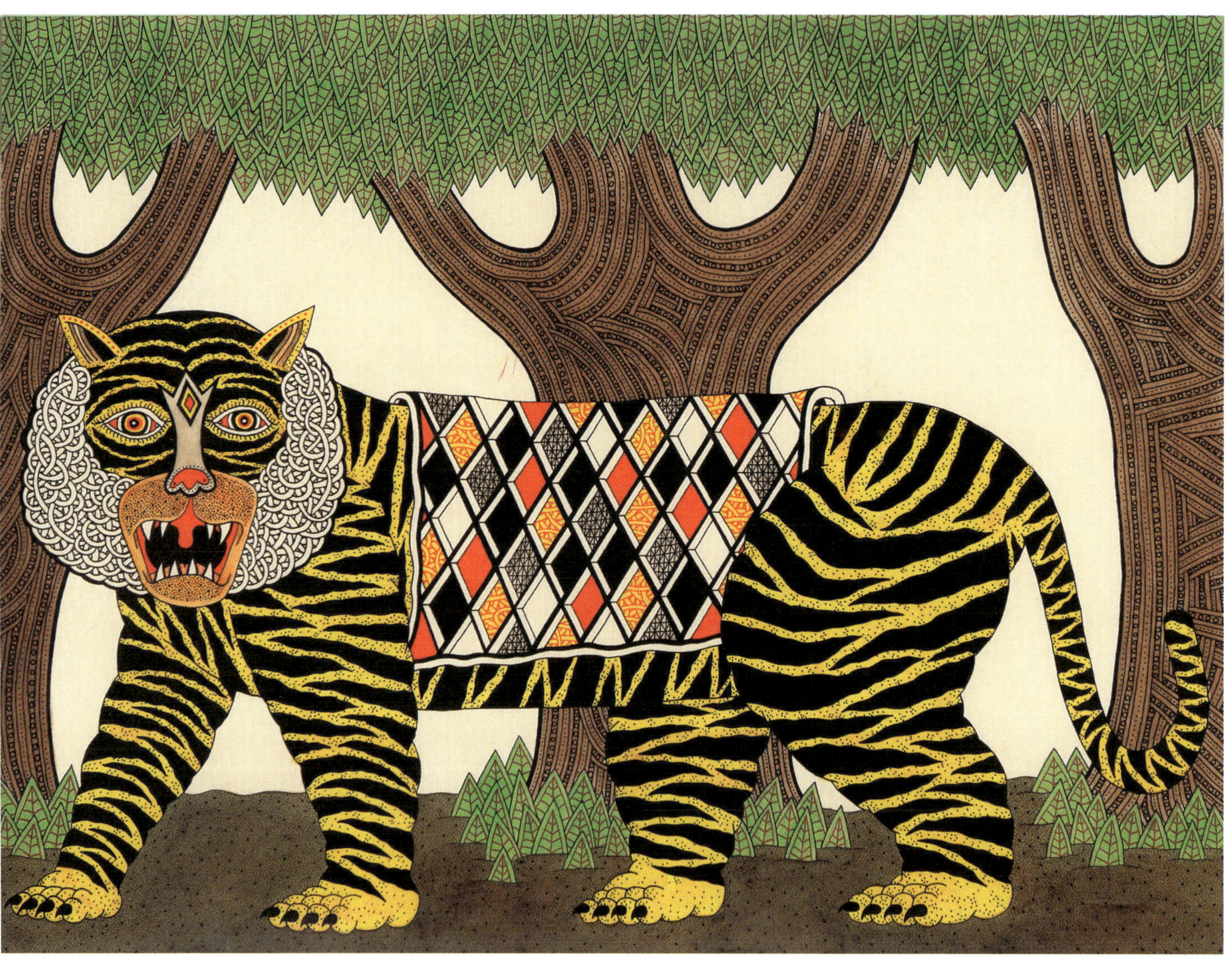

84

Matt Leines

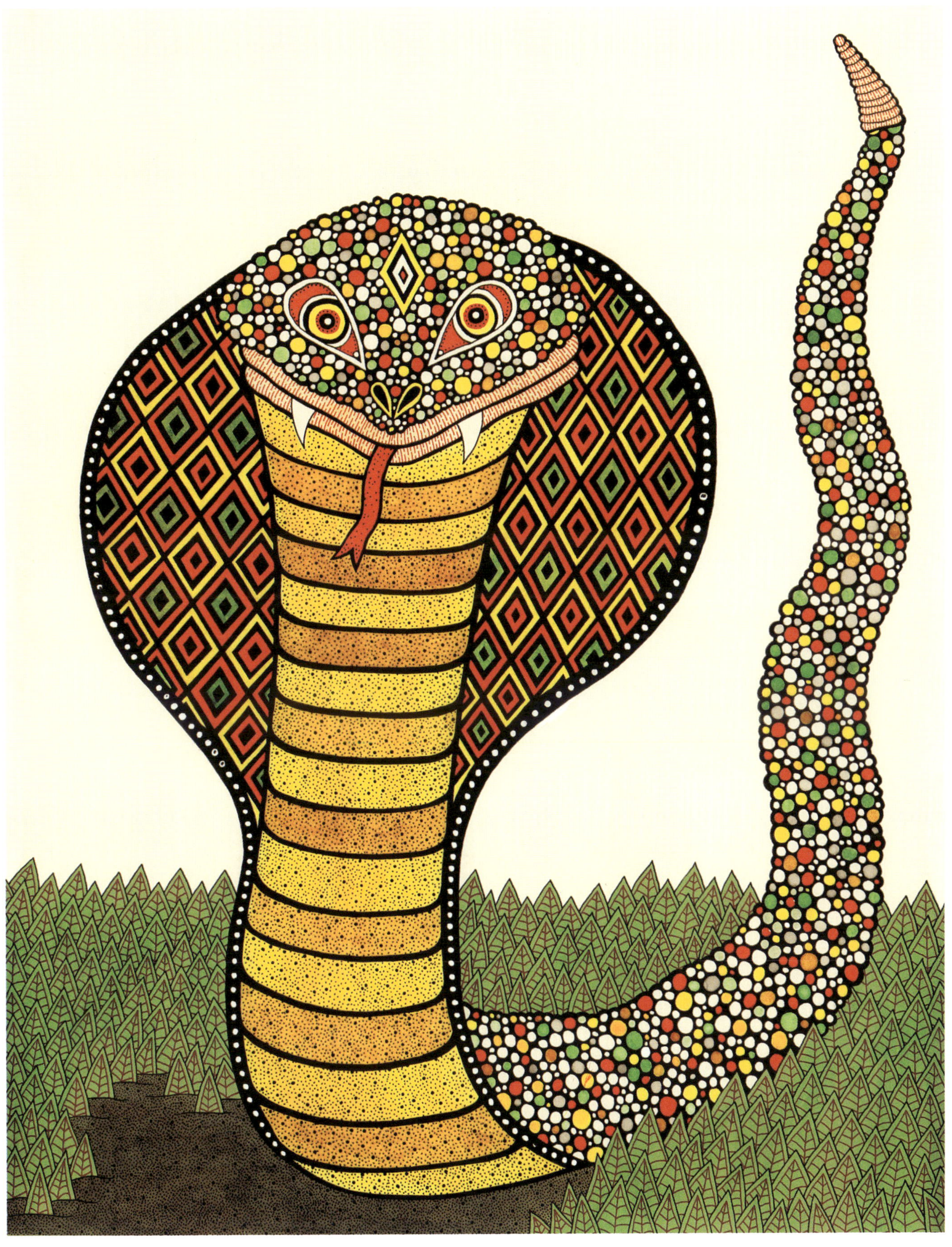

You Are Forgiven

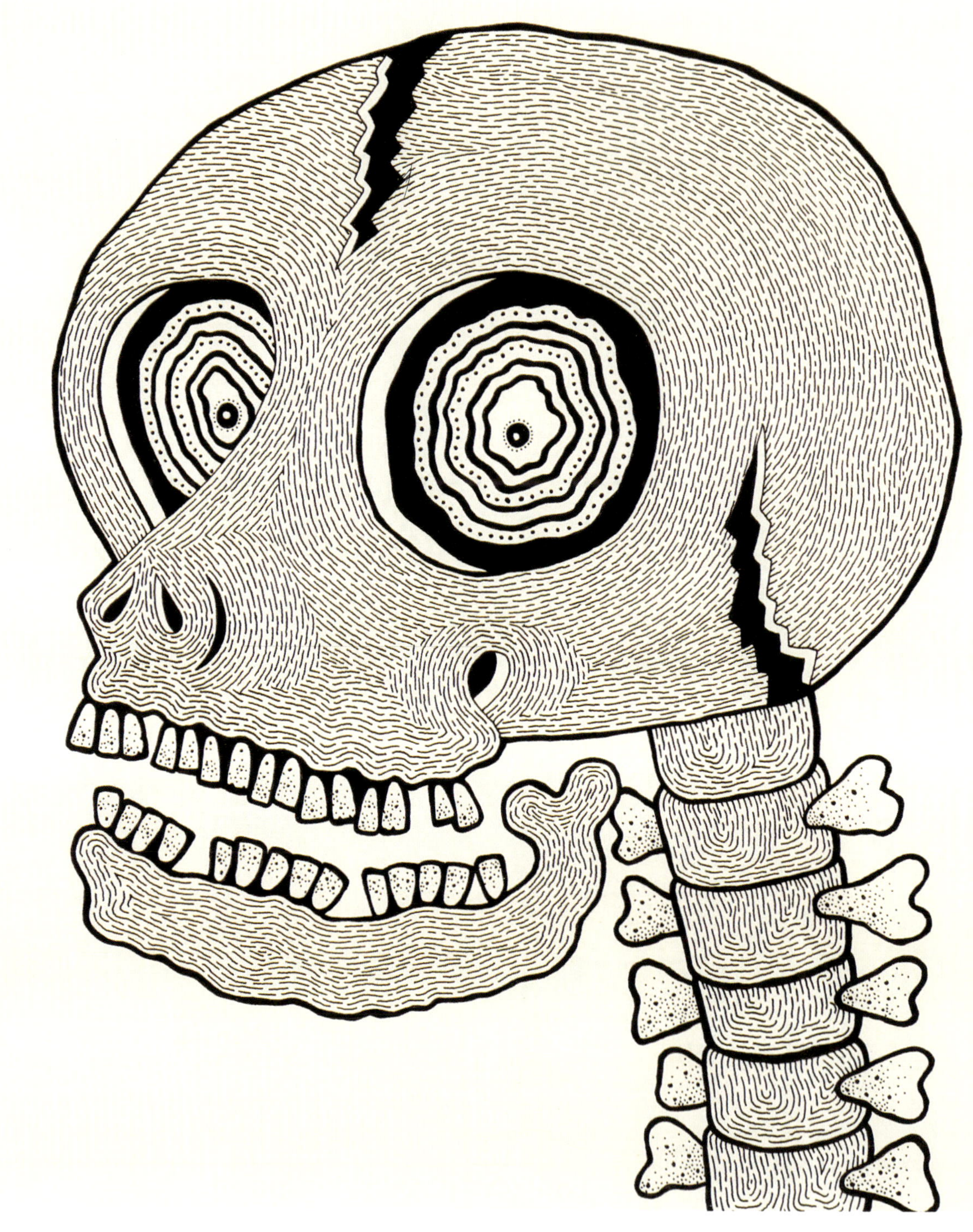

Matt Leines

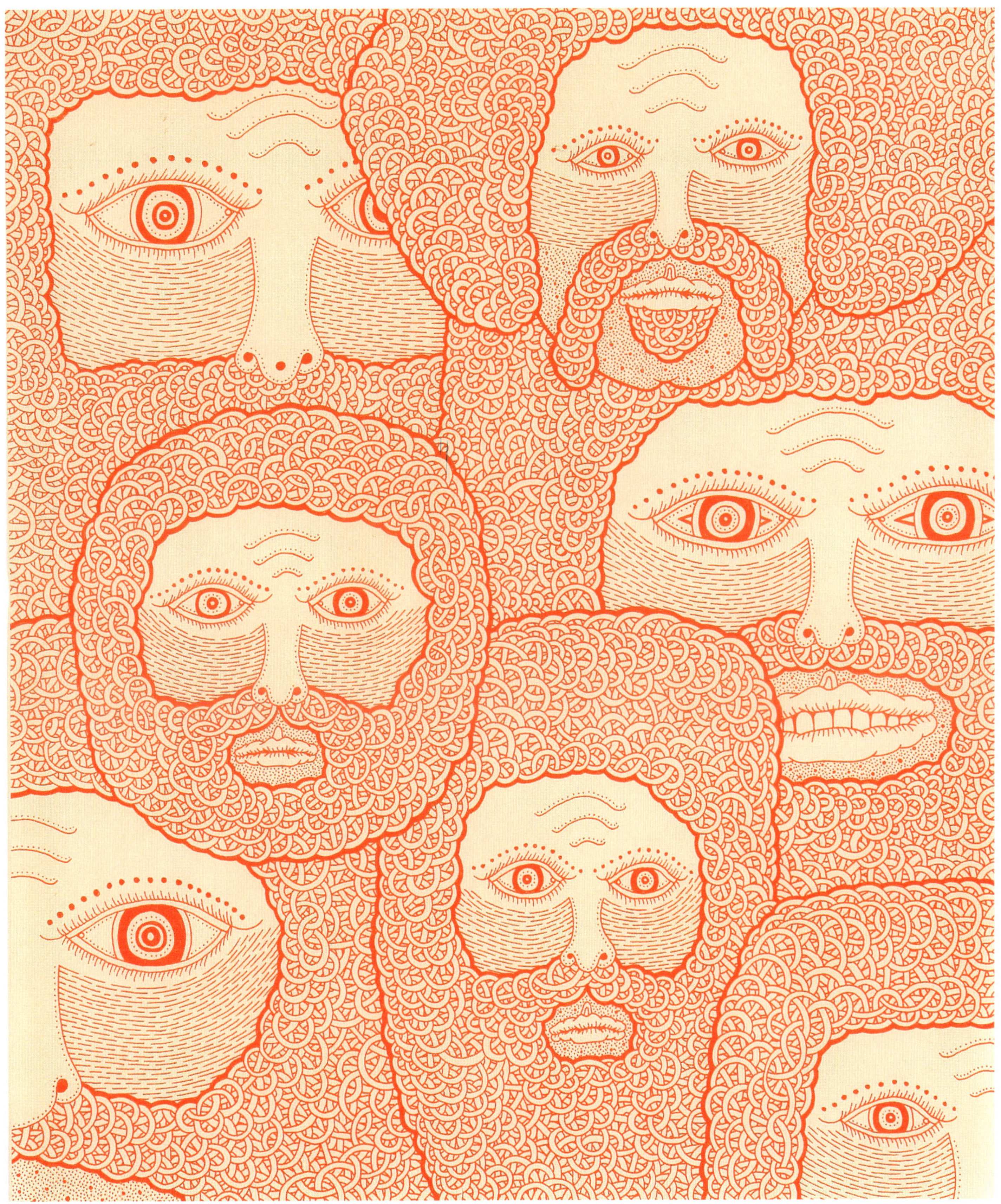

You Are Forgiven

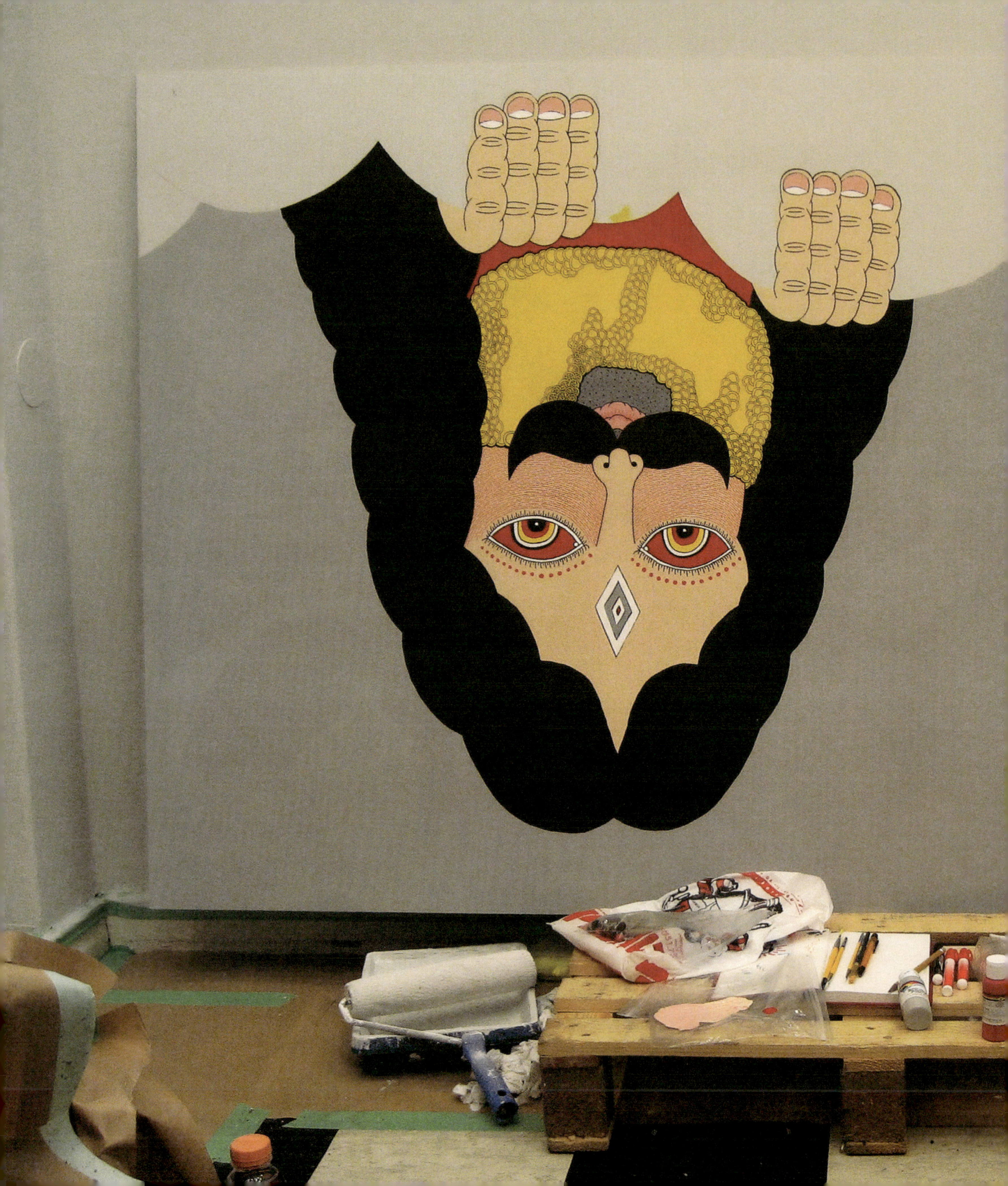

You Are Forgiven

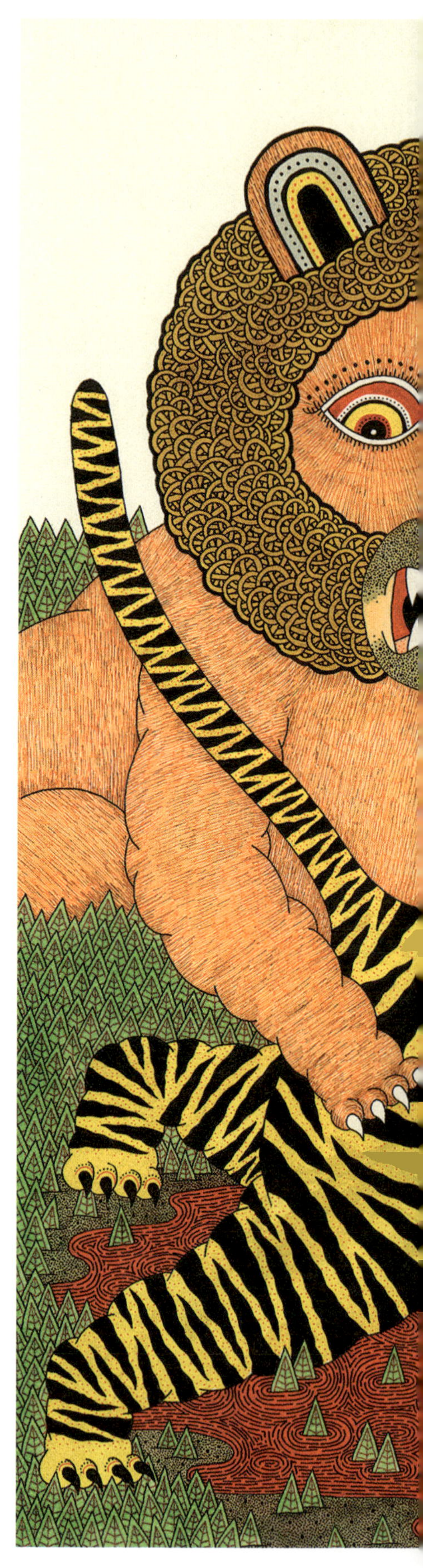

Matt Leines

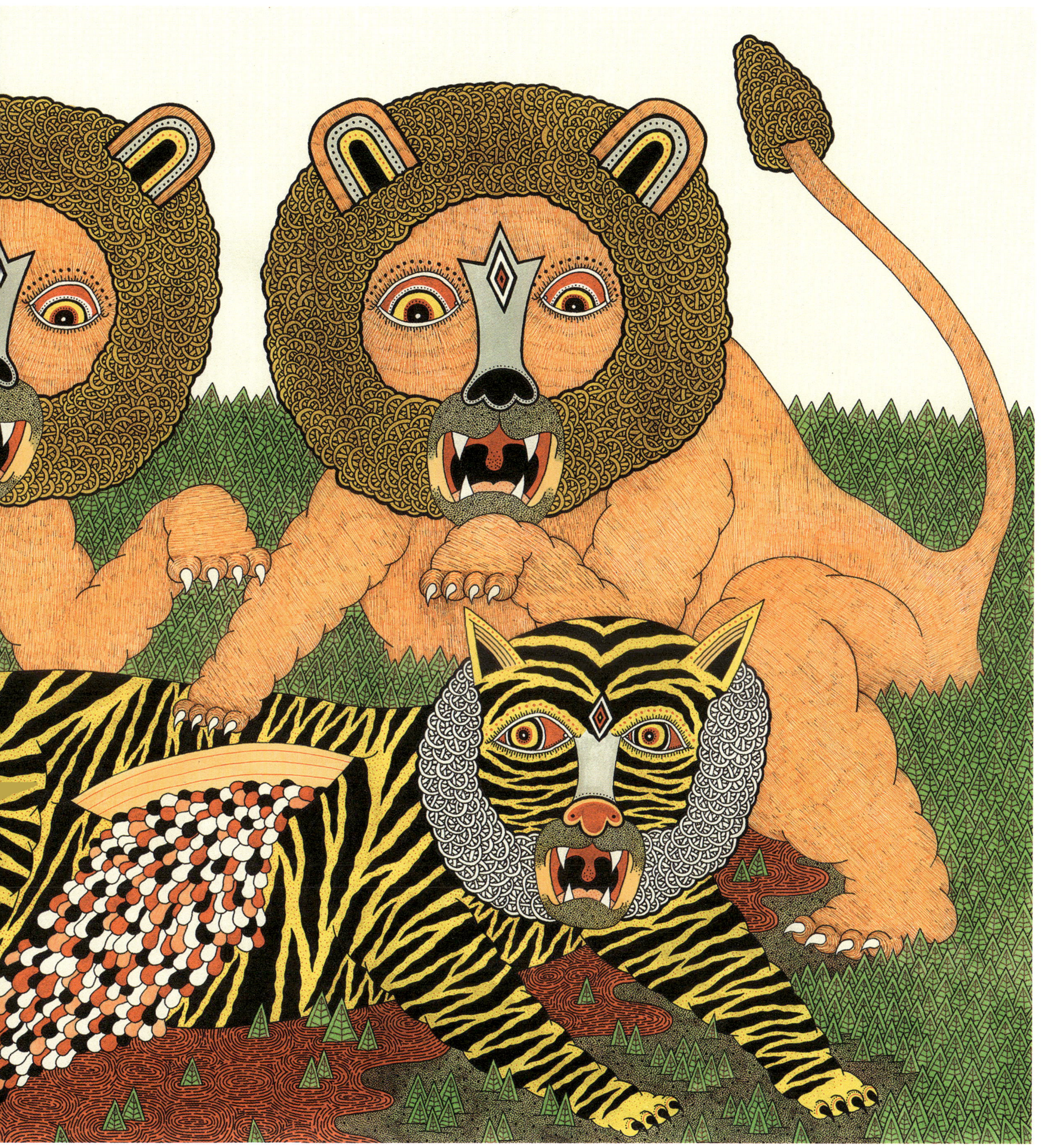

You Are Forgiven

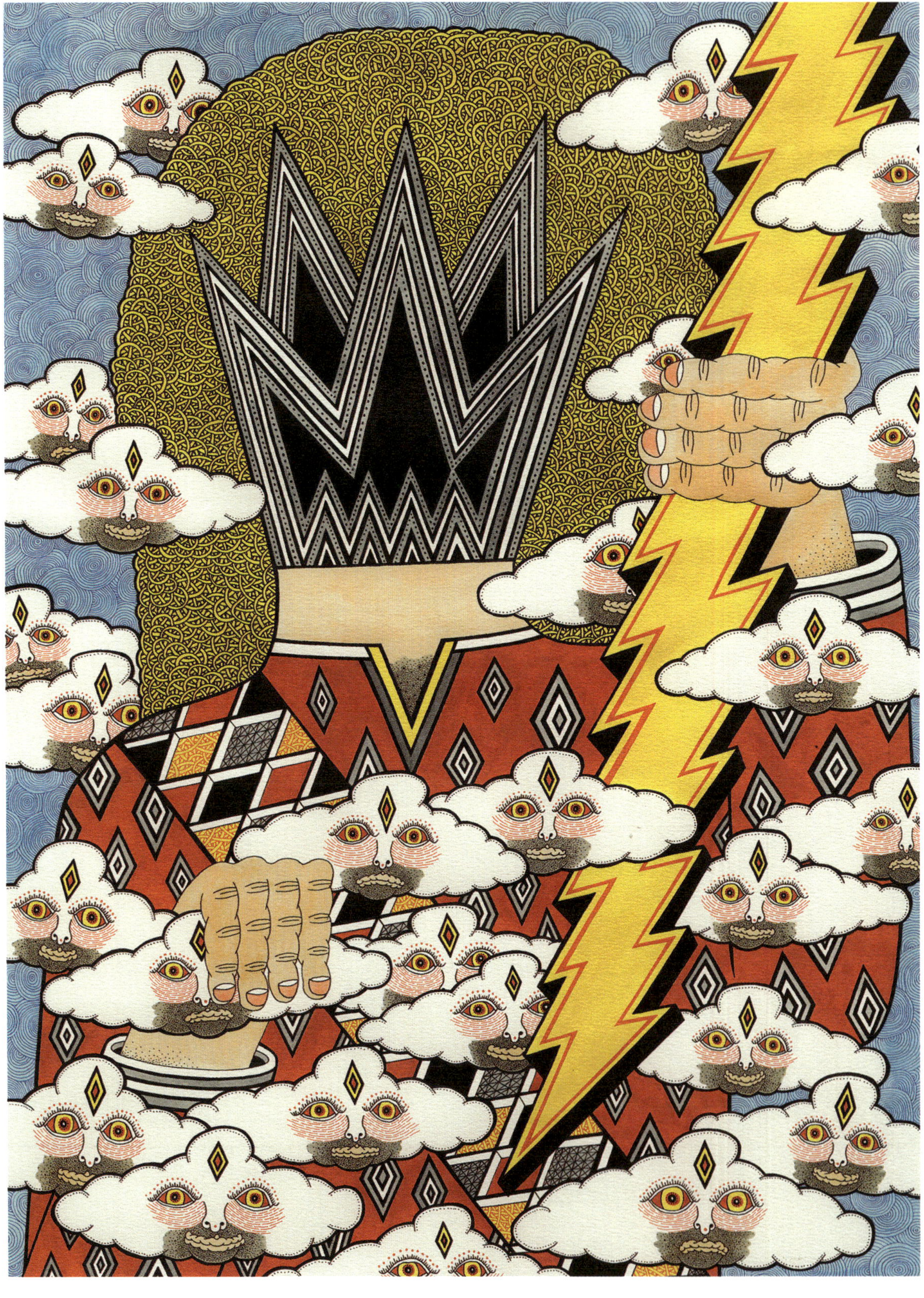

Matt Leines

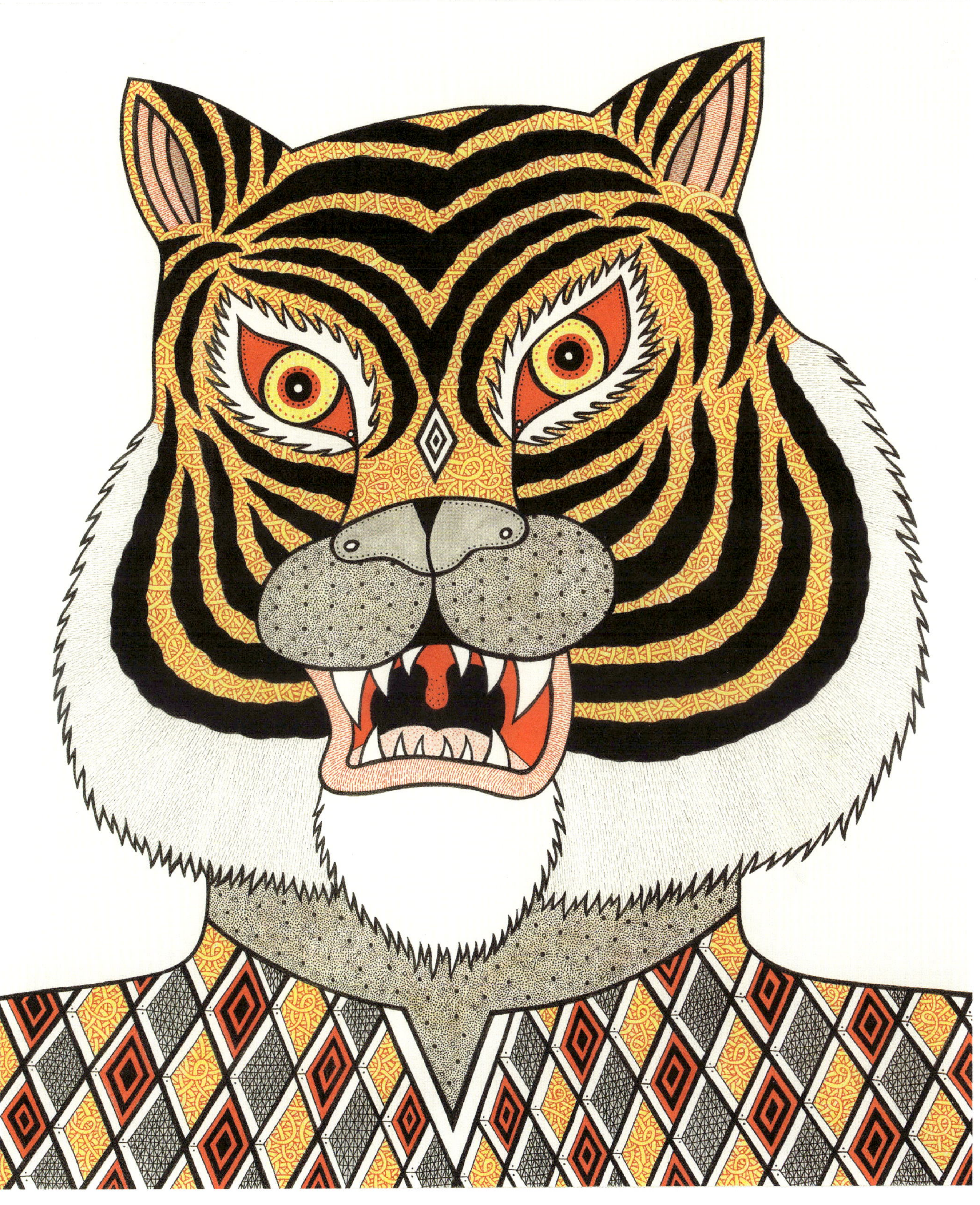

93

You Are Forgiven

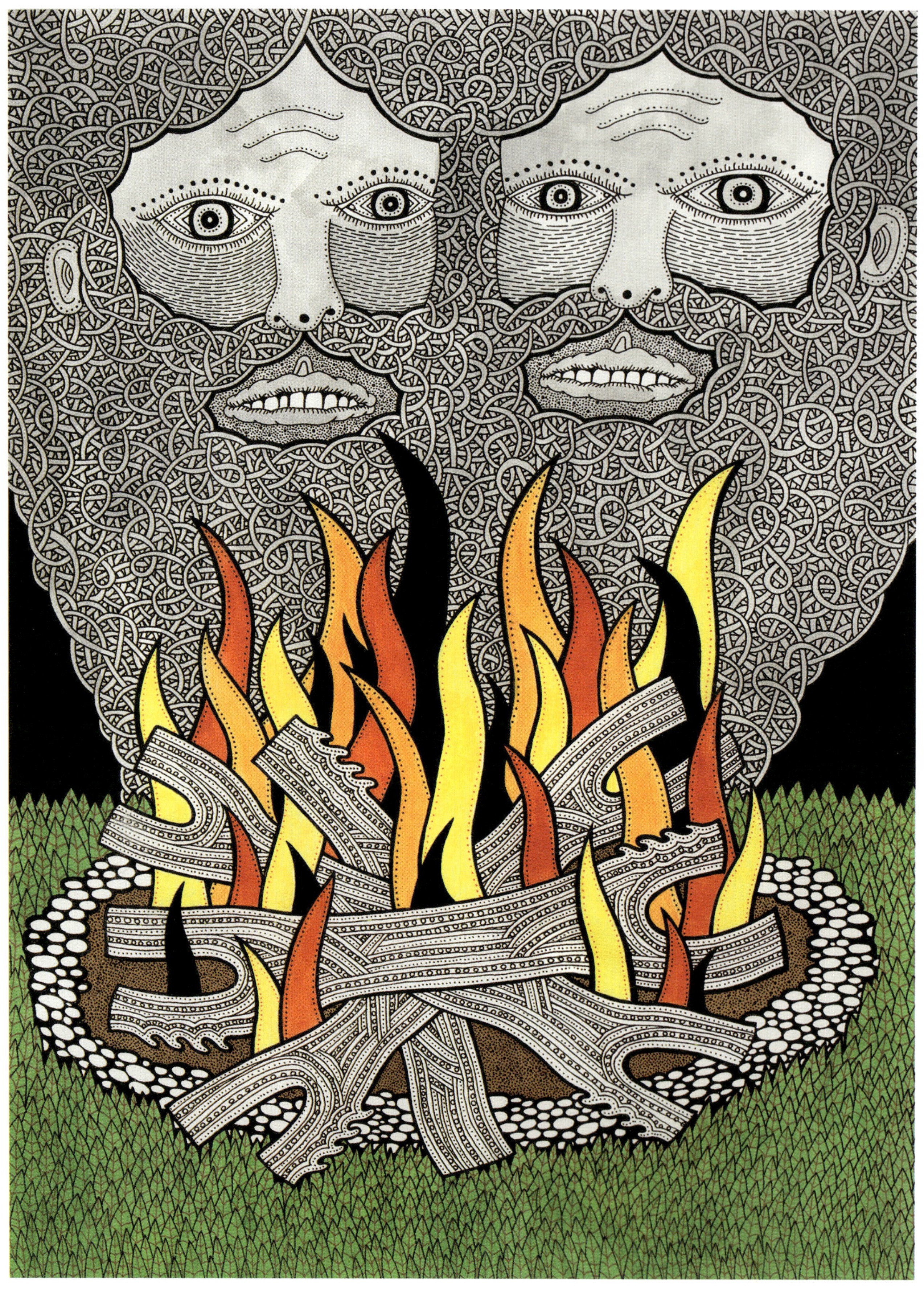

94

Matt Leines

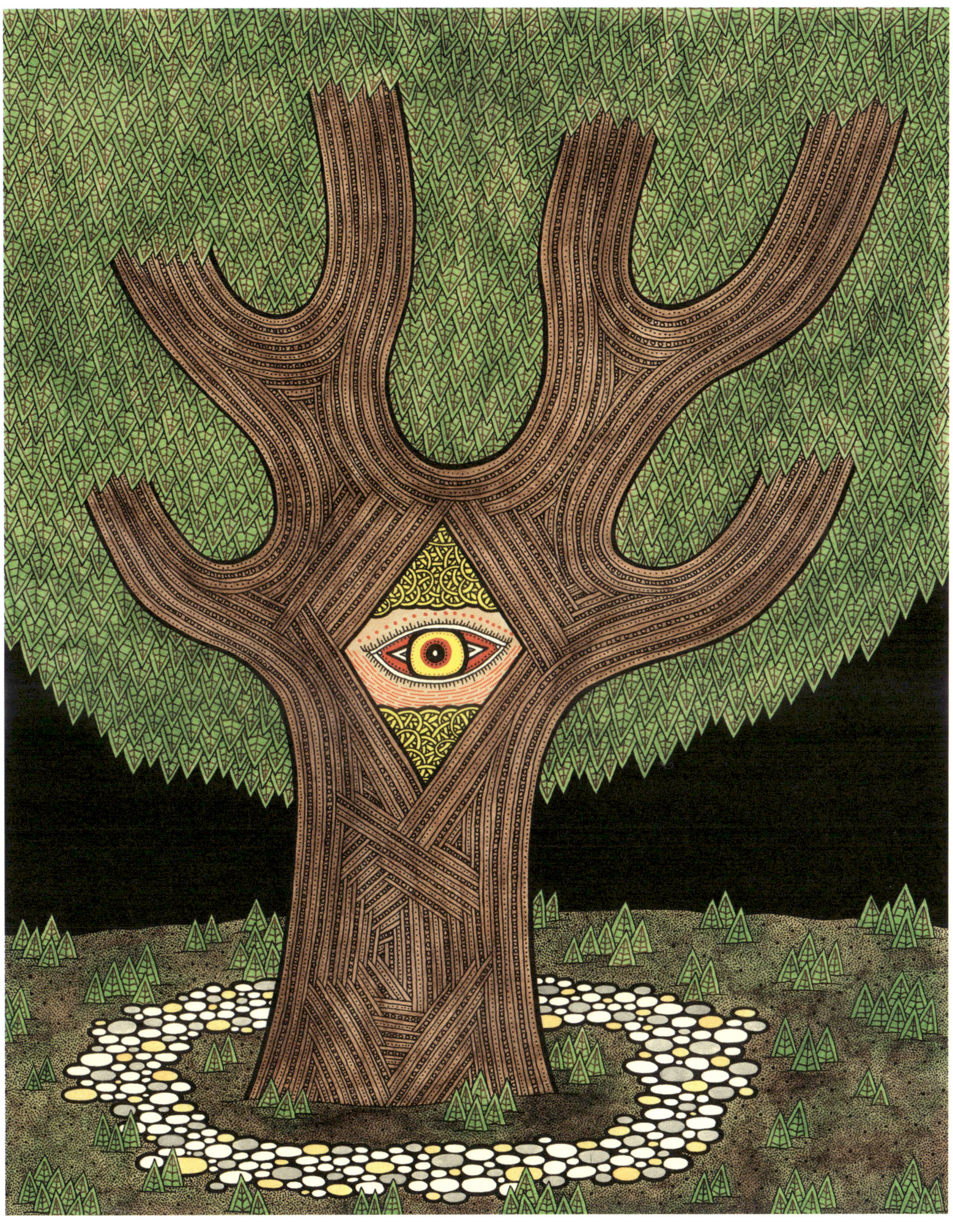

You Are Forgiven

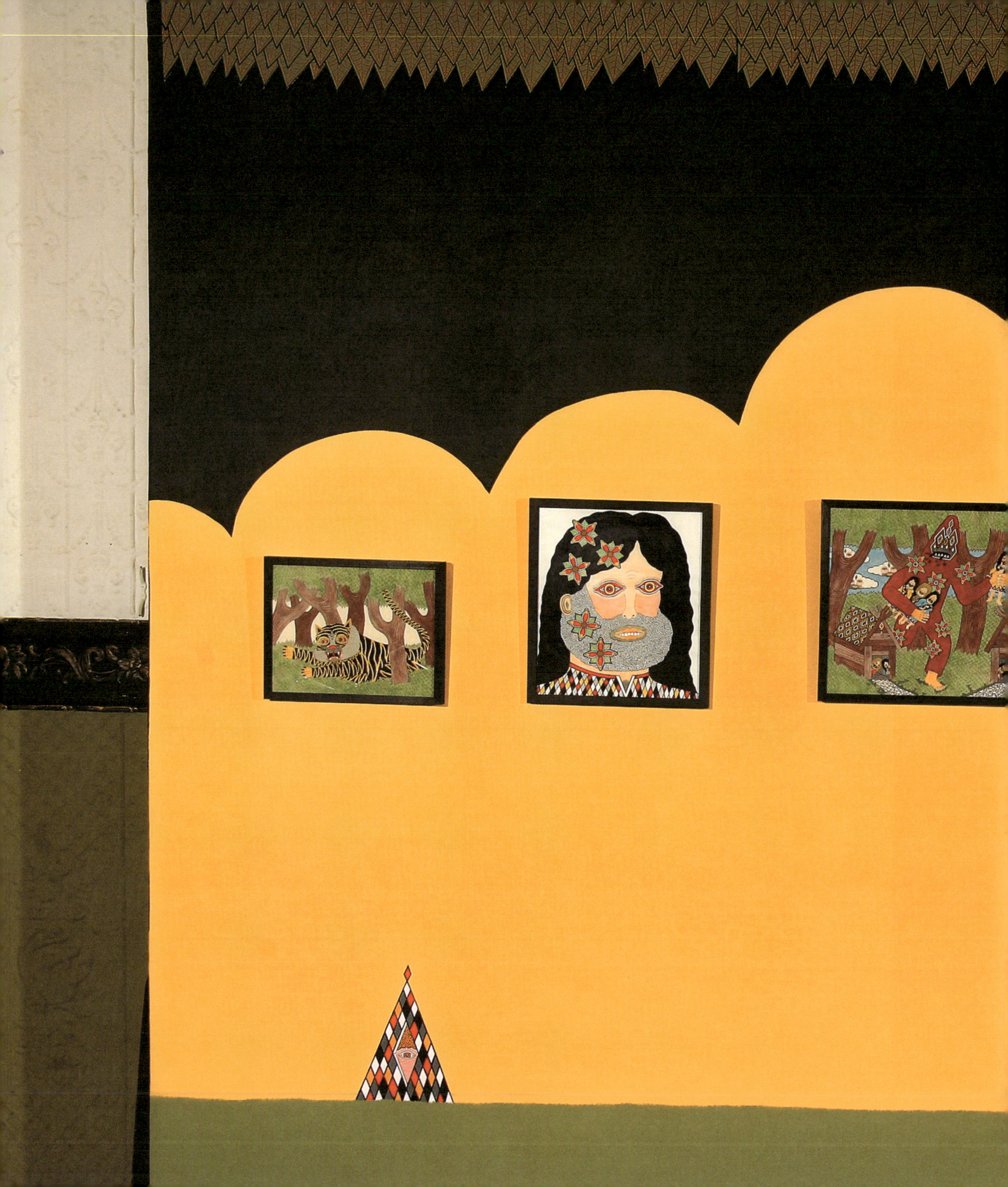

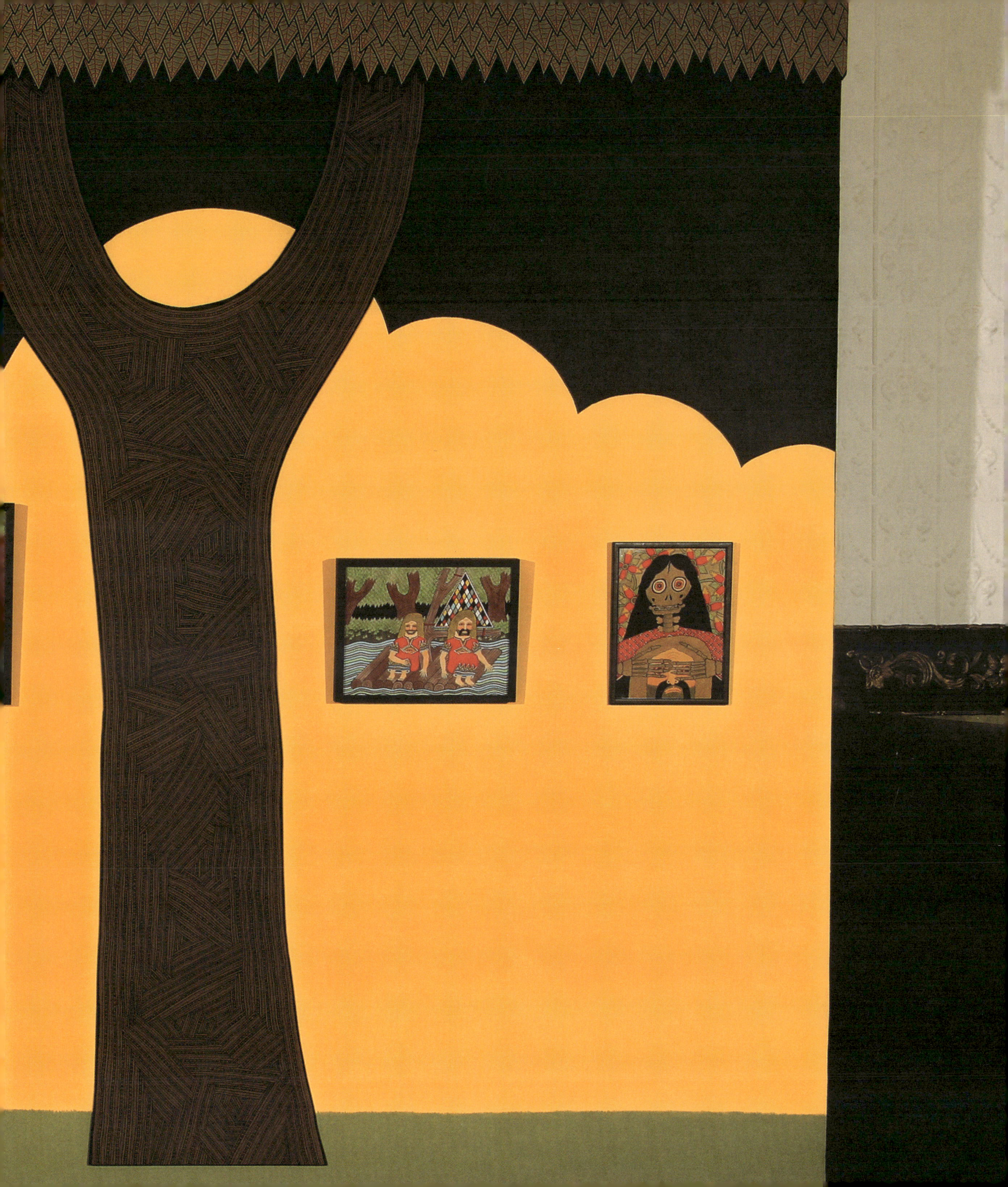

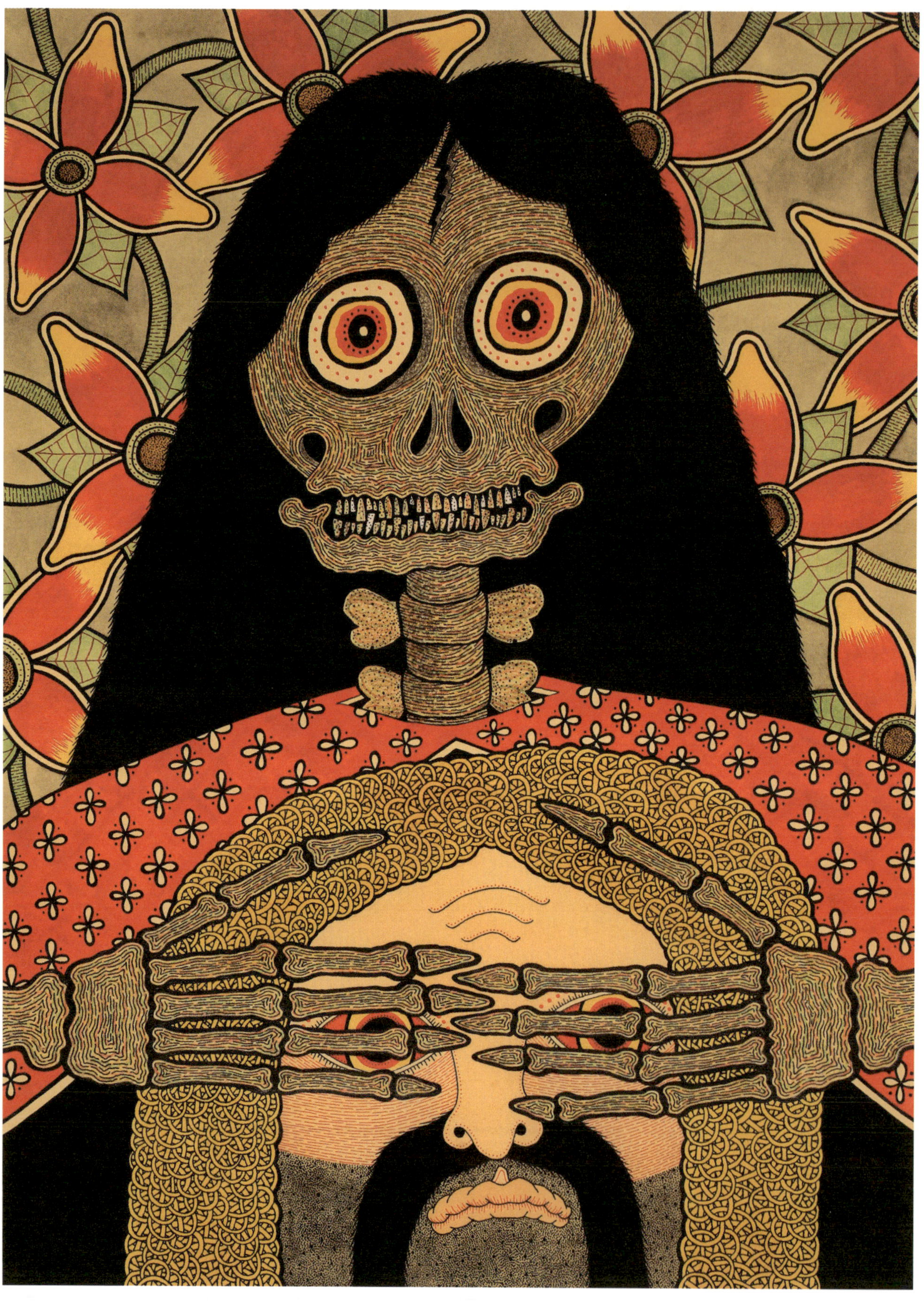

98

Matt Leines

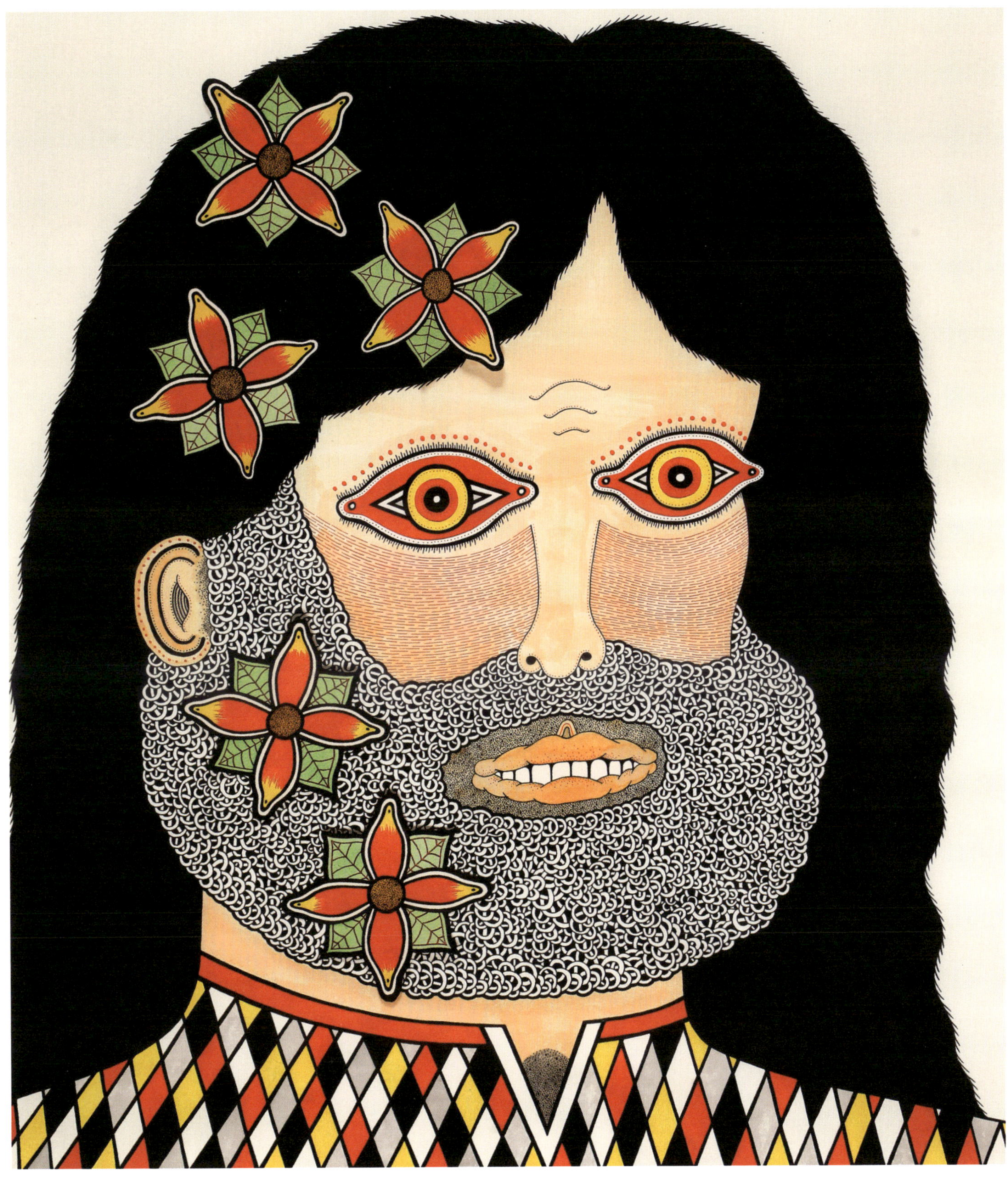

You Are Forgiven

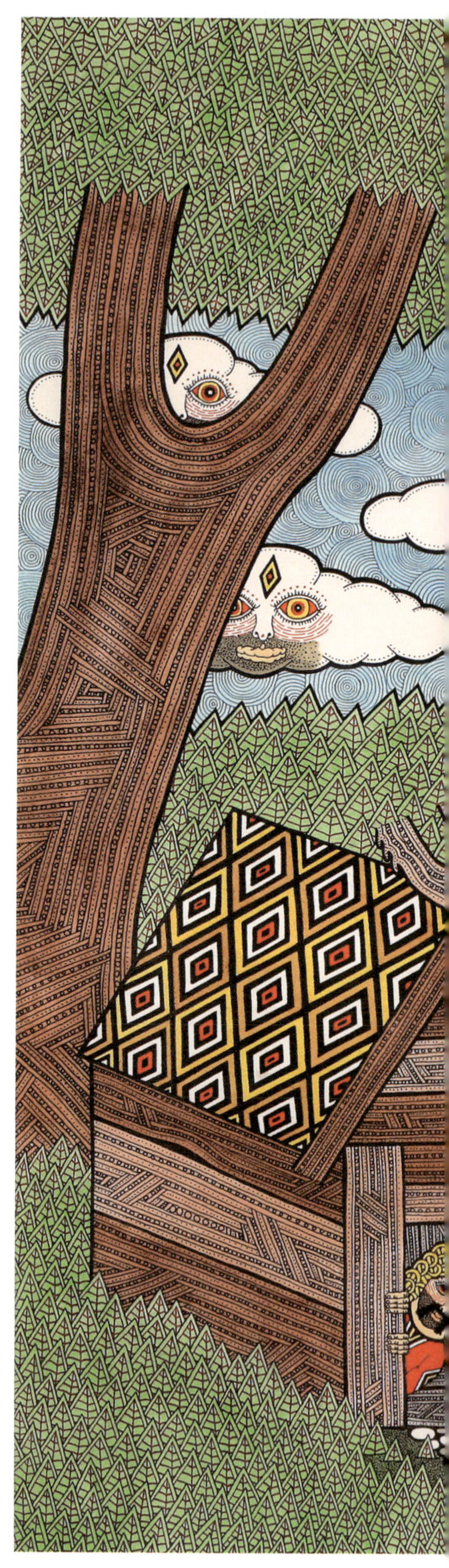

Matt Leines

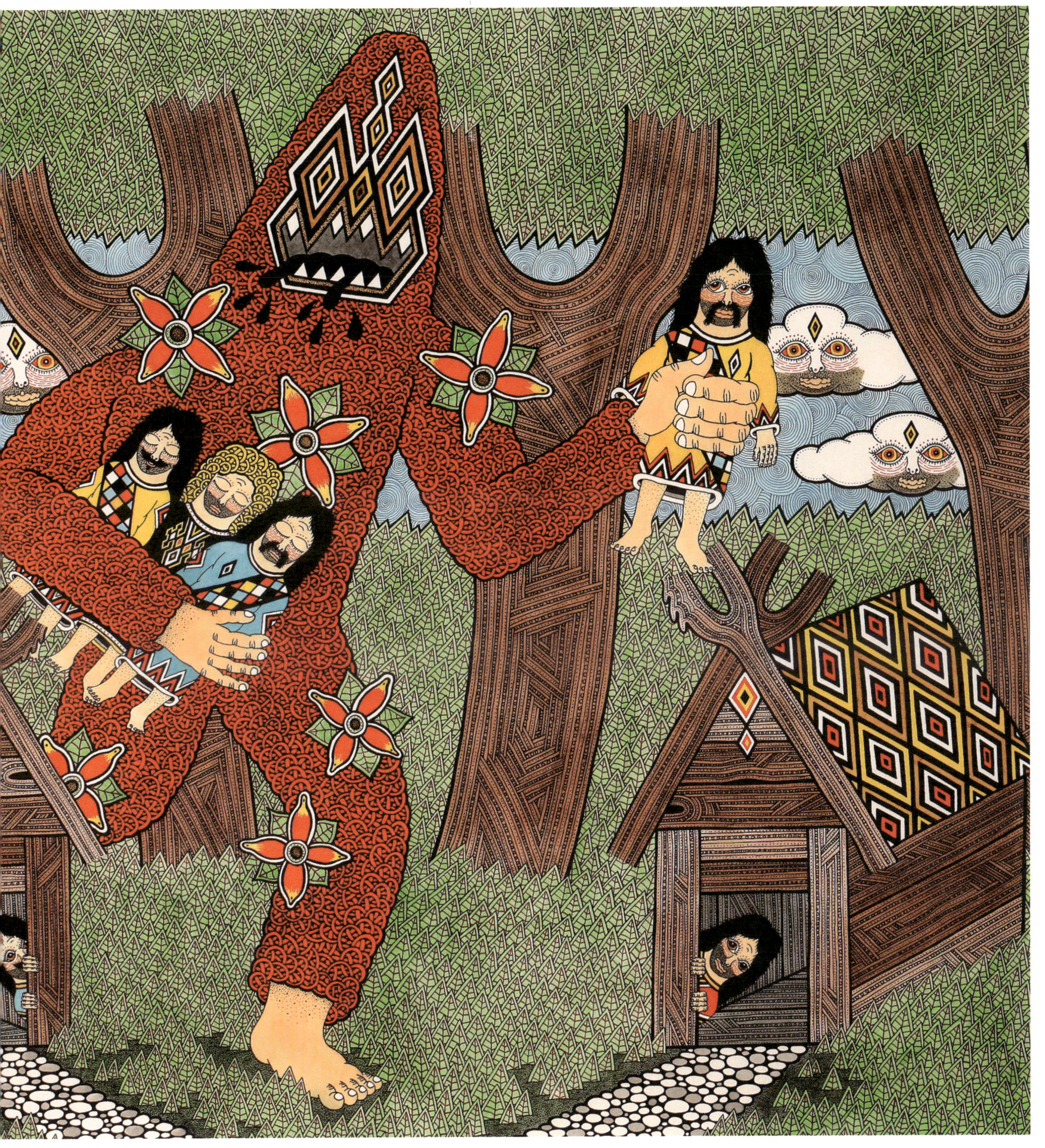

You Are Forgiven

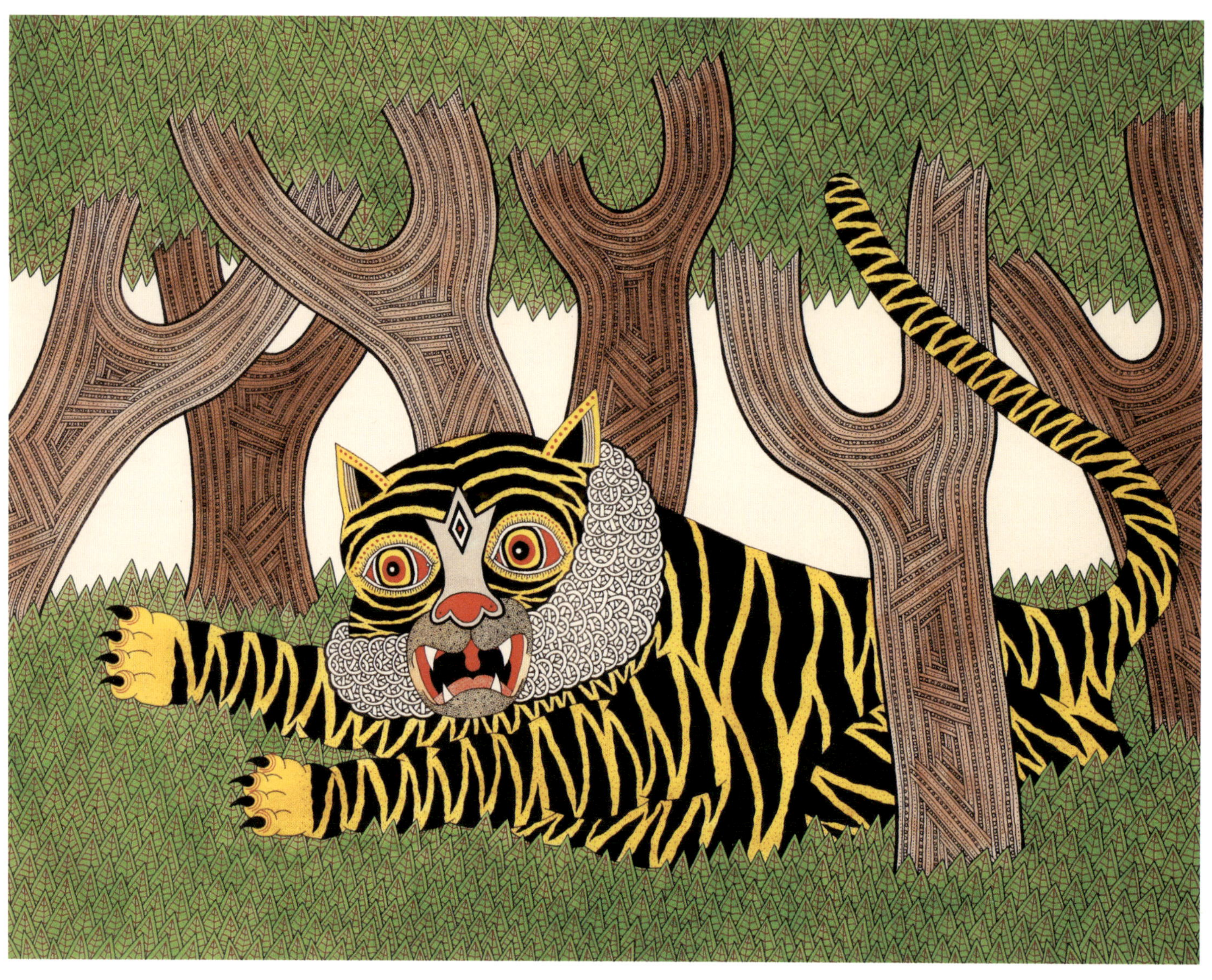

102

Matt Leines

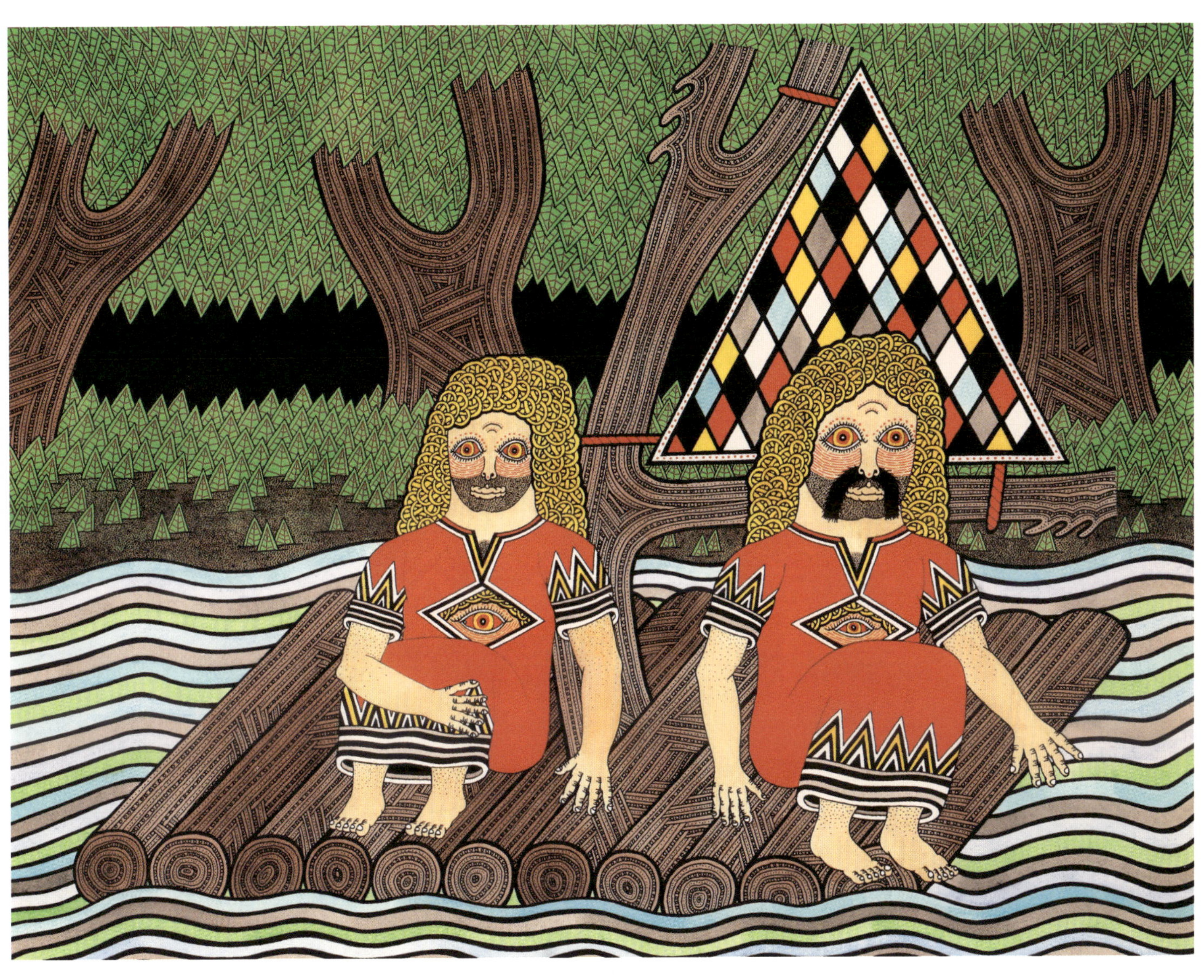

You Are Forgiven

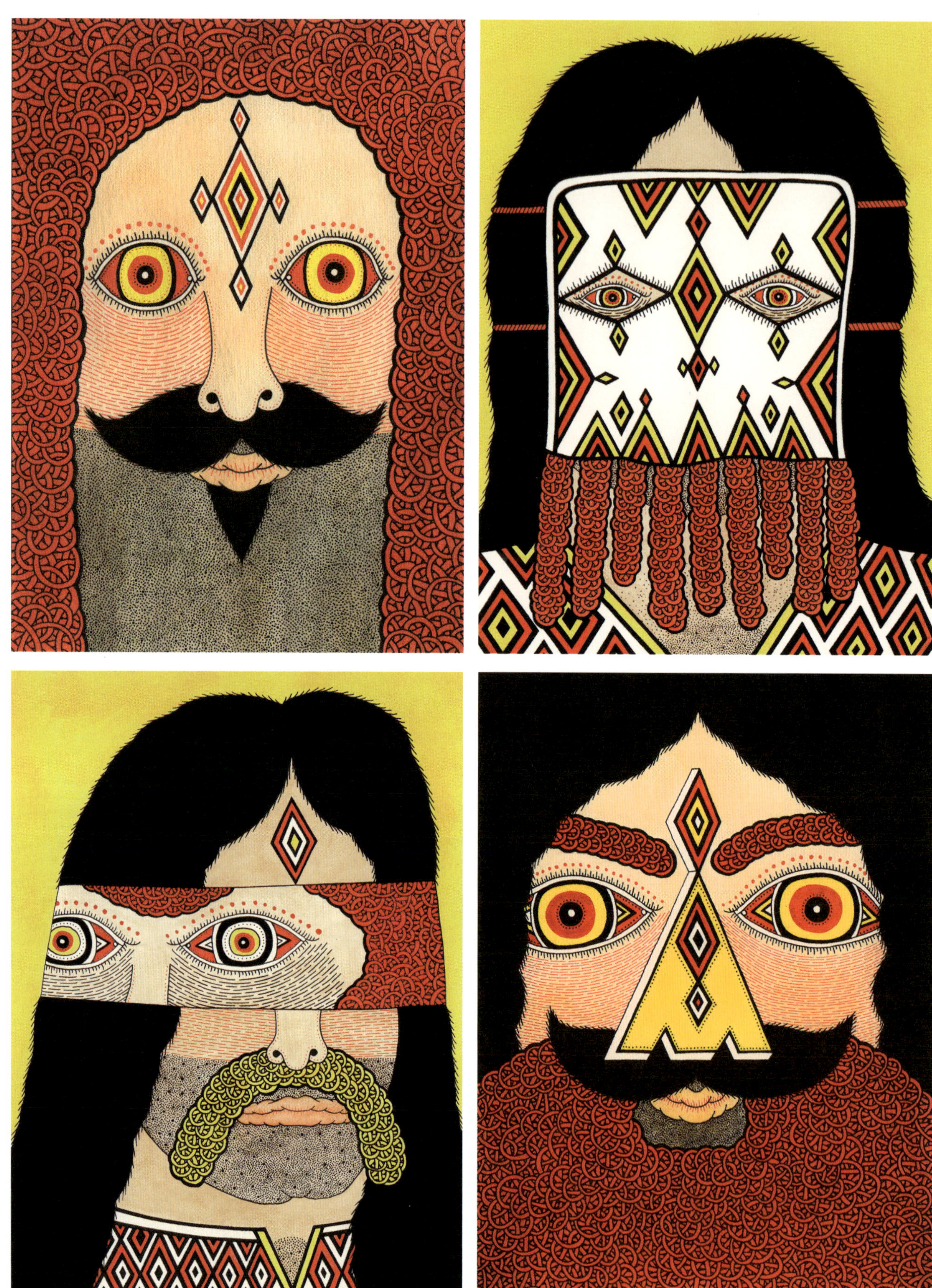

104

Matt Leines

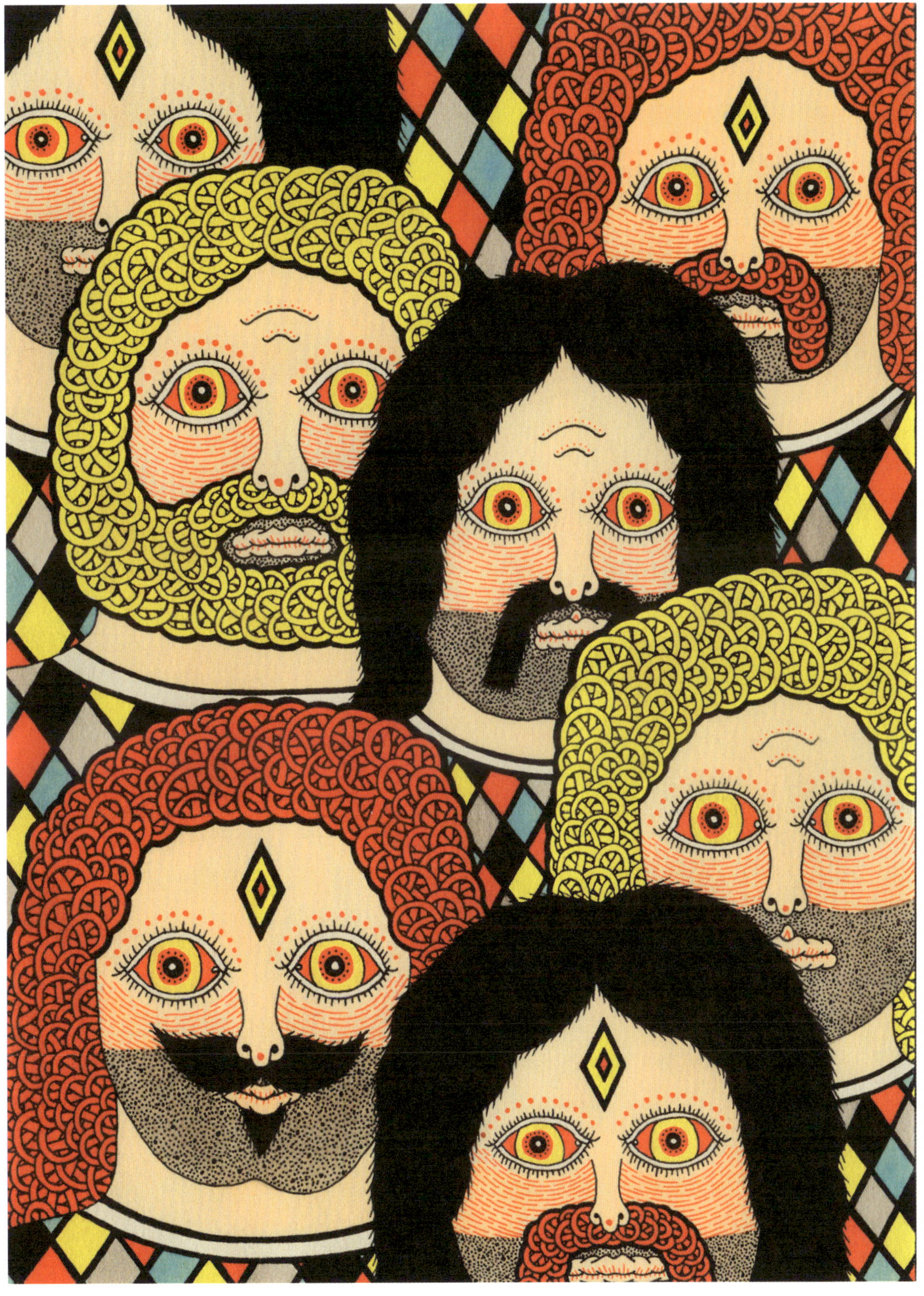

You Are Forgiven

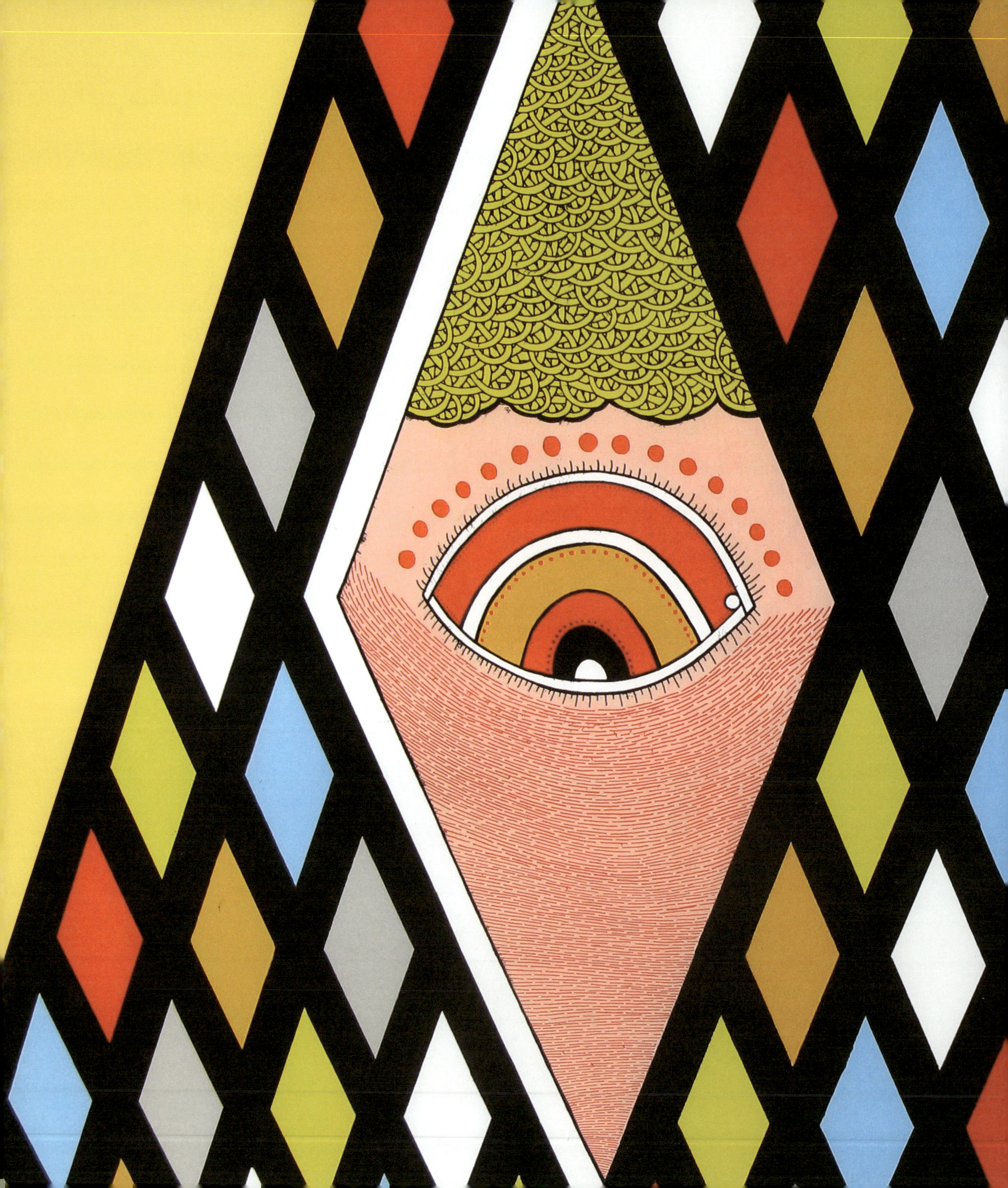

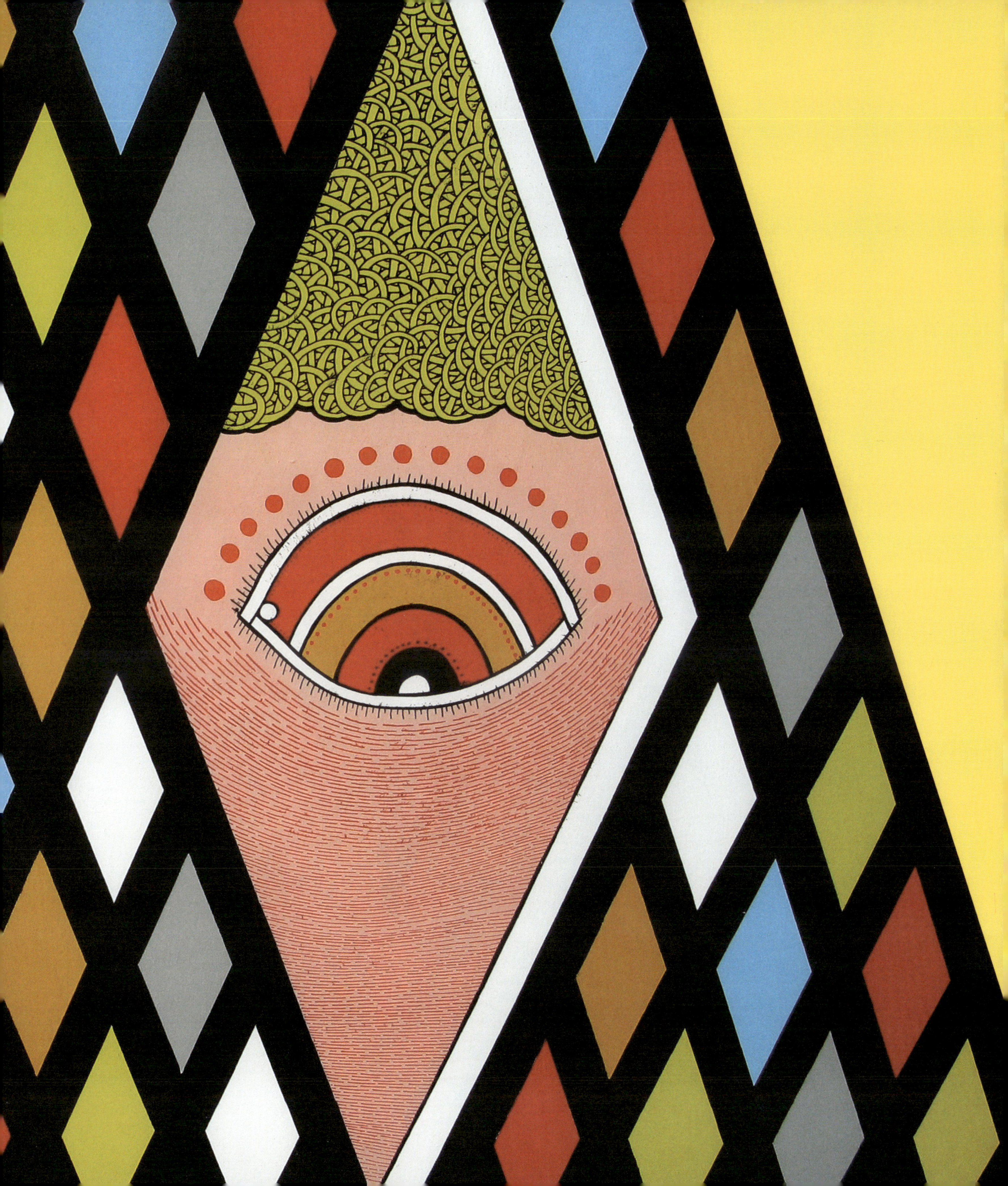

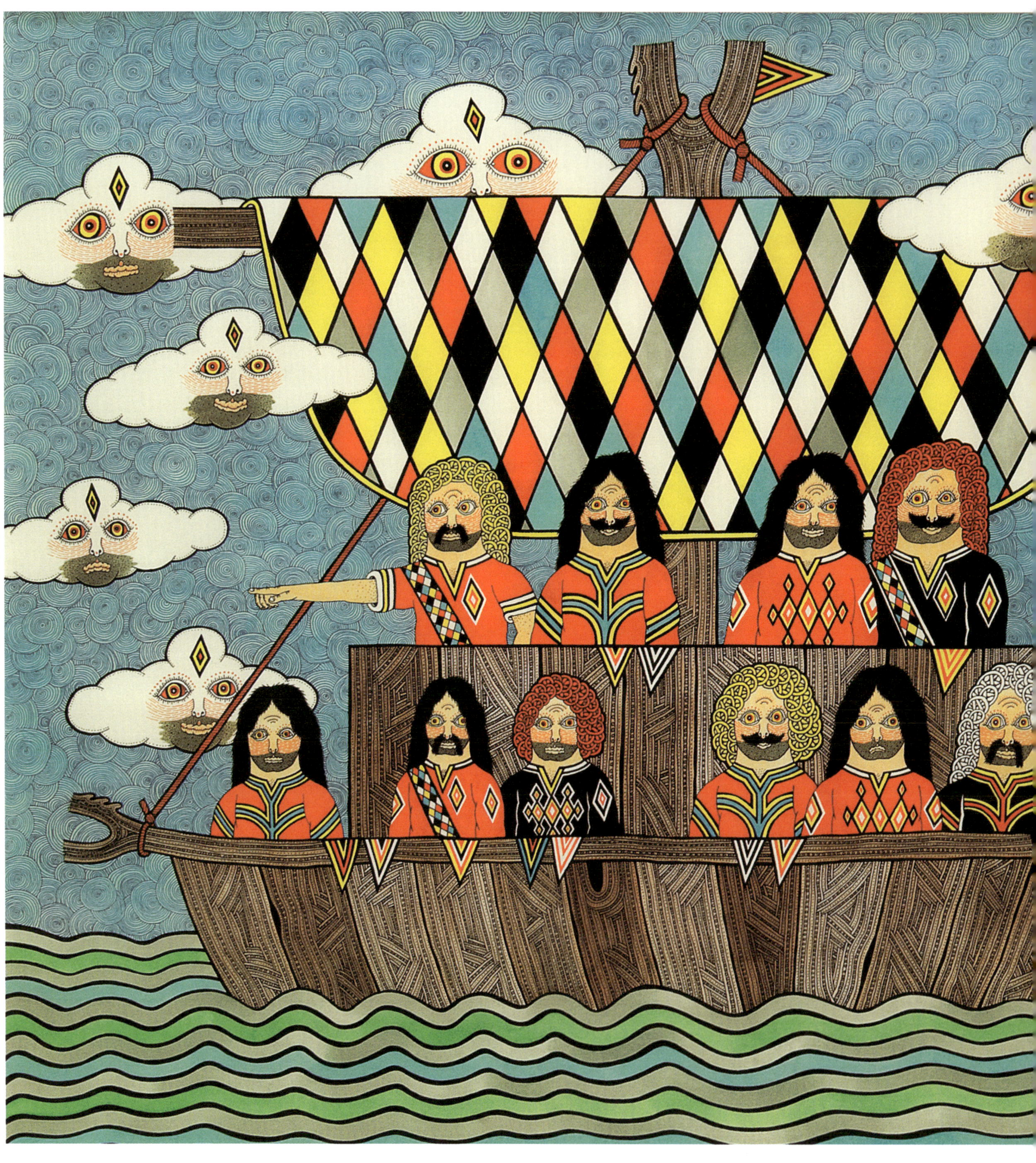

Matt Leines

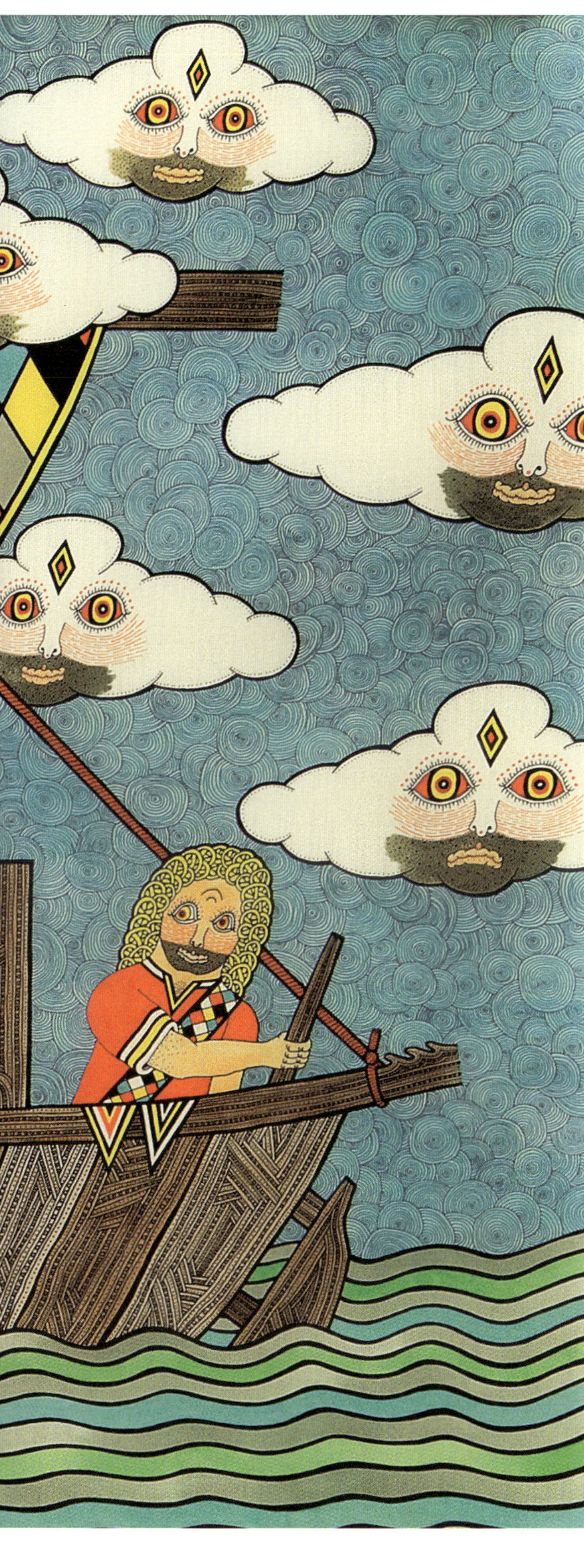

You Are Forgiven

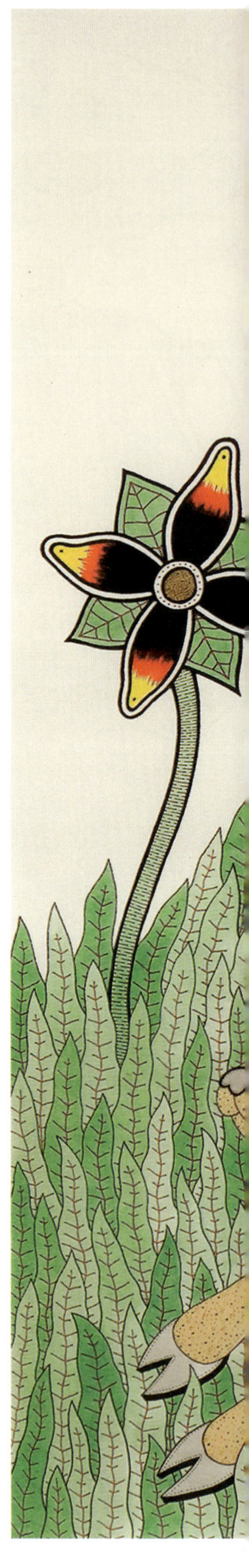

Matt Leines

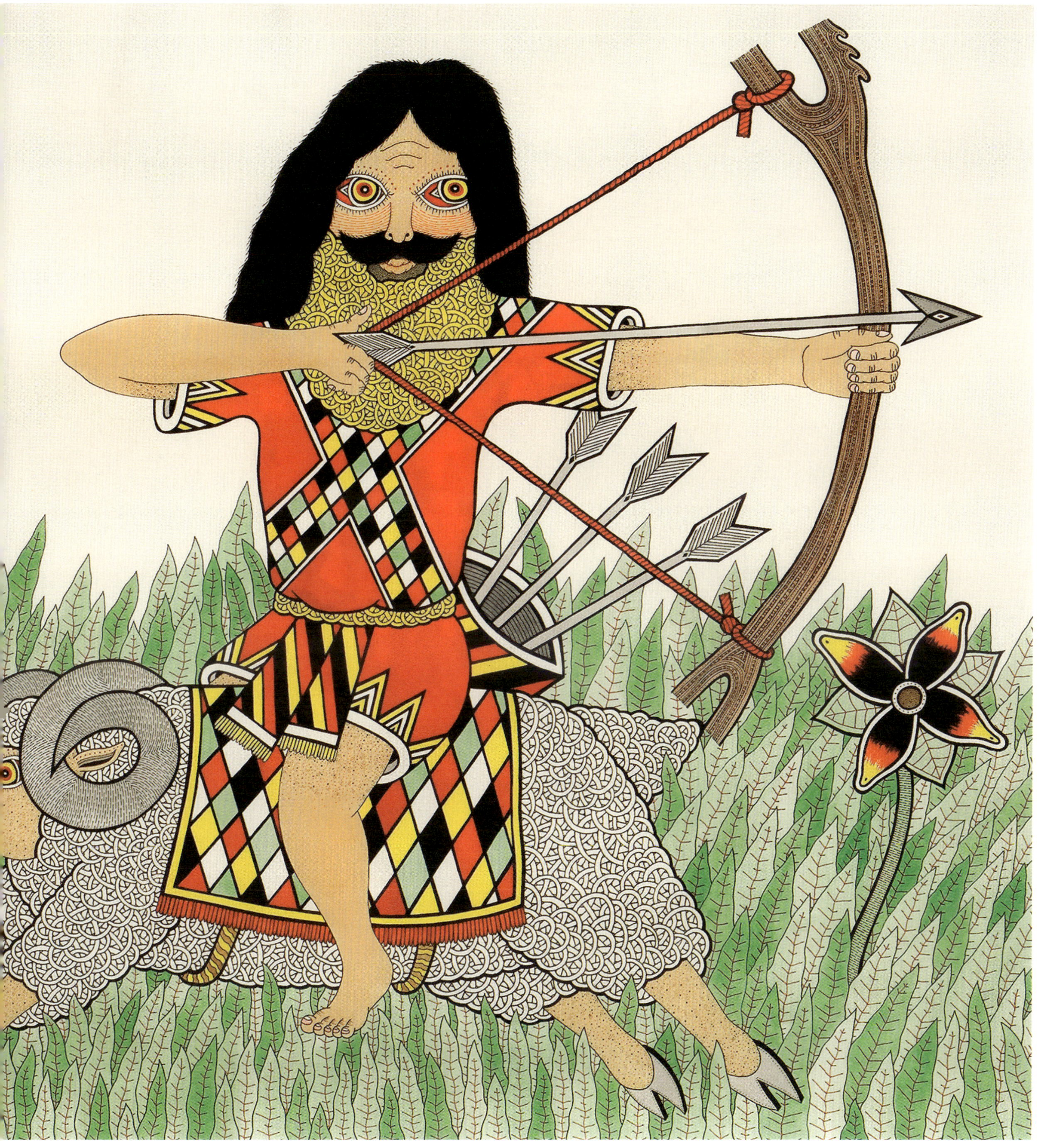

You Are Forgiven

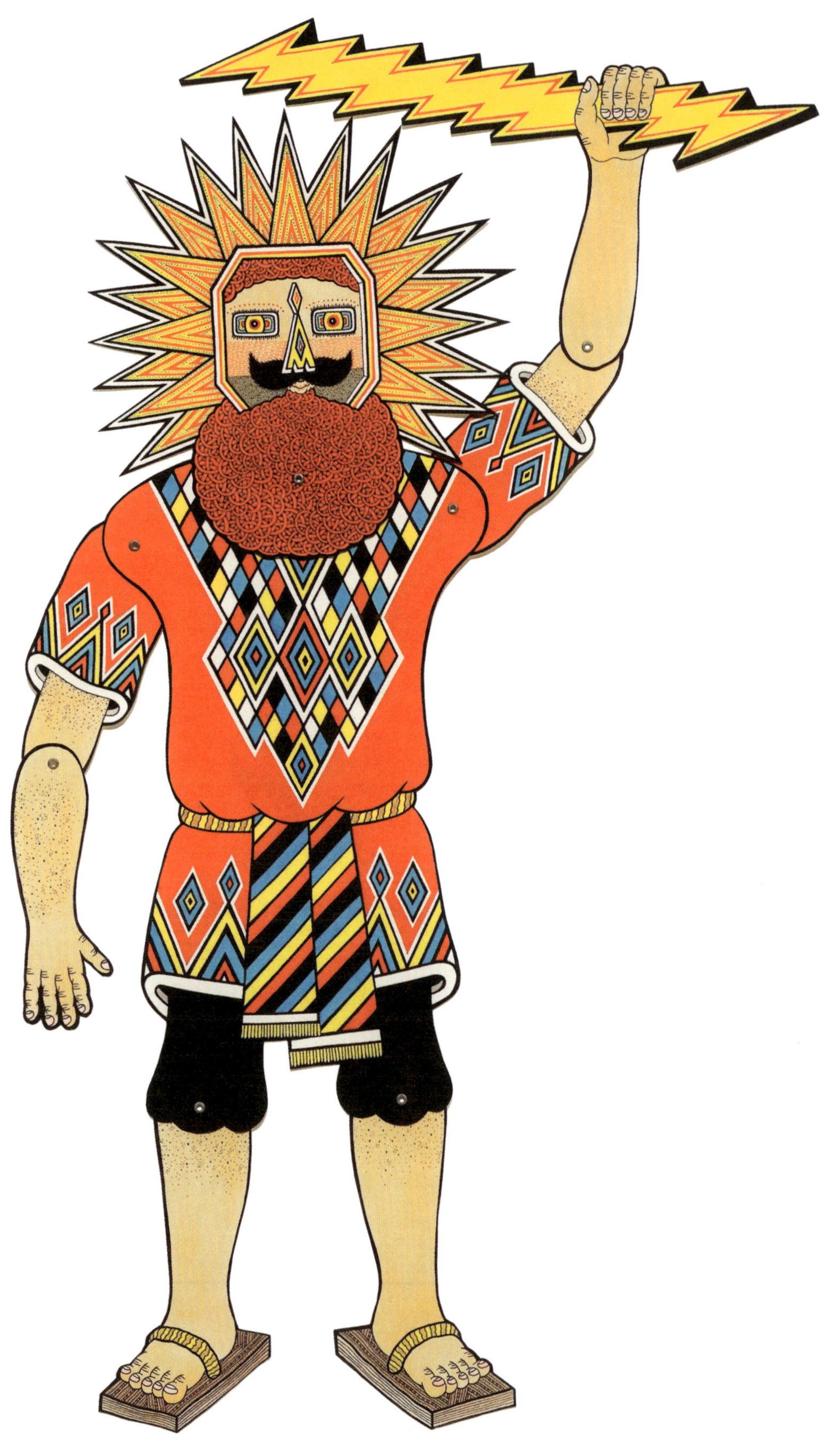

Matt Leines

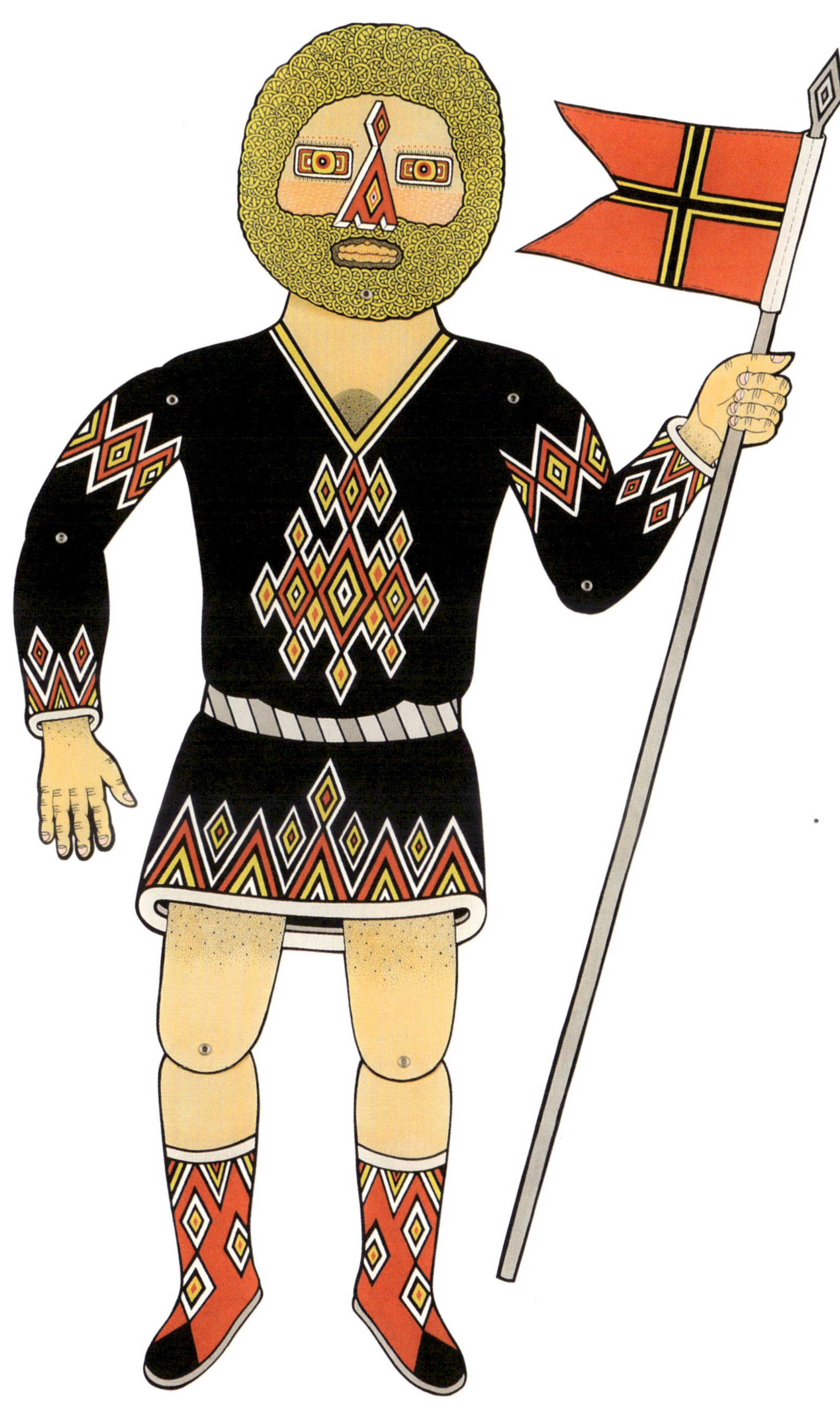

You Are Forgiven

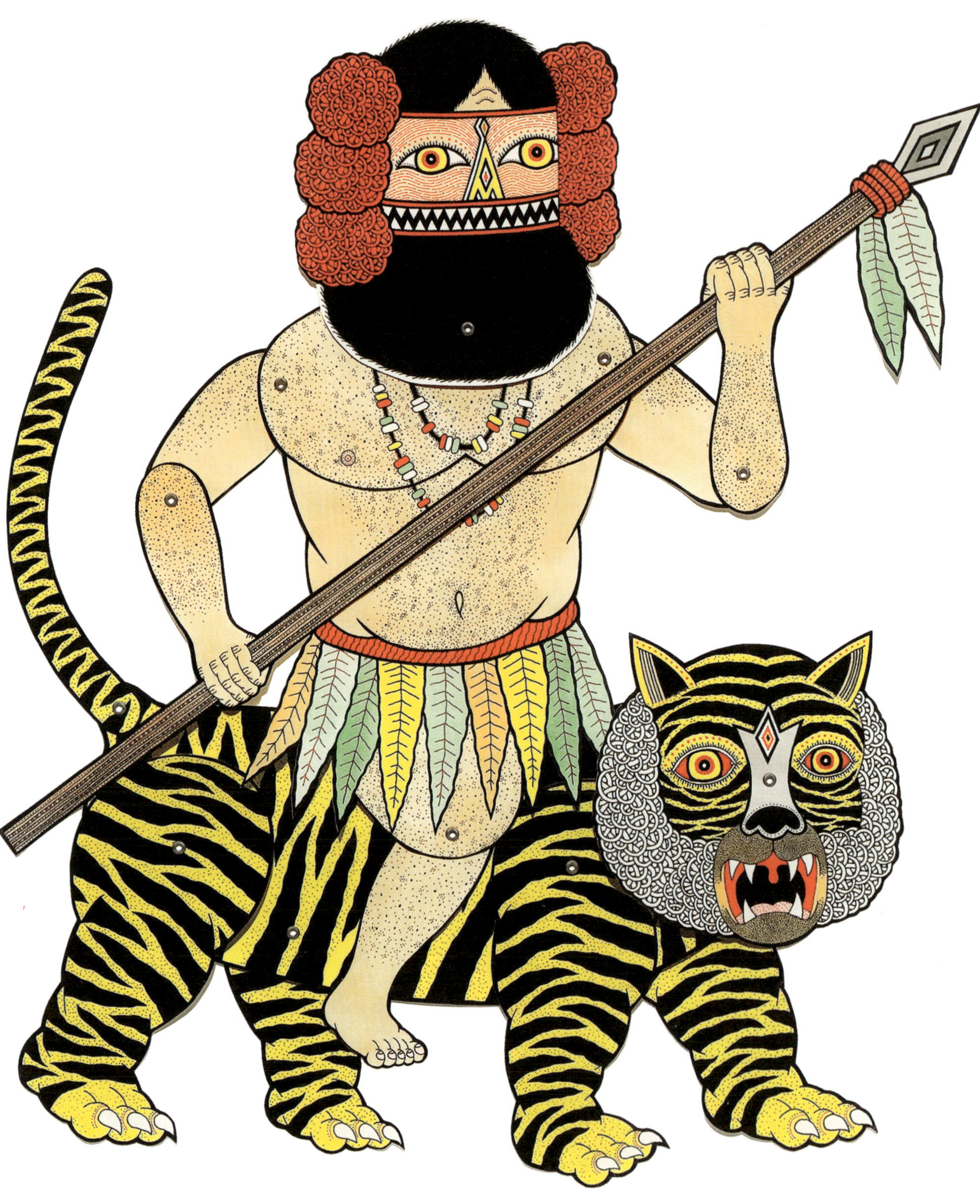

Matt Leines

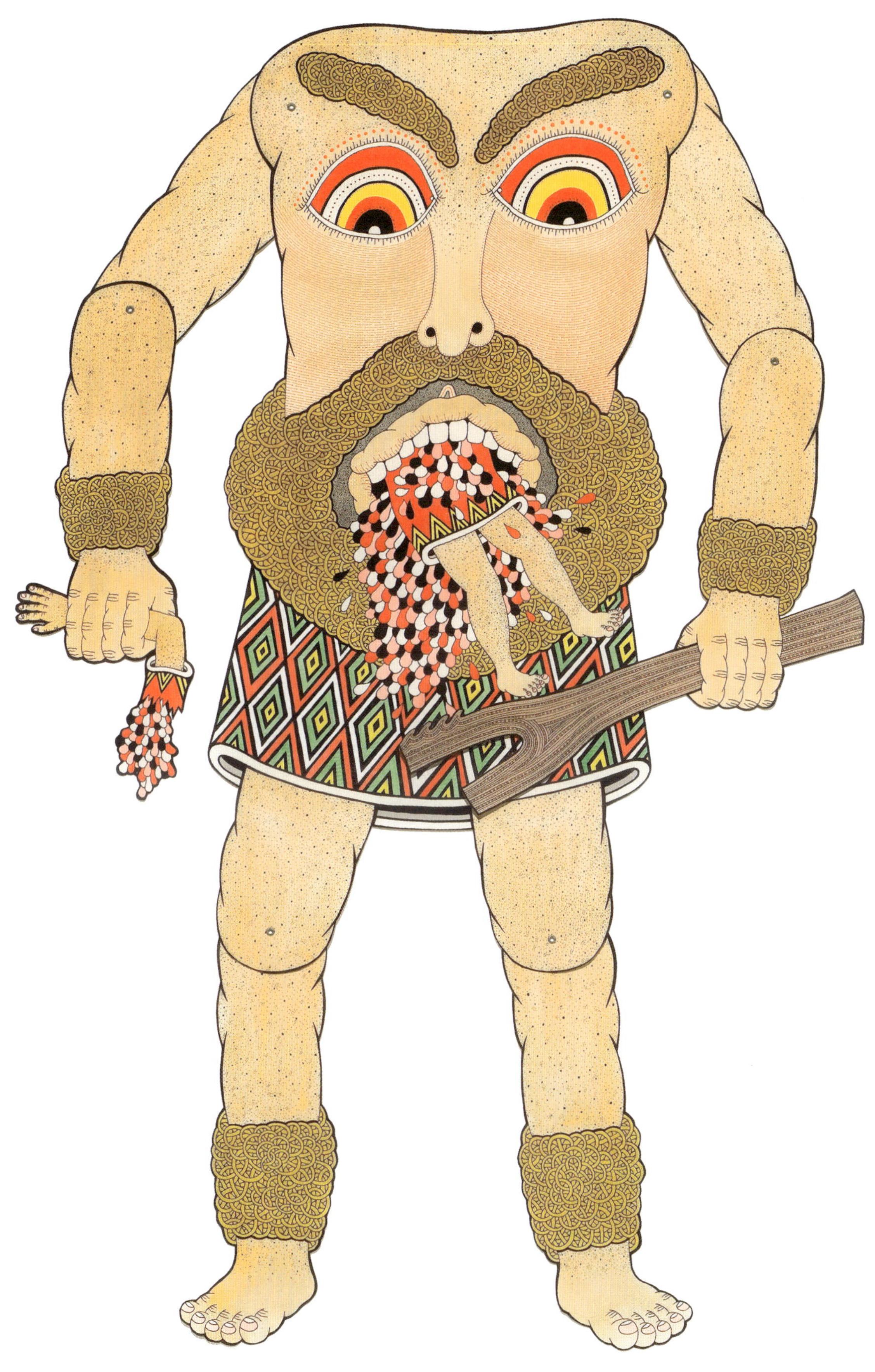

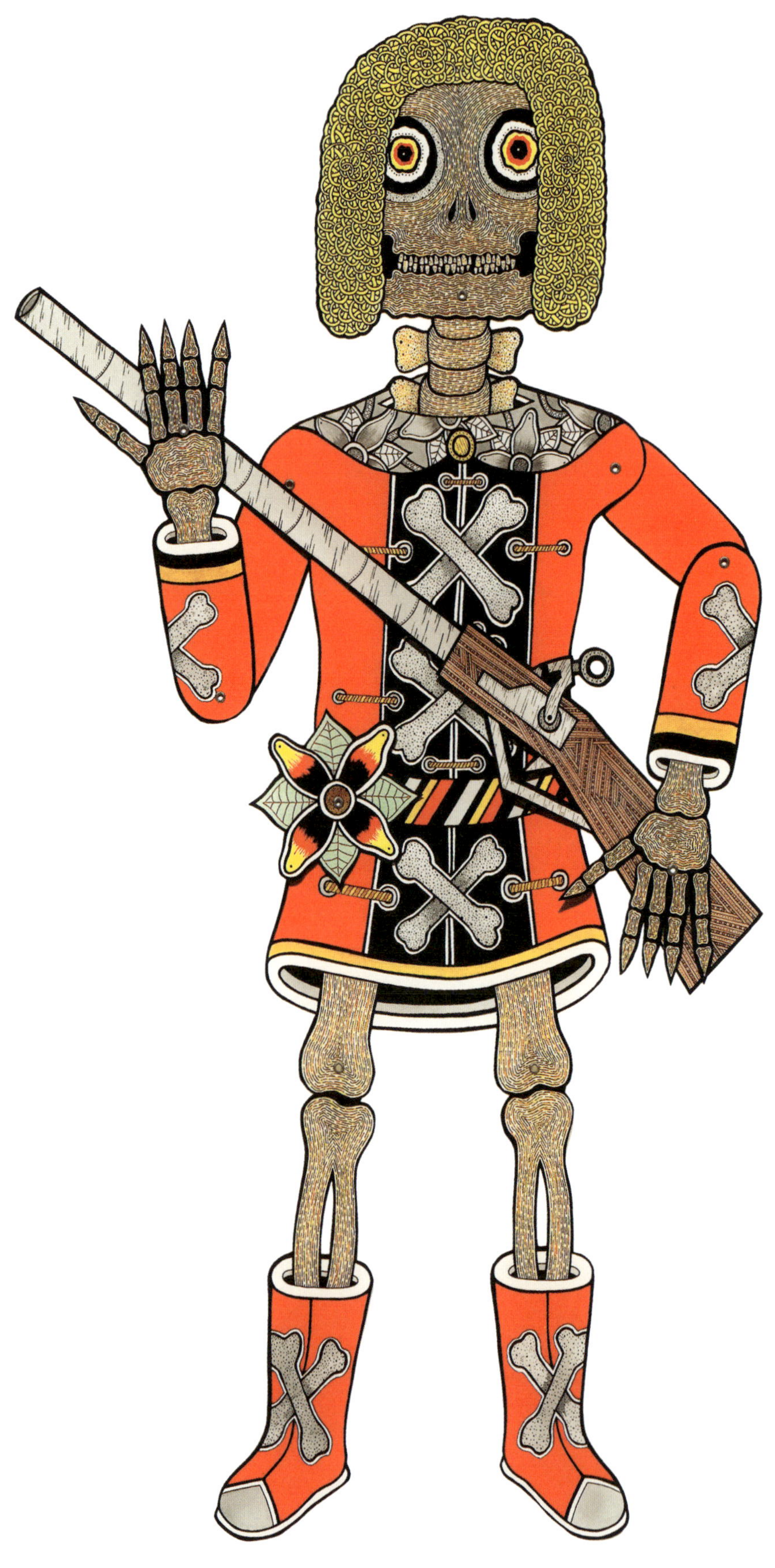

116

Matt Leines

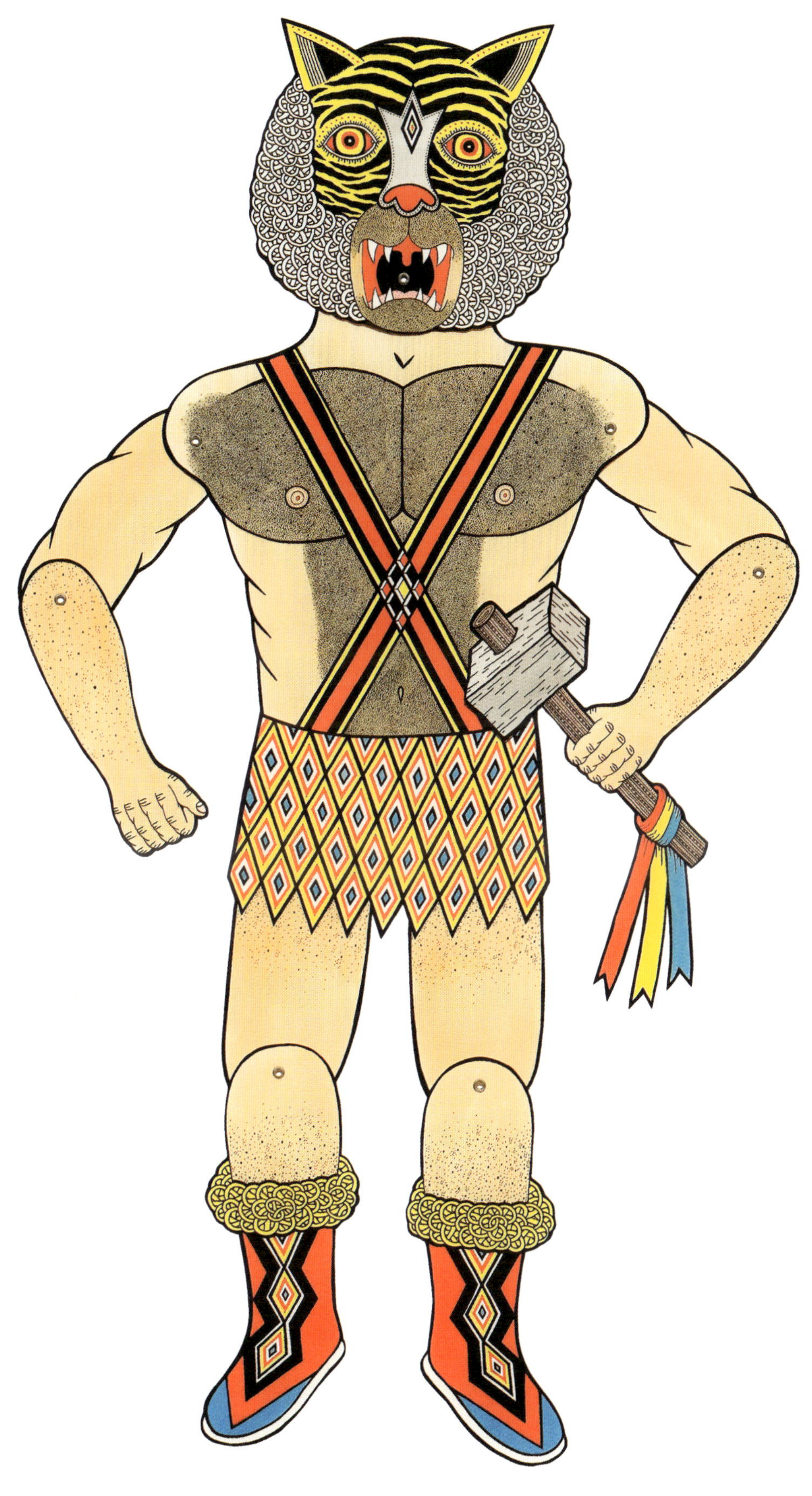

You Are Forgiven

Matt Leines

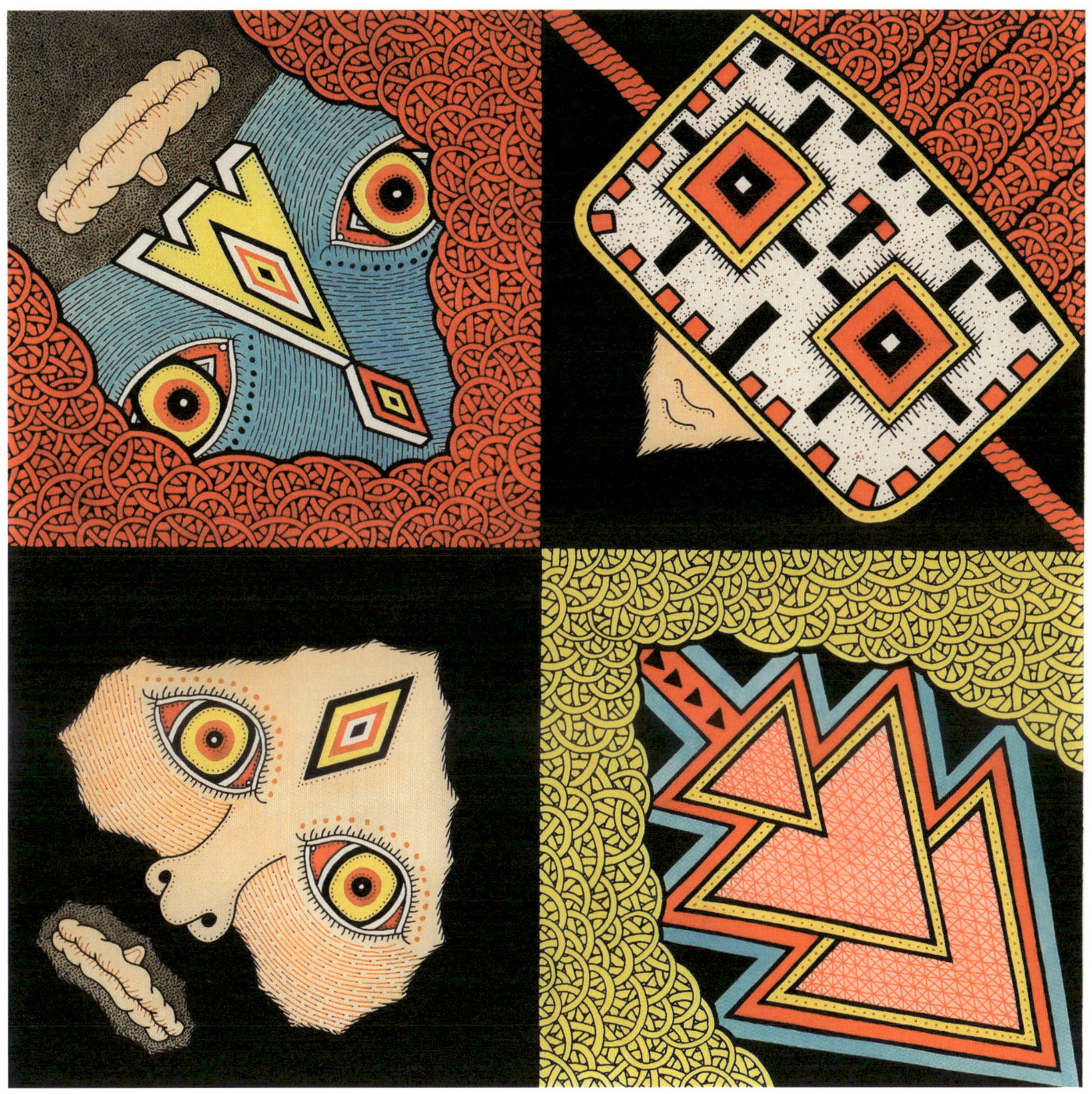

You Are Forgiven

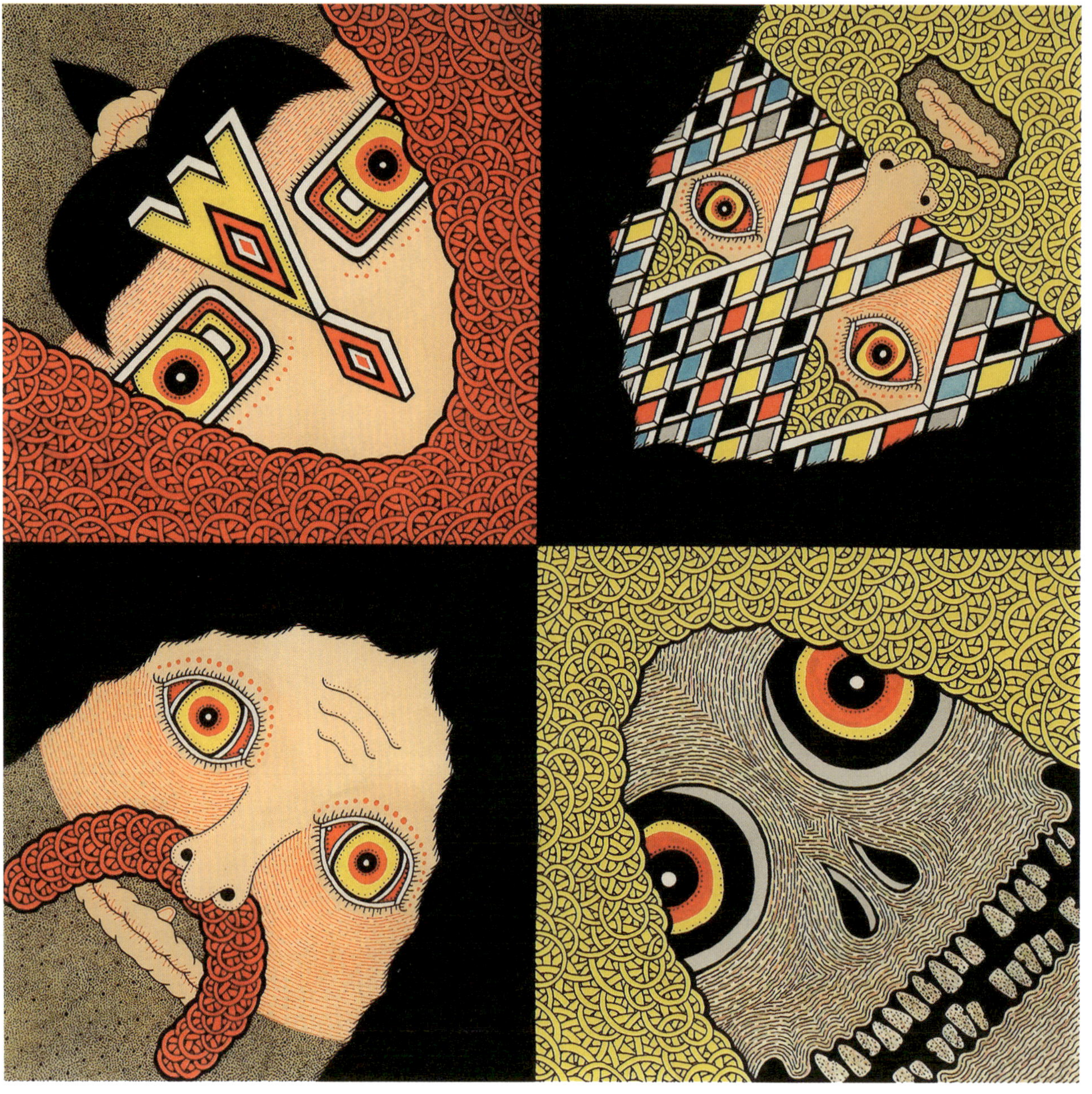

Matt Leines

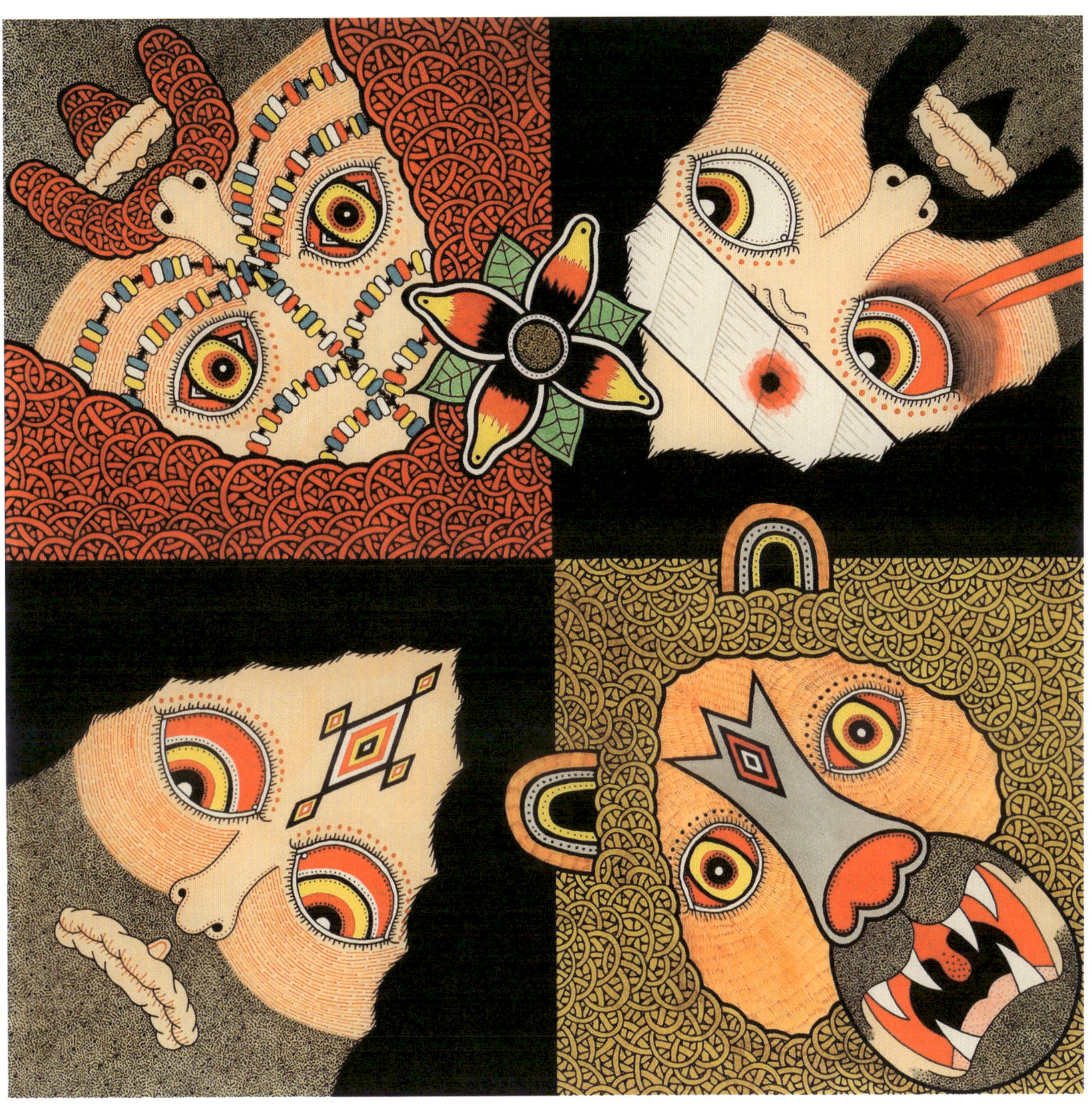

You Are Forgiven

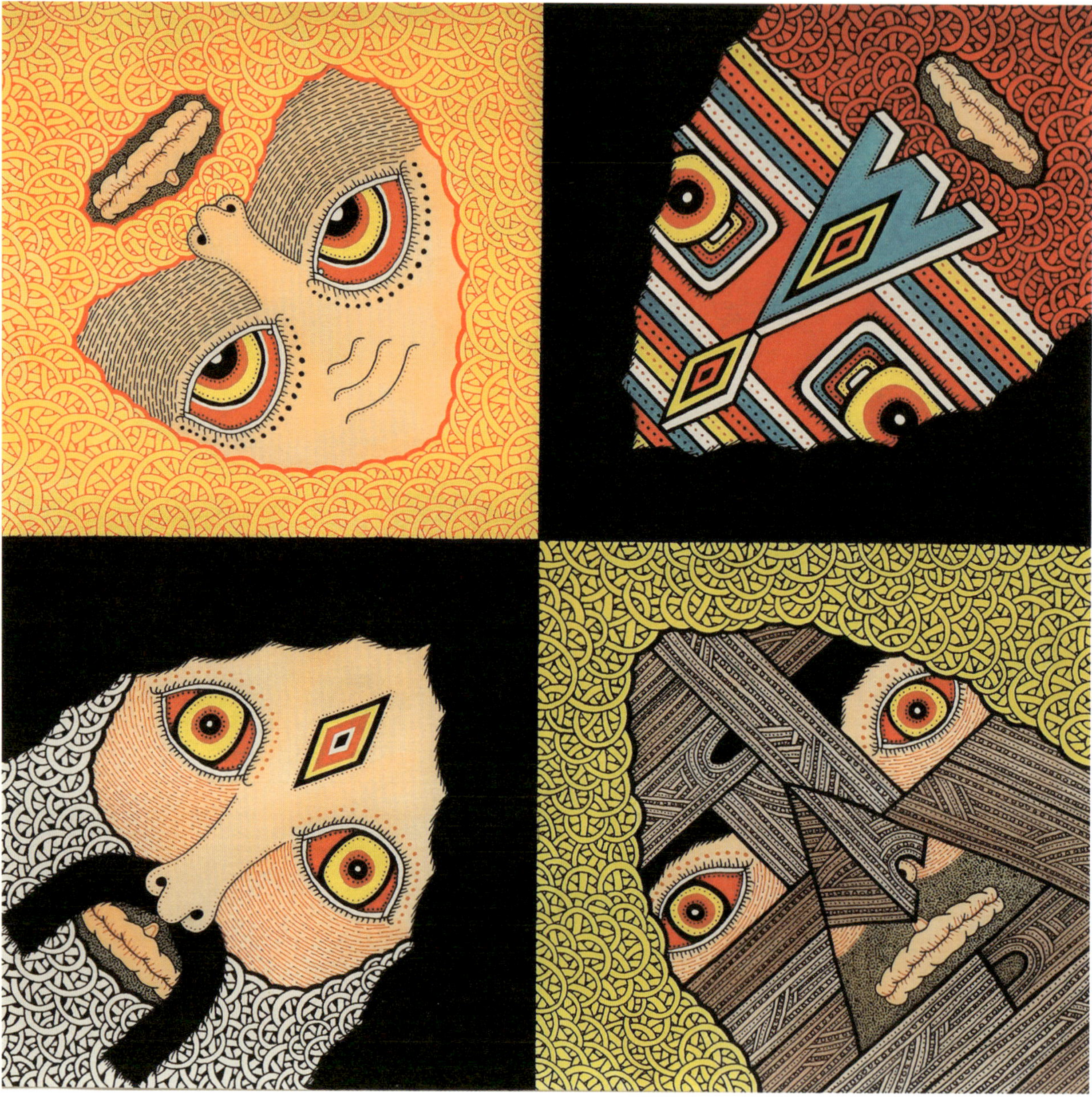

Matt Leines

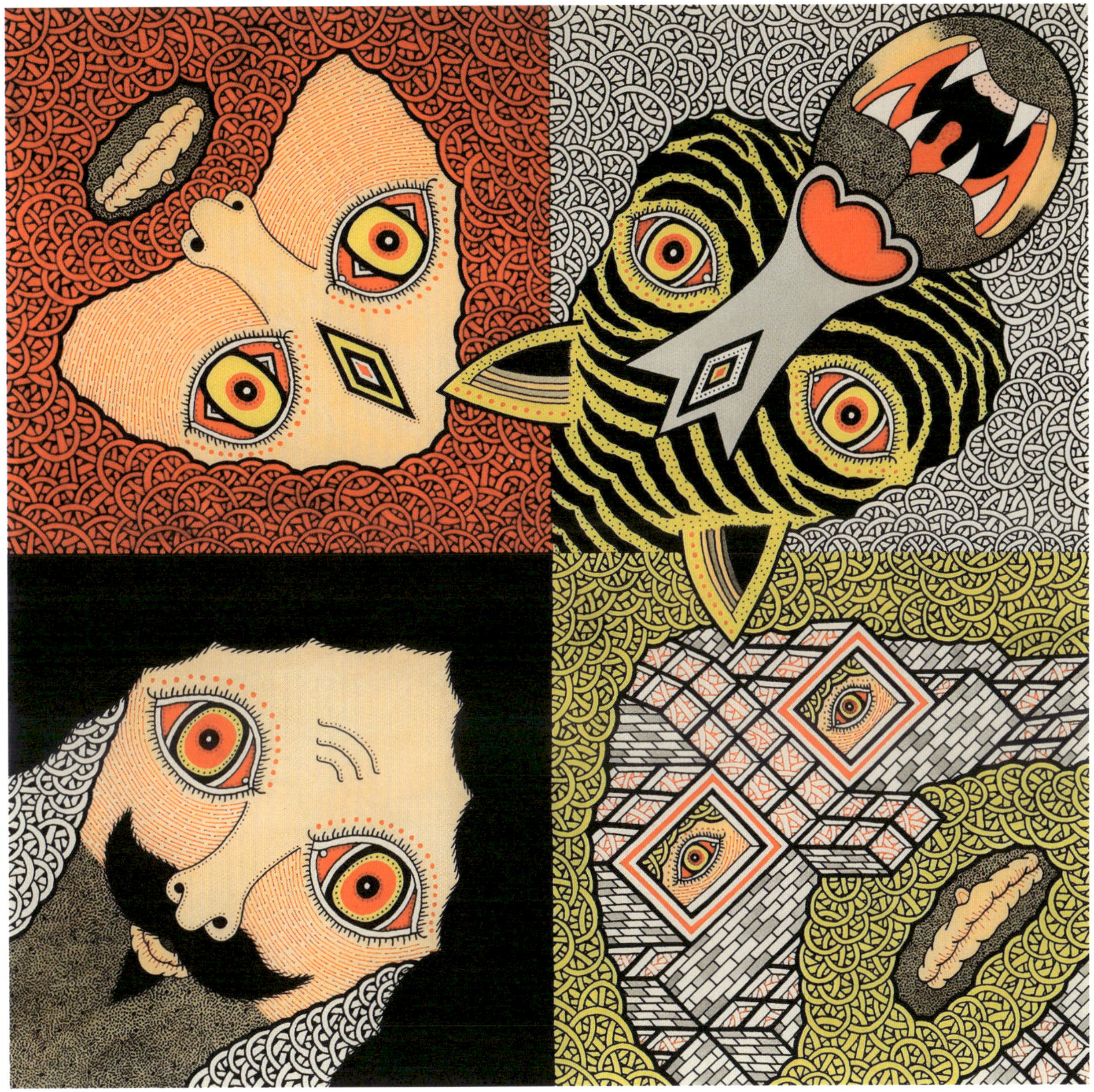

You Are Forgiven

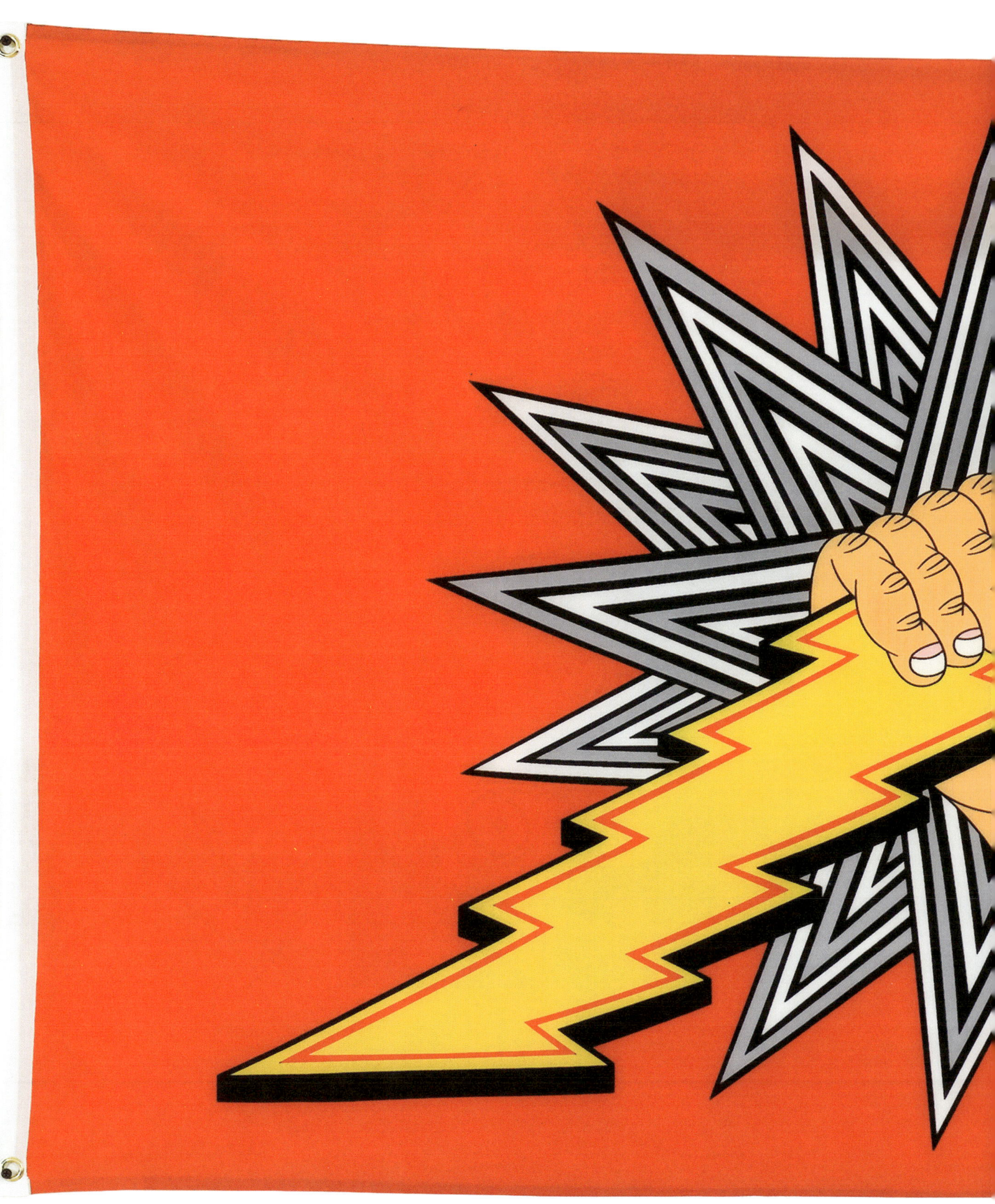

Matt Leines

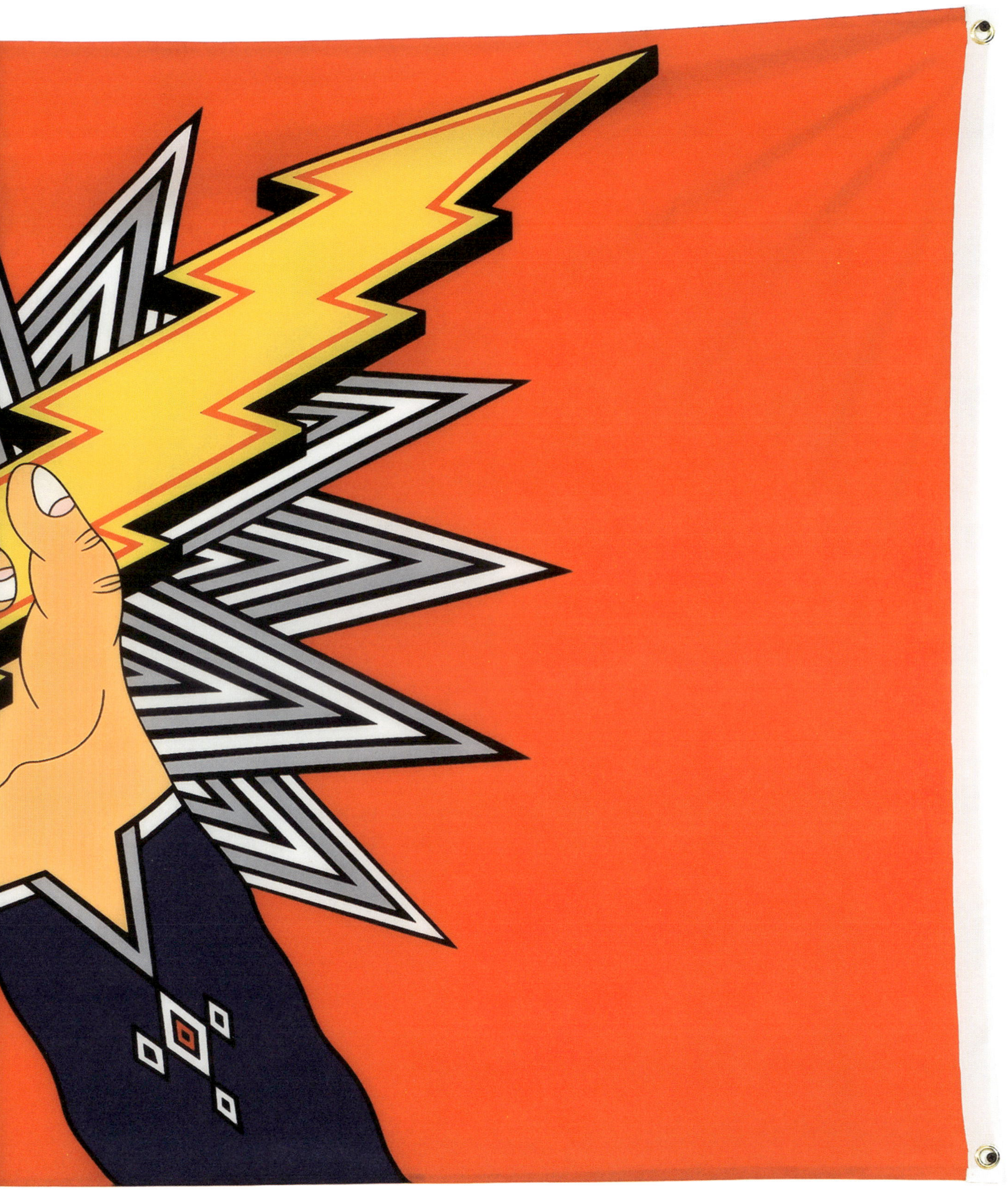

You Are Forgiven

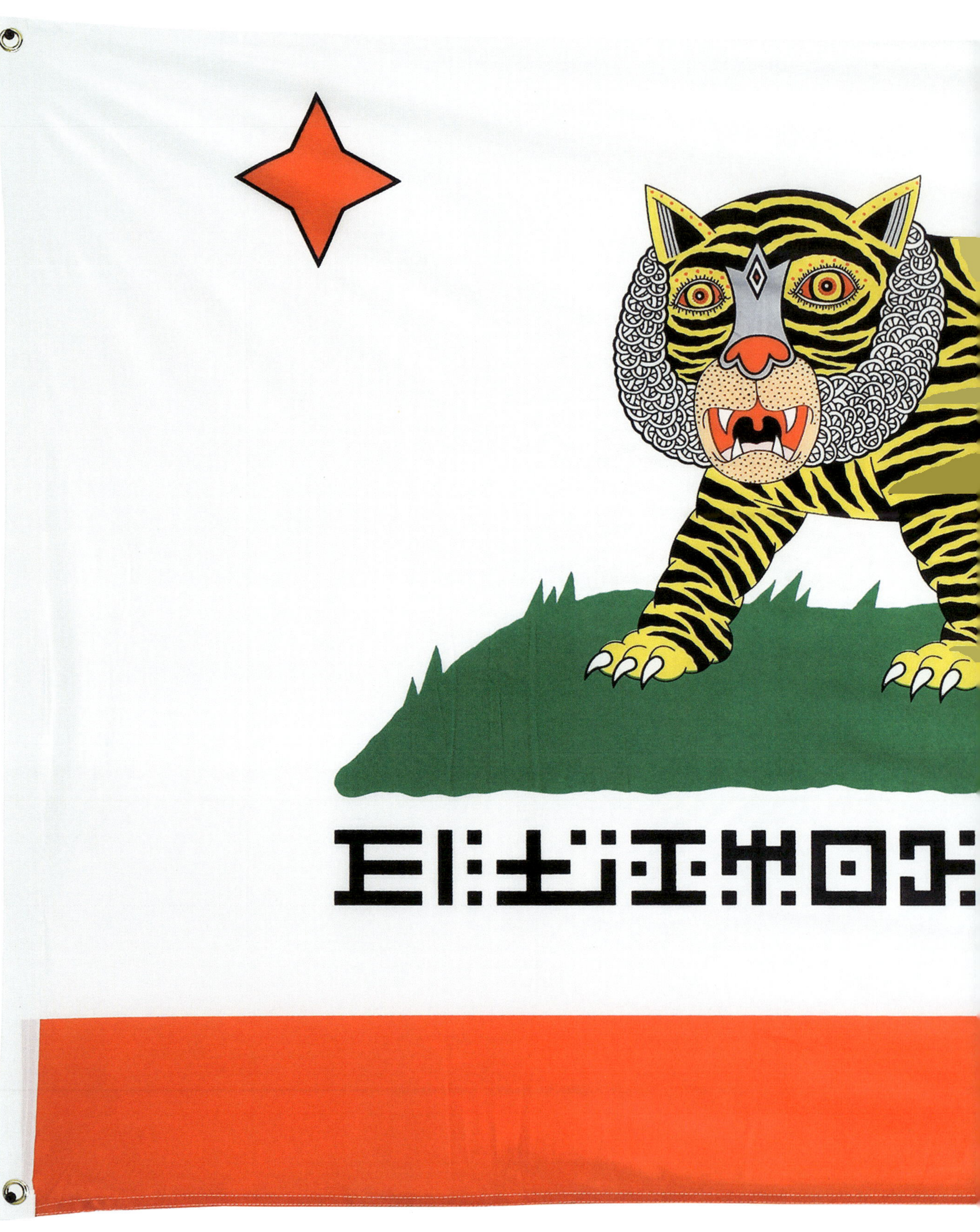

Matt Leines

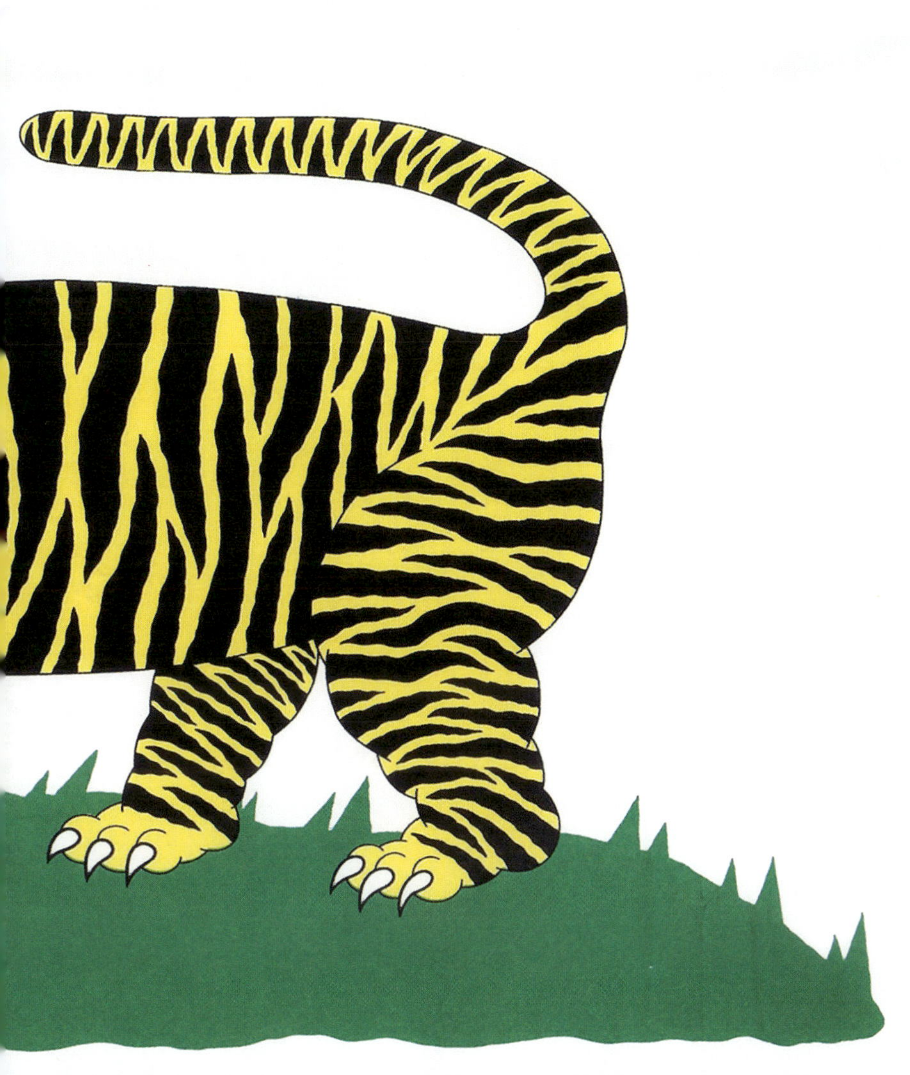

You Are Forgiven

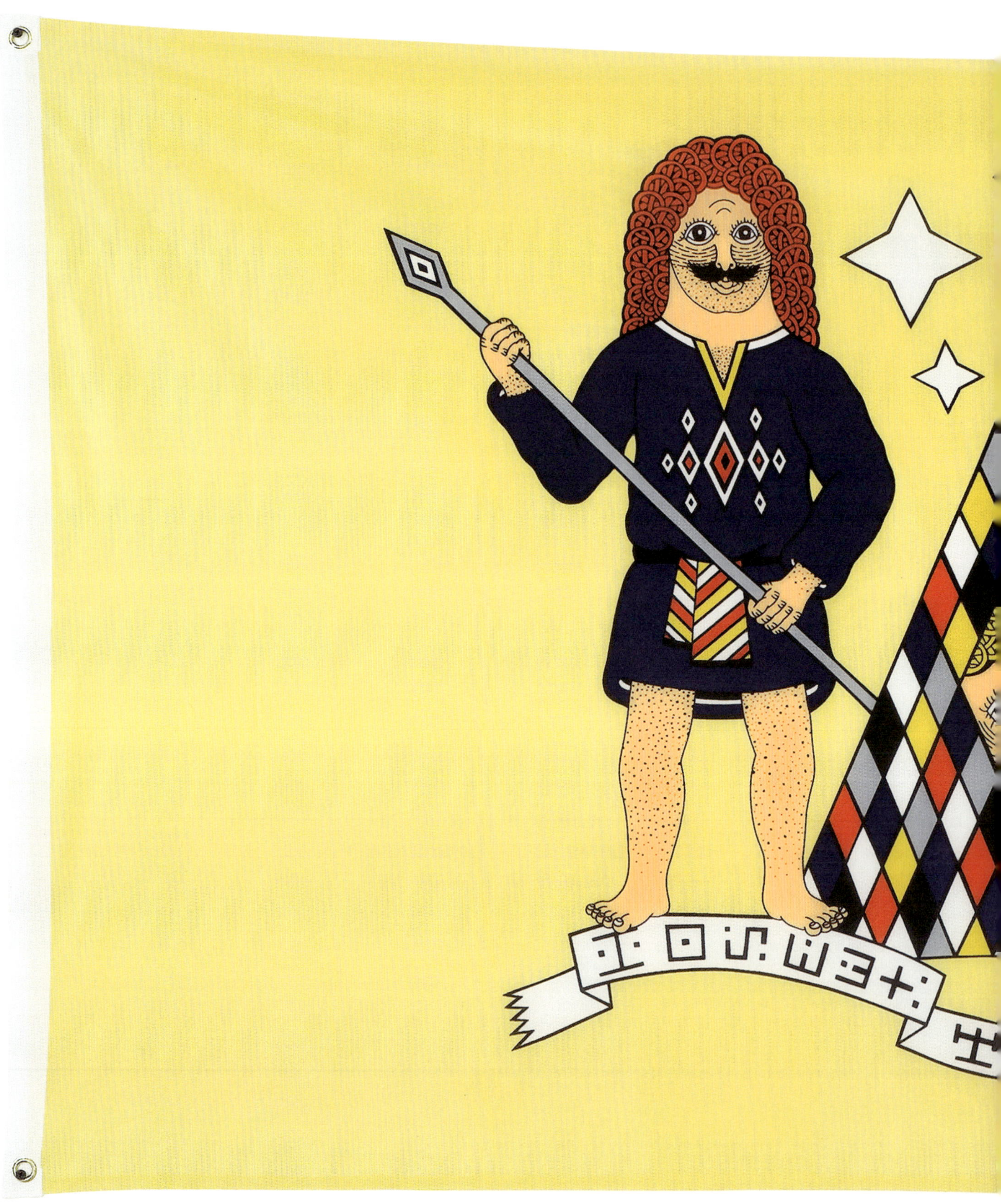

Matt Leines

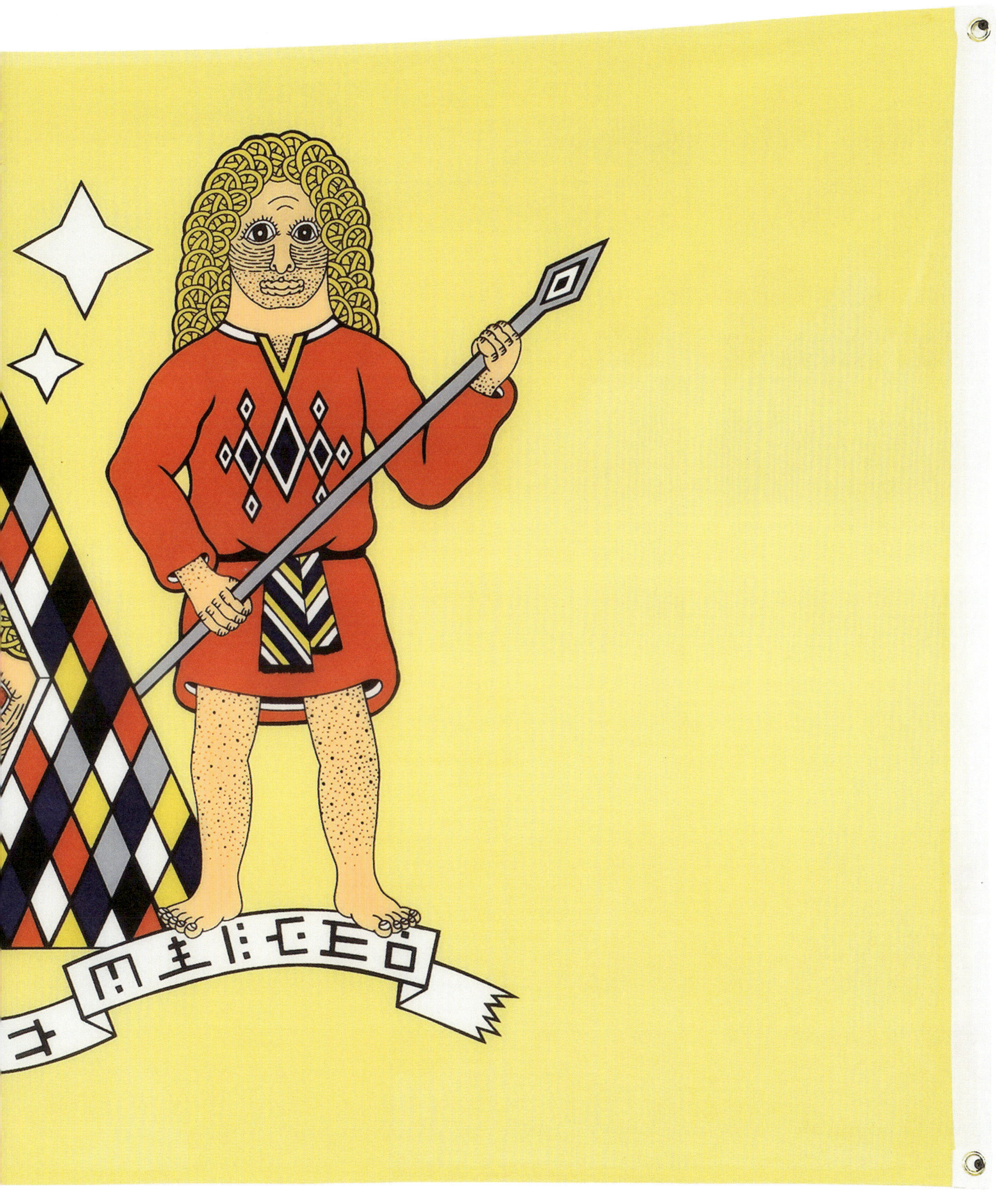

You Are Forgiven

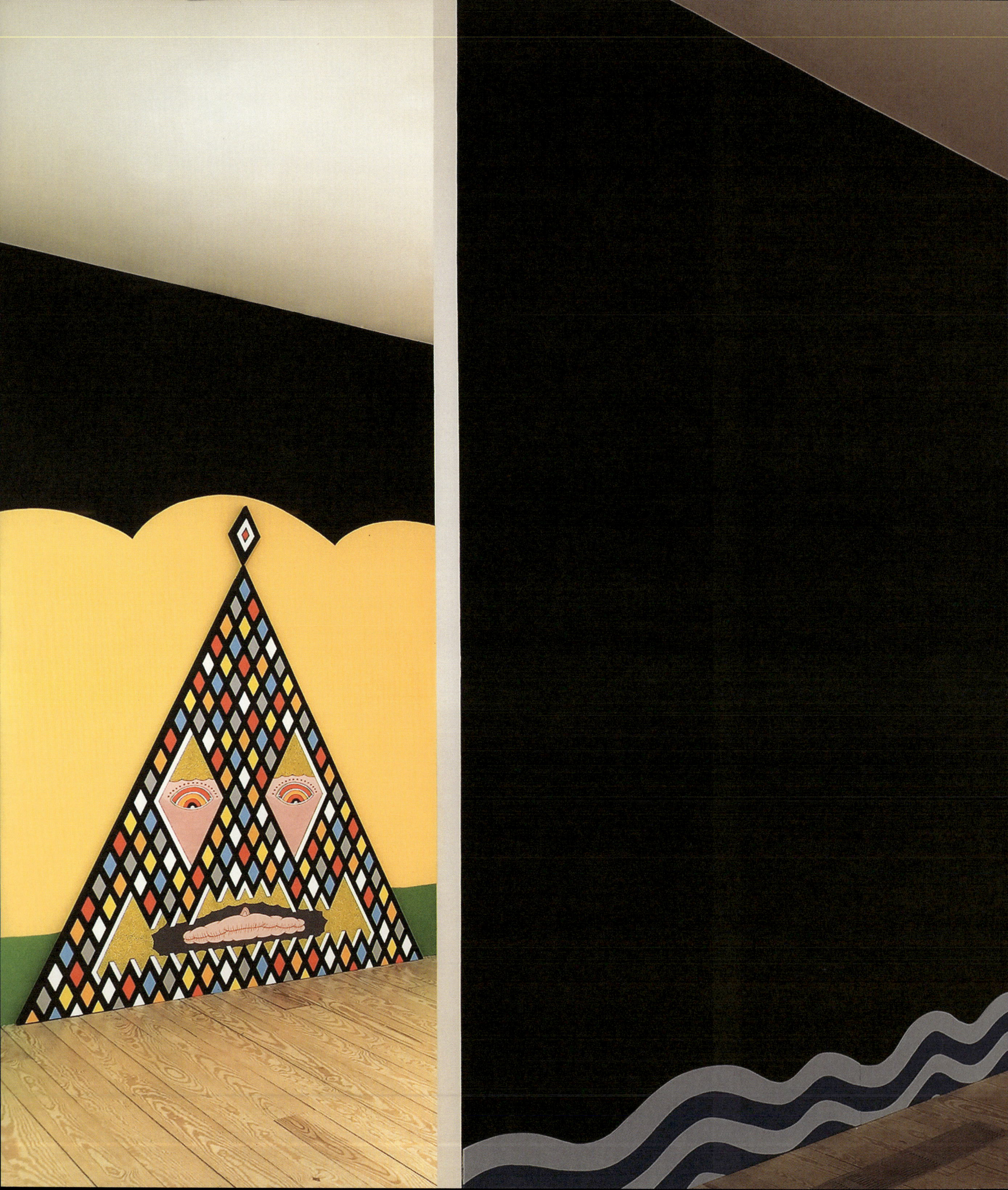

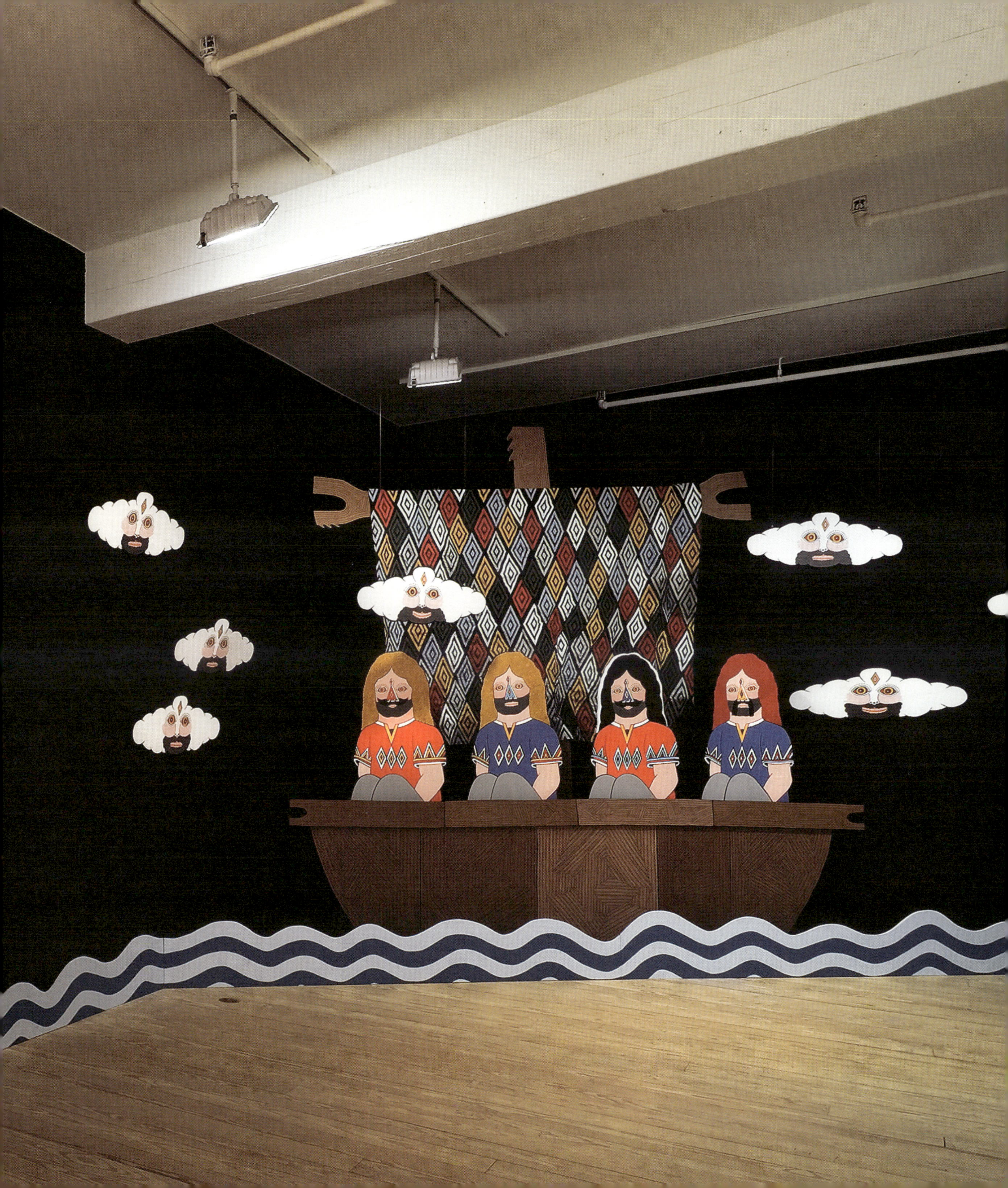

Matt Leines

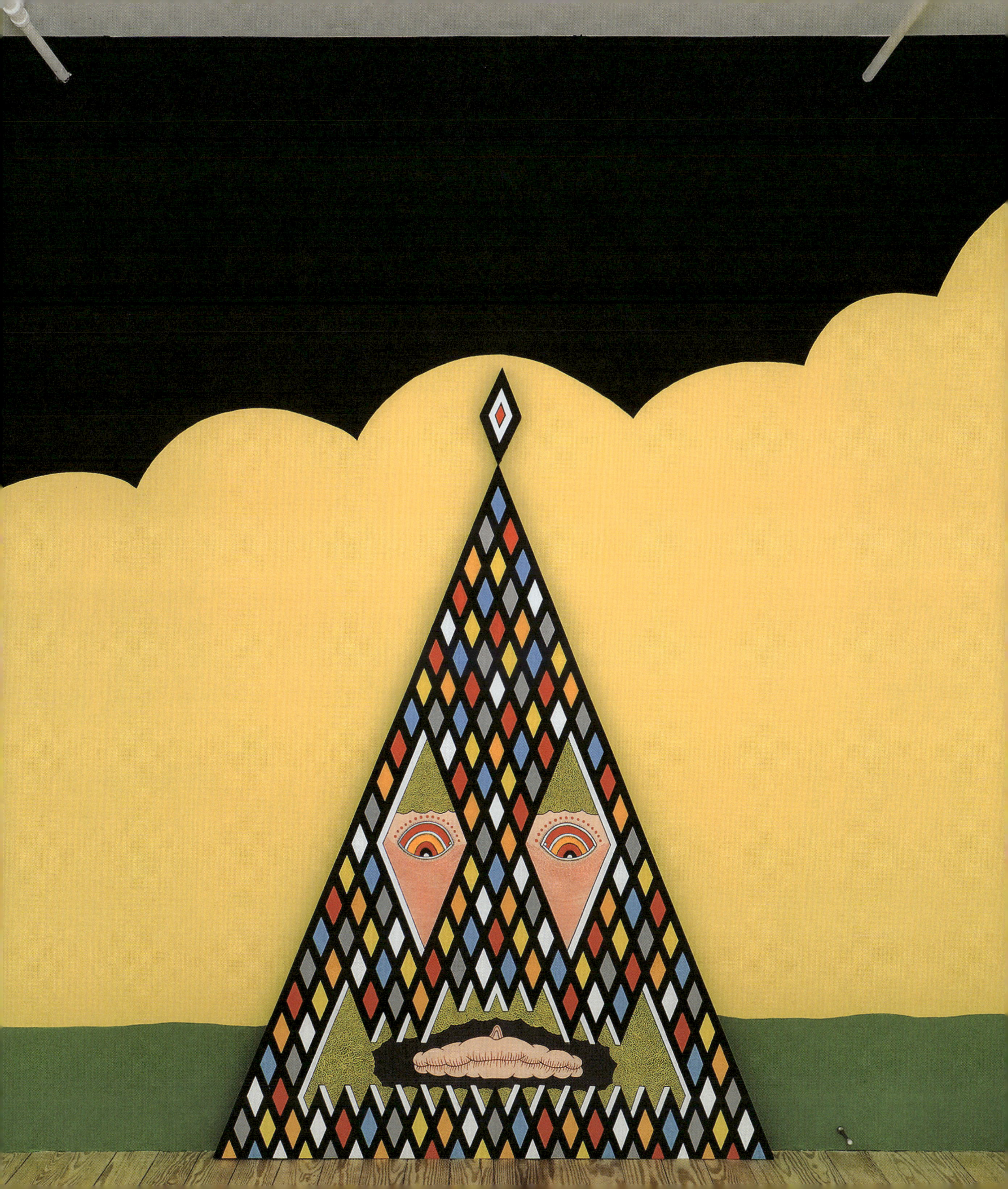

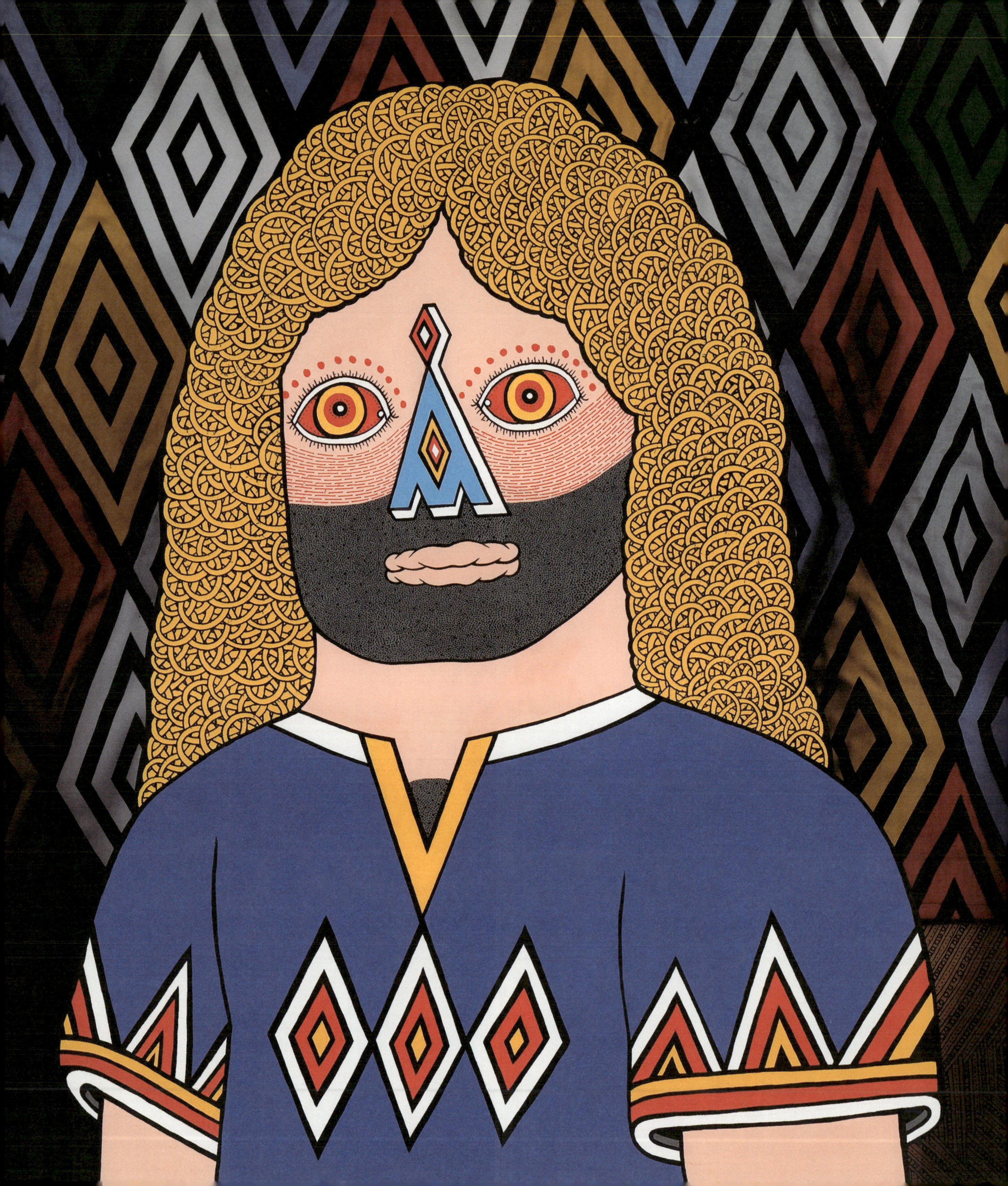

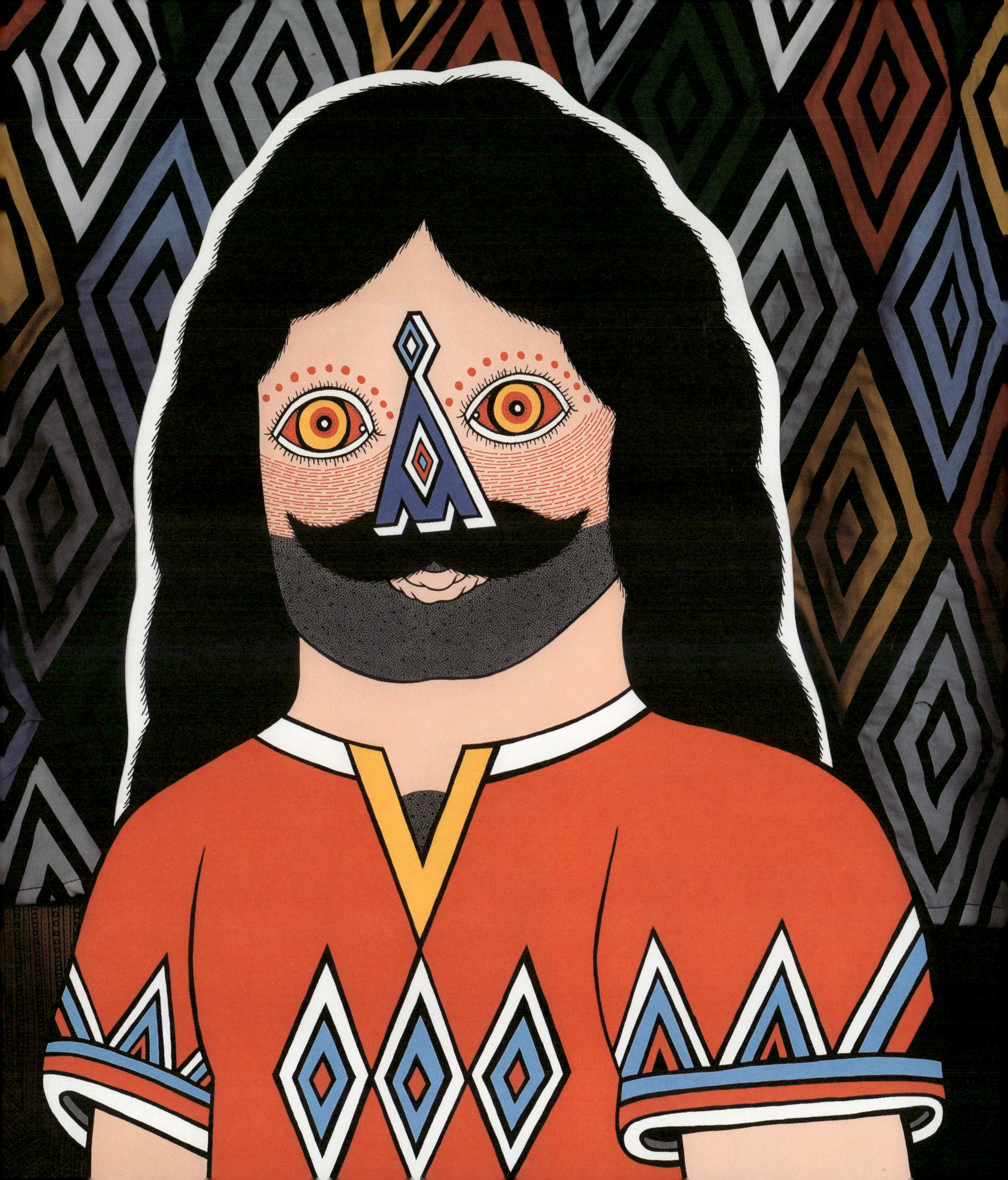

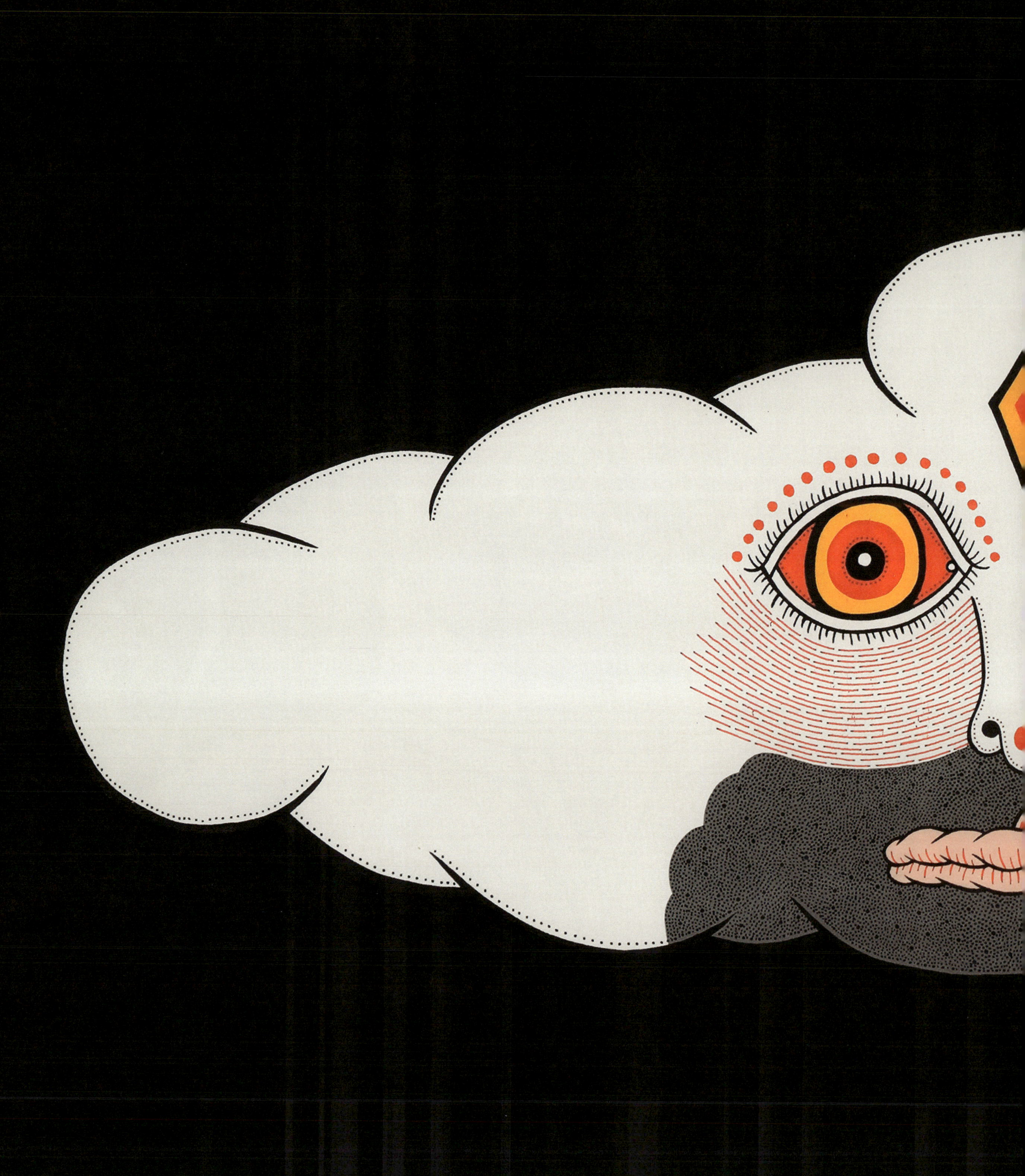

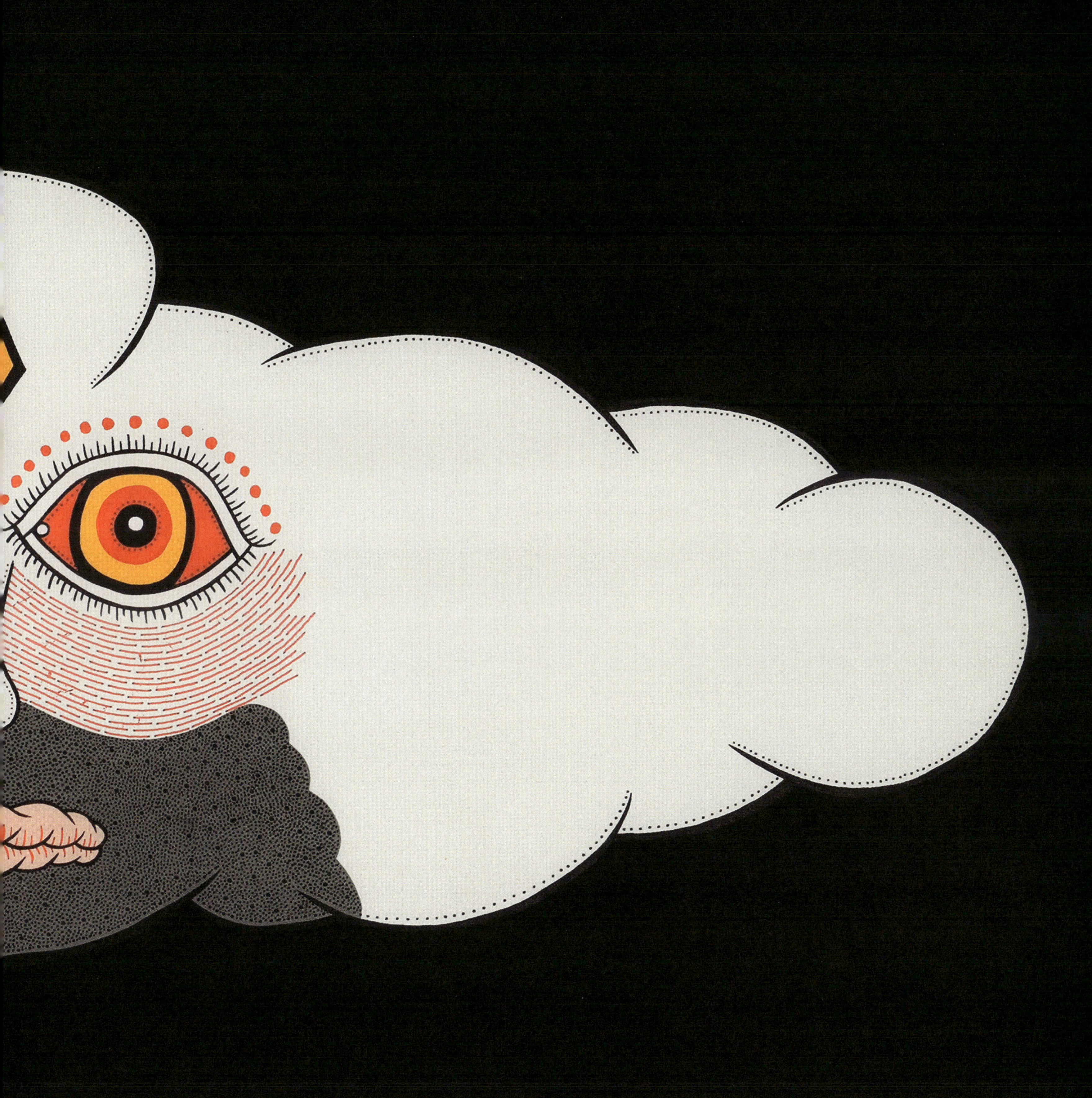

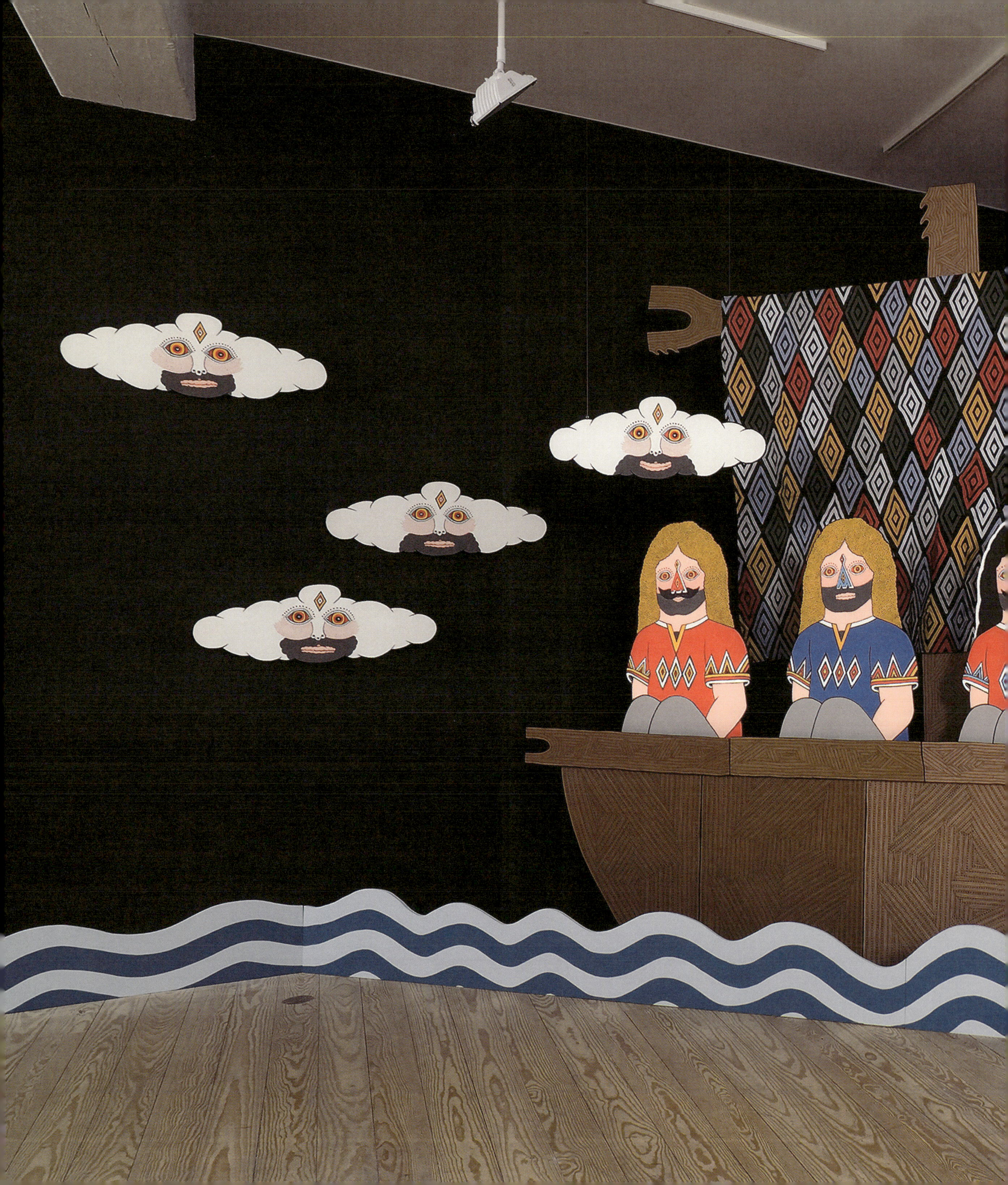

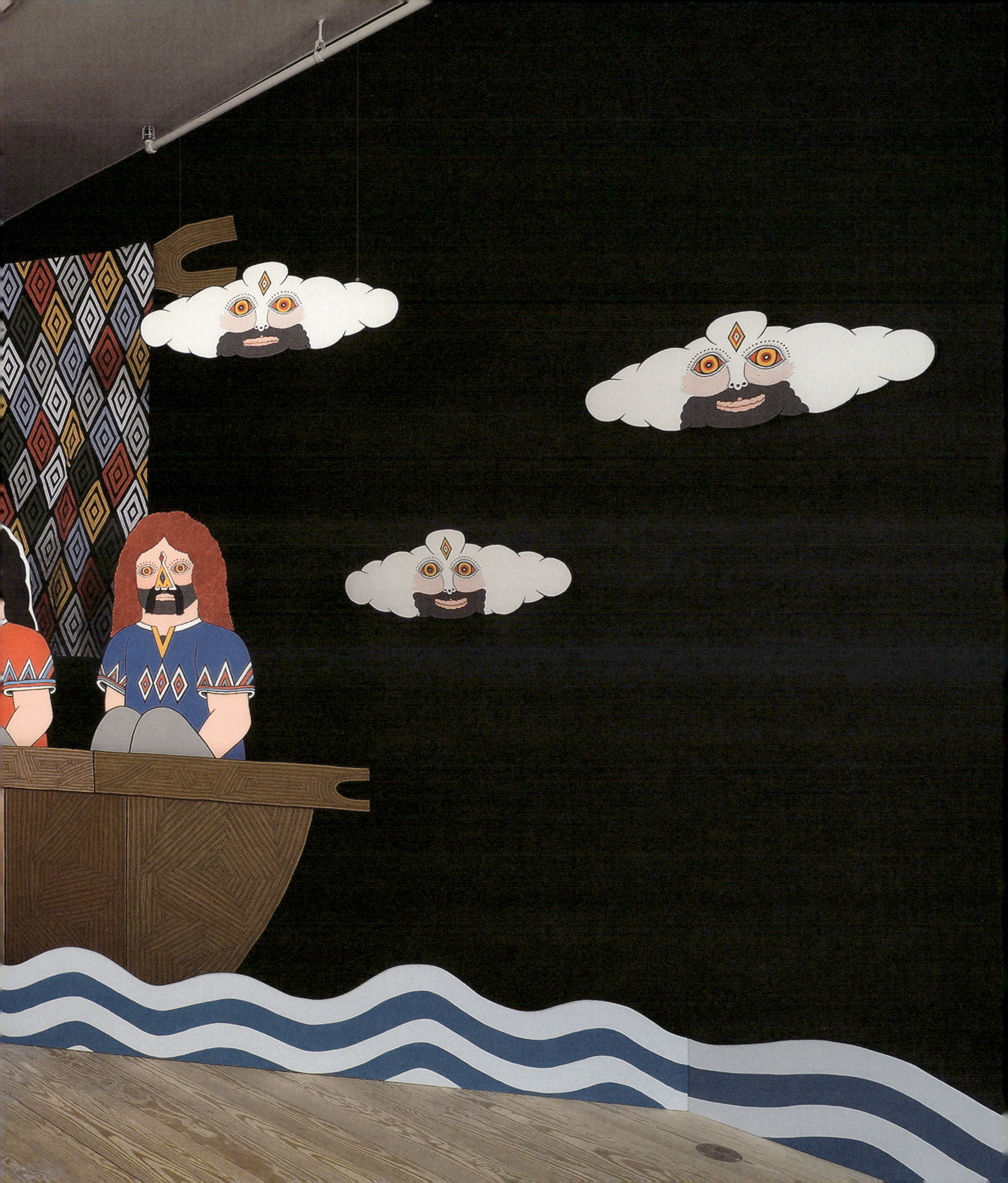

LIST OF WORKS

3. *Untitled (Temple)*
2004
Acrylic on paper
13 3/4 x 13 3/4 inches

9. *The Observation Room*
2002
Acrylic on wood

10. *Untitled*
2001
Acrylic on wood

11. *Untitled (Tiger Plane)*
2002
Acrylic on wood

12-13. *Tiger's Revenge*
2001-2002
Acrylic on panel
6 panels, each 5 x 7
inches

14. *Bolts to the Head*
2001
ink on paper

15. *Untitled*
2002
ink and pencil on paper

16. Top: *Untitled*
2002
Acrylic on wood

Bottom: *Tiger with Sword*
2002
Acrylic on wood

17. *Untitled*
2002
Acrylic on panel
5 x 7 inches

18. *Tiger Rider*
2003
Acrylic on wood

20-21. *Anteater*
2003
Ink and watercolor
on paper

22-23. *Untitled (Boxheads
Carrying Man)*
2003
ink and pencil on paper

24. *Boxhead*
2003
Mixed media sculpture

25. *Boxheads*
2002
Acrylic on wood

26-27. *Untitled (Tree)*
2003
Mixed media

28. *Man with
Lightning Eye*
2003
Ink, watercolor, and
pencil on paper
8 1/2 x 11

29. *Untitled*
2004
Ink, watercolor, and
pencil on paper
8 1/2 x 11

30-31. *Untitled*
2003
Ink and acrylic on paper,
acrylic and enamel on
aluminum

33. *Untitled (Arcade)*
2002
Ink on paper

34. *Machine*
2002
Ink and pencil on paper

35. *Machine Heads*
2002
Ink on paper

36. Left: *Building
With Tree*
2003
Ink and pencil on paper

Right: *Building*
2003
Ink and pencil on paper
5 x 7 inches

37. *Building*
2003
Ink and pencil on paper
8 1/5 x 11 inches

38-41. *Building Series*
2003
Ink and pencil on paper
each 5 x 7 inches

42-43. *Untitled*
2003
Acrylic on wood

44. *Ambassador of the Men
with Lightning Fists*
2004
Ink, watercolor, and
pencil on paper

45. *Untitled*
2004
Ink, watercolor, and
pencil on paper

46-47. *Lion Guarding the
Tower of the Men with
Lightning Fists*
2003
Acrylic on paper
12 x 15 1/2 inches

48-53. *Building Head Series*
2003-2004
Ink, watercolor, and
pencil on paper
each 8 1/2 x 11 inches

54-55. *Building Heads*
2004
Ink, watercolor, and
pencil on paper
11 x 17 inches

56. *Flag of the Men of
the Great Tiger*
2004
Acrylic on paper

57. *Flag of the Men with
Lightning Fists*
2004
Acrylic on paper

59. *Untitled (Installation)*
"Trunk of Humours"
2004, Deitch Projects,
New York, NY
Acrylic on wood
Dimensions variable
Courtesy of Deitch
Projects

60. *Untitled (Stabbing
Tiger)*
2004
Acrylic on paper
12 x 10 inches
Courtesy of Deitch
Projects, New York, NY

61. *Untitled (three knights)*
2004
Acrylic on paper
12 1/2 x 13 1/2 inches
Courtesy of Deitch
Projects, New York, NY

62-63. *Untitled (Anteater)*
2004
Acrylic on paper
18 x 20 inches
Courtesy of Deitch
Projects, New York, NY

64. *Untitled (Tiger Head)*
2004
Acrylic on paper
12 3/8 x 10 1/4 inches
Courtesy of Deitch
Projects, New York, NY

65. Left: *Untitled
(Diamond Face)*
2004
Acrylic on paper
8 3/8 x 6 3/8 inches
Courtesy of Deitch
Projects, New York, NY

Right: *Untitled
Face Orange)*
2004
Acrylic on paper
8 3/8 x 6 3/8 inches
Courtesy of Deitch
Projects, New York, NY

66-67. *Untitled
(Ghost Bucket)*
2004
Acrylic on board
9 3/4 x 23 3/4 inches
Courtesy of Deitch
Projects, New York, NY

68-69. *Untitled (Large
Diamonds)*
2004
Acrylic on board
11 1/8 x 16 3/4 inches
Courtesy of Deitch
Projects, New York, NY

70. *Untitled (Land
Mollusk)*
2004
Acrylic on paper
9 x 12 inches

71. *Wolfrat attacked
by Tiger Pack*
2004
Acrylic on paper
8.5 x 11 inches

72. *Untitled*
2005
Ink and watercolor on
paper

73. Left: *Portrait of a
Warrior in Helm*
2005
Ink and watercolor
on paper
5 x 7 inches
Courtesy of Galleri Loyal,
Stockholm, Sweden

Right: *Portrait of a Man
in a Pointy Hat*
2005
Ink and watercolor
on paper
Courtesy of Galleri Loyal,
Stockholm, Sweden

74. *Untitled (Fort)*
2006
Ink and watercolor
on paper
18 1/2 x 22 inches
Courtesy of Roberts &
Tilton, Culver City, CA

75. *Lion Warrior*
2006
Ink and watercolor
on paper
7 x 5 inches
Courtesy of Roberts &
Tilton, Culver City, CA

76. *The Elder*
2006
Ink and watercolor
on paper
11 x 8 1/2 inches
Courtesy of Roberts &
Tilton, Culver City, CA

77. *Untitled (Shaman)*
2006
Ink and watercolor
on paper
11 x 8 1/2 inches
Courtesy of Roberts &
Tilton, Culver City, CA

78. *Casualty (Head)*
2006
Ink and watercolor
on paper
8 1/2 x 11 inches
Courtesy of Roberts &
Tilton, Culver City, CA

79. *(Untitled) Beast*
2006
Ink and watercolor
on paper
11 x 8 1/2 inches
Courtesy of Roberts &
Tilton, Culver City, CA

80. *The Casualty*
2006
Ink and watercolor
on paper
8 1/2 x 11 inches
Courtesy of Roberts &
Tilton, Culver City, CA

81. *Mounted Warrior*
2006
Ink and watercolor
on paper
11 x 8 1/2 inches
Courtesy of Roberts &
Tilton, Culver City, CA

82. *Untitled (Man with Diamond Face)*
2006
ink and watercolor
on paper
10 1/2 x 10 1/2 inches
Courtesy of Galleri Loyal,
Stockholm, Sweden

83. *Untitled (Shaman in Wooden Mask)*
2006
Ink and watercolor
on paper
8.5 x 8 1/2 inches
Courtesy of Roberts &
Tilton, Culver City, CA

84. *Untitled (Tiger in Forest)*
2006
Ink and watercolor
on paper
8 1/2 x 11 inches
Courtesy of Roberts &
Tilton, Culver City, CA

85. *Untitled (Cobra)*
2006
Ink and watercolor
on paper
11 x 8 1/2 inches
Courtesy of Roberts &
Tilton, Culver City, CA

86. *Untitled (Skull)*
2006
Ink and watercolor
on paper
8.5 x 8 1/2 inches
Courtesy of Roberts &
Tilton, Culver City, CA

87. *Untitled (Red Heads)*
2006
Ink and watercolor
on paper
10.25 x 8 1/2 inches
Courtesy of Roberts &
Tilton, Culver City, CA

88-89. *Man In The Sky in progress*
Galleri Loyal, Stockholm,
Sweden
Photo by Amy Giunta

90-91. *Young Lions*
2006
ink and watercolor
on paper
16 x 13 inches
Courtesy of Galleri Loyal,
Stockholm, Sweden

92. *King of the Men in the Sky*
2006
ink and watercolor
on paper
16 x 12 inches
Courtesy of Galleri Loyal,
Stockholm, Sweden

93. *Untitled (Tiger)*
2006
ink and watercolor
on paper
13 x 11 inches
Courtesy of Galleri Loyal,
Stockholm, Sweden

94. *Untitled (Fire Visions)*
2006
ink and watercolor
on paper
8 x 11 inches
Courtesy of Galleri Loyal,
Stockholm, Sweden

95. *Fortune Tree*
2006
ink and watercolor
on paper
8 1/2 x 11 inches
Courtesy of Galleri Loyal,
Stockholm, Sweden

96-97. Installation view
"Jungleland" 2007, Space
1026, Philadelphia, PA

98. *The Death Messenger*
2007
Ink, watercolor, and
colored pencil on paper

99. *Untitled*
2007
Ink and watercolor
on paper
14 x 16 inches

100-101. *Invading the Village*
2007
Ink and watercolor
on paper

102. *Untitled (Tiger)*
2007
Ink and watercolor
on paper
11 x 14 inches

103. *Night Landing*
2007
Ink and watercolor
on paper
11 x 14 inches

104. Top Left: *Untitled*
2007
ink and watercolor
on paper
7 x 5 inches

Top Right: *Untitled (Shaman in Mask)*
2006
Ink and watercolor
on paper
7 x 5 inches
Courtesy Roberts &
Tilton, Culver City, CA

Bottom Left: *Untitled (Shaman in Blindfold)*
2006
Ink and watercolor
on paper
7 x 5 inches
Courtesy Roberts &
Tilton, Culver City, CA

Bottom Right: *Untitled (Gypsy)*
2006
Ink and watercolor
on paper
7 x 5 inches
Courtesy Roberts &
Tilton, Culver City, CA

105. *Untitled (Group of Men)*
2007
Ink and watercolor
on paper
7 x 5 inches

106-107. *Diamond Temple* (detail)

108-109. *Untitled (Ship)*
2007
ink and watercolor
on paper
18 x 24 inches
Courtesy of Clementine
Gallery, New York, NY

110-111. *Archer Riding Ram*
2008
ink, watercolor, and
colored pencil on paper
18 x 24 inches
Courtesy of Clementine
Gallery, New York, NY

112. *King of the Lightning Men (Cut-Out)*
2008
ink, watercolor, and
colored pencil on paper
with metal hardware
26 1/2 x 16 inches
Courtesy of Clementine
Gallery, New York, NY

113. *Flag Bearer (Cut-Out)*
2008
Ink and watercolor
on paper with metal
hardware
22 x 13 in
Courtesy Roberts &
Tilton, Culver City, CA

114. *Native Riding Tiger (Cut-Out)*
2008
ink and watercolor
on paper with metal
hardware
18 x 15 1/2 inches
Courtesy of Clementine
Gallery, New York, NY

115. *Monster (Cut-Out)*
2008
ink, watercolor, and
gouache on paper with
metal hardware
33 x 22 inches
Courtesy of Clementine
Gallery, New York, NY

116. *Skeleton Soldier (Cut-Out)*
2008
ink, watercolor, and
colored pencil on paper
with metal hardware
26 1/2 x 16 inches
Courtesy of Clementine
Gallery, New York, NY

117. *Tiger Hero (Cut-Out)*
2008
ink and watercolor on
paper with metal hard-
ware
26 1/2 x 16 inches
Courtesy of Clementine
Gallery, New York, NY

119-123. *Twenty Heads*
2007-08
ink, watercolor, and
colored pencil on paper
5 pieces, each 11 x 11
inches
Courtesy of Clementine
Gallery, New York, NY

124-125. *Untitled (Red Flag)*
2008
Dye transfer release
on woven polyester
3 x 5 feet
signed, numbered
edition of 50
Courtesy of Clementine
Gallery, New York, NY

126-127. *Untitled (White Flag)*
2008
Dye transfer release on
woven polyester
3 x 5 feet
signed, numbered
edition of 50
Courtesy of Clementine
Gallery, New York, NY

128-129. *Untitled (Yellow Flag)*
2008
Dye transfer release
on woven polyester
3 x 5 feet
signed, numbered
edition of 50
Courtesy of Clementine
Gallery, New York, NY

130-131. Installation view
"The Righteous Age" 2008,
Clementine Gallery, New
York, NY

133. *Diamond Temple*
2007-2008
Acrylic on board
102 x 68 inches
Courtesy of Clementine
Gallery, New York, NY

134-137. *Untitled (Boat)* details

138-139. *Untitled (Boat)*
2007-2008
Mixed Media Installation
Dimensions variable
Courtesy of Clementine
Gallery, New York, NY

Dust Jacket:
You Are Forgiven (Diptych)
2008
Ink and watercolor
on paper
each 18 x 24 inches

BIOGRAPHY

MATT LEINES
Born: 1980, Totowa, NJ
Resides: Philadelphia, PA

EDUCATION
2002
BFA, Rhode Island School of Design

SOLO EXHIBITIONS
2008
The Righteous Age, Clementine Gallery, New York, NY

2006
The Promise of the North, Roberts and Tilton,
Los Angeles, CA

SELECTED GROUP EXHIBITIONS
2008
Macrocosm, Roberts and Tilton, Culver City, CA
Crocodile Tears, Giant Robot, New York, NY
Road Works, Adam Baumgold Gallery, New York, NY
**I Think He Said "Until We Meet Again, But Under
Different Circumstances" (Or Something Like That)**
Nog Gallery, London, England
Move 16: Don't Paint Your Teeth, curated by Rich Jacobs,
Cinders Gallery, Brooklyn, NY
Group Sects, Giant Robot, San Francisco, CA
Draw, Stolen Space Gallery, London, England
**Something Old, Something New, Something Borrowed,
Something Blue**, curated by Aaron Rose, Primo Marella
Gallery, Milan, Italy

2007
On Line, Adam Baumgold Gallery, New York, NY
Hey You Guyyyyys!, Community Outreach, Toronto, Canada

Snack Isle, Giant Robot, New York, NY
In Full Cry, curated by Matt Leines and Taylor McKimens,
New Image Art, Los Angeles, CA
Tiger in a Tropical Storm, Riviera, Brooklyn, NY
Dream & Trauma - Works from The Dakis Joannou
Collection, Kunsthalle Wien and MUMOK, Wien, Austria
4 Large Works, Community Outreach, London, Canada
Brain Bashers, curated by AJ Fosik, Andenken Gallery,
Denver, CO
Jungleland, Space 1026, Philadelphia, PA
Look Behind You, Giant Robot, New York, NY
Crystal Crunch, Perugi Arte Contemporanea. Padova, Italy
Move 15: These Bagels Are Gnarly, curated by Rich Jacobs,
Cinders Gallery, Brooklyn, NY

2006
Panic Room - Works from The Dakis Joannou Collection,
curated by Kathy Grayson and Jeffrey Deitch,
Deste Foundation, Athens, Greece
A Piece Apart, curated by Jordin Isip, Aidan Savoy Gallery,
New York, NY
Do Not Stack, Roberts & Tilton, Los Angeles, CA
HENTEKO Pop & Psychedelic, curated by Taylor McKimens
and Misaki Kawai, The Watari Museum of Contemporary
Art, Tokyo, Japan
If You Want To Hear Something Just Yell, curated by Rich
Jacobs, and Julia Schonlau, Neurotitan, Berlin, Germany
Young Lions Galleri Loyal, Stockholm, Sweden
Oval, The Front Room, Brooklyn, NY
Fine Line, Adam Baumgold Gallery, New York, NY

2005
Sometimes I Just Want a Hug, Jonathan Levine Gallery,
New York, NY
Loyal and His Band: Hand Painted Covers, Galleri Loyal,
Stockholm, Sweden
Carry On, curated by Rich Jacobs and Abigail Scholar,
Feigen Contemporary, New York, NY

Mystery Meat, Future Prospects Gallery, Quezon City, Philippines
Some Of My Best Friends Are American, New Image Art, Los Angeles, CA
Move 13, curated by Rich Jacobs, Clementine Gallery, New York, NY
Everybody Knows This Is Nowhere, Galleri Loyal, Stockholm, Sweden
New Image Art@ RVCA, RVCA Clothing, Costa Mesa, CA
Drone, Vilma Gold, London, UK
Move 12: Raw Dogs, curated by Rich Jacobs, New Image Art, Los Angeles, CA

2004
Move 11, curated by Rich Jacobs, 96 Gillespie, London, UK
Eye of The Needle, Roberts and Tilton, Los Angeles, CA
Trunk of Humors, Curated by Kathy Grayson, Deitch Projects, New York, NY
Dreamland Artists Club, Creative Time, Coney Island, NY
Majority Whip, Curated by Kathy Grayson and Laura Tepper, White Box, New York, NY
Good World, Publico, Cincinnati, OH
Untitled, Wrong Gallery, New York NY

2003
Today's Man, curated by John Connelly, Hiromi Yoshii Gallery, Tokyo, Japan
Beam Me Up, New Image Art, Los Angeles, CA
Dirt Wizards, curated by Kathy Grayson, Brooklyn Fire Proof, Brooklyn, NY
Move 9: Lead Poisoning, curated by Rich Jacobs & Marsea Goldberg, New Image Art, Los Angeles, CA
Crazy Bastard, New Image Art, Los Angeles, CA
Dimebag, curated by Jordin Isip and Rodger Stevens, The Front Room, Brooklyn, NY
Assembly, curated by Jordin Isip and Rodger Stevens, The Front Room, Brooklyn, NY

2002
Monster Mash, 5024SF. San Francisco CA
The Giant Electric, New Image Art, Los Angeles, CA
Panorama Project, curated by Jordin Isip and Rodger Stevens,
The **Front Room**, Brooklyn, NY
Panorama Project, curated by Jordin Isip and Rodger Stevens, 69a, San Francisco CA

RESIDENCIES
2007
Watermill Center, Watermill, NY

THANK YOU

Alex Lukas, Rich Jacobs, Taylor Mckimens, Liz Zanis, Erin Coughlin, Phil Brychta, Evan Wraga, Zac Smith, "Hollywood" Tom Breen, Rob and Maria Czyzewski, Jack Long, Caitlin Keegan, Julia Rothman, Ethan Hayes-Chute, Joseph Hart, Misaki Kawai, Eric White, Ashley Macomber, Jim Houser, Rebecca Westcott, Bennet and Julie Roberts, Lindsay Charlwood, Elizabeth Burke, Abby Messitte, Emily Wiggins, Aaron Rose, Kathy Grayson, Martin Lilja, Amy Giunta, Kristian Bengtsson, Marsea Goldberg, Jeffrey Deitch, Paul Bright, Adam Baumgold, Jonathan LeVine, Kyra Byrne, Pat Byrne, Rob Ross, Anthony Mongiardo, Jesse Jenkins, Neil and Jamie Sabatino, Christian "Jam Bro" Jacobs, Casey Holland, Liz Rice, Pat Tenore, Chris Johanson, Jo Jackson, William Buzzell, AJ Fosik, Marc Bell, James Benjamin Franklin, Robyn O'Neil, Barry Mcgee, Thomas Campbell, Cheryl Kaminsky, Matt Furie, Ben Jones, Andrew Jeffery Wright, Crystal Stokowski, Jeff Ladoucer, Brian Gibbs, Jonah Takagi, Ben Koch, Allen Spetnagle, Lee Kosa, Joel Speasmaker, Kevin Christy, James Hughes, Benjamin Schmidt, Noah Khoshbin and the Watermill Center, Koji Shimizu, James Towers, Julie Machado, Parnell Corder, Philip Paratore, Michael Landrum, The Deste Foundation, Chet Parlavecchio, Alex Raymond, Sir Peter Blake, Bruce Springsteen… and Tony Smyrski, Meg Kemner, Max Lawrence, Adam Wallacavage, and Gary Panter for making this book a reality.

SPECIAL THANKS

Virginia Leines, Patty Leines, Richard Stewart, the Vanderbergs, the Rikers, Jordin Isip, Robert Brinkerhoff, Polly Becker, James Mercadante, Carrie Ingraham, and William DeGroot

DEDICATED

to the loving memory of Carl Leines and Bridie Stewart

Matt Leines

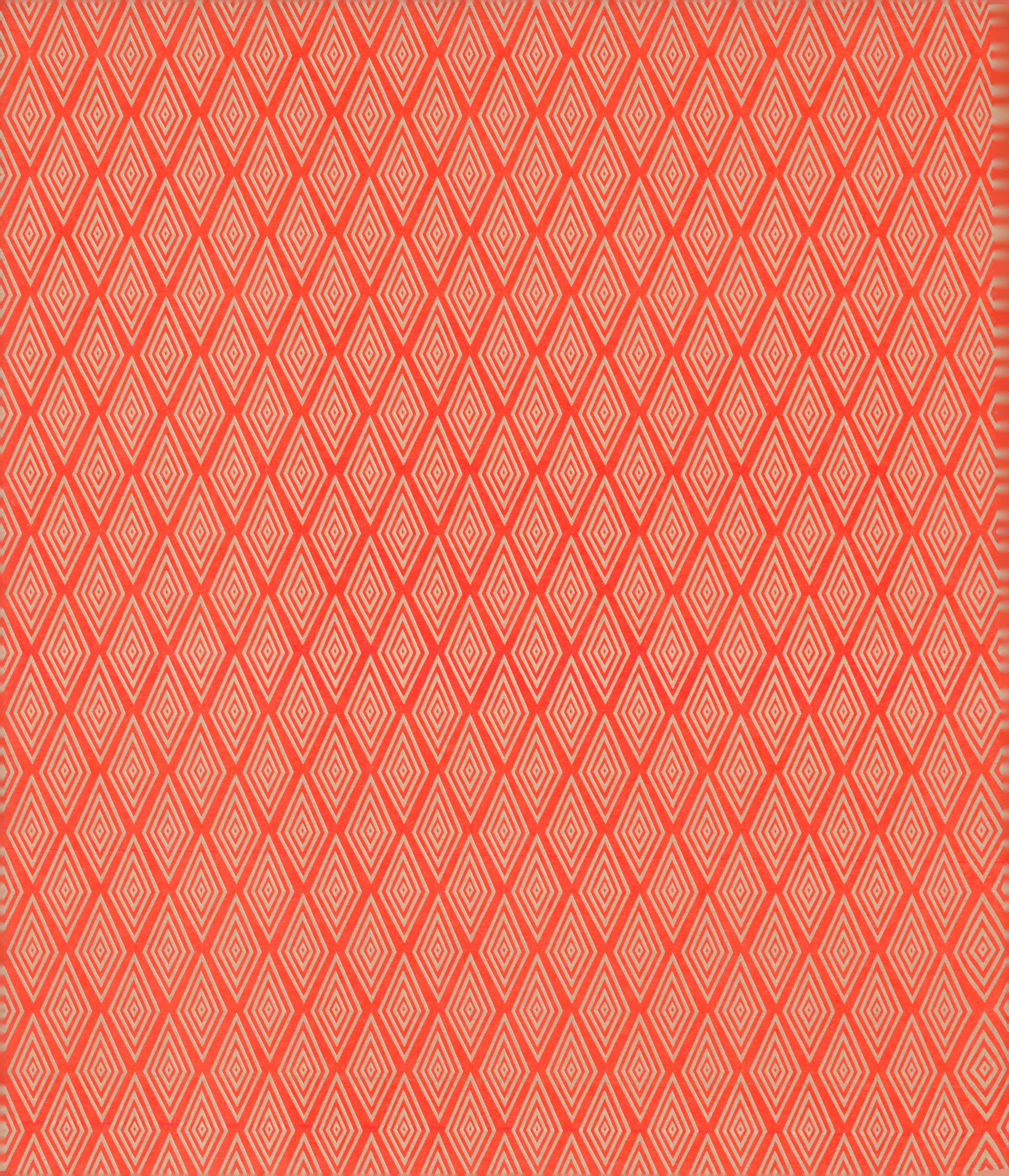